Societal Accounting

Societal Accounting

TREVOR GAMBLING

Professor of Accounting at the University of Birmingham

London · George Allen & Unwin Ltd

Ruskin House Museum Street

First published in Britain in 1974

ISBN 0 04 330242 4

Printed in Great Britain
in 11 on 13pt Times Roman
by The Aldine Press, Letchworth, Herts

Contents

Preface

The thesis of this book is that classical accounting theory is based on a mistaken premise, so that the current attempts, on both sides of the Atlantic, to refine its content are largely in vain. Moreover, this inadequacy in the basic underpinning of the subject has profound effects which are not by any means confined to academia, but result in an artificial limitation of the scope of real-life accounting practice. It is only in recent years that society has turned its attention to social betterment as an independent goal from purely economic advance; the criticisms that our theoreticians are at present trying to counter will be demonstrated to be essentially of the failure of accounting practice to take account of this broader interest. What is needed is nothing less than the redefinition, or clarification of 'accounting' as the data-base for *all* aspects of social measurement and control.

This is because accounts are attempts to make statements about success or failure in achieving the goals of the organisation in question; these goals are dictated by the system of values entertained by the society in which it operates, and the value system is an integral part of the culture of that society. Anthropologists demonstrate the differing value systems that are found in various parts of the world, primarily, it is true, among what we might call its less sophisticated societies. However, Chapter 2 of the book adduces subtle variations in the goals (and hence the values) of more developed societies, from their well-documented differences of approach to the preparation of National Income Accounts. Even between societies whose values are not dissimilar, it is possible to find basically different approaches to income recognition; primarily between those who are prepared to take account of managerial intentions (as in Germany and the Netherlands) and those who seek some internal accounting standards (as in Great Britain and the United States). It follows that the book is seeking to apply to accounting the distinction between the 'formal' and 'substantive' approach that is such a feature of anthropological economics; these arguments are discussed in detail in Chapter 3.

Briefly, the formal approach is a formal logical deduction about human behaviour based on first principles and which assumes that the behaviour of the group can be looked upon as a straightforward aggregation of the deduced individual behaviour. The substantive approach views human society as a complex 'system,' and takes the position that no sensible conclusions can be taken about groups or individuals except in the context of the system of which they are part.

The particular method used to arrive at profit is seen as proceeding from the culture itself. It is simply not possible to claim that 'our' viewpoint is more correct than any other in absolute terms, but this does not imply that every method is equally efficient in achieving the goals of its society, even in its own terms. It matters little whether we measure profit as cash flow, as accruals-adjusted net income, or as return on investment, if there are significant areas of welfare (and hence 'wealth') which are not encompassed by our accounting system. The first thesis of this book, therefore, is that academic accountants have been misled by this confusion of formal and substantive and thus neglect the more important issue of what it is that a given society is trying to achieve, and whether its accounting methods give it much help in this.

Since accounting has a history of some 700 years in very much its present form, it must be supposed that, by and large, it has proved adequate for the purposes of the societies it served. It may be that the case is now altered. The problems facing a large section of the world seem to be of a social rather than a purely economic nature. In the developed nations, technological advances enable a comparatively small part of the available labour force to produce enough goods and services to maintain themselves adequately, and also support the balance of the population permanently 'on welfare.' It could be hypothesised that if the whole of the able-bodied population of all such societies were to work flat out, the result would be a disastrous exhaustion of natural resources and pollution of the environment; also, underdeveloped nations would find themselves deprived of access to natural resources to an even greater extent than at present. If it is true that the world is now pressing against the boundaries of its ecological possibilities, we cannot look forward to great enhancement of the *economic* standard of life, but whatever standards can be achieved will be obtainable with a much slighter sacrifice of leisure. In short we in this country are probably witnessing the death-throes of the old-style 'working class.' Who should be surprised at our present climate of industrial disturbance at a time when a whole section of our culture is being swept away? This is especially the case when the speed of the underlying technological change is also very great.

Moreover, this comparative stagnation of economic wealth would force attention on the possibility of finding other ways of enhancing the 'quality of life.' Except in most deviant personalities, economic wealth is in any case just a means of increasing 'welfare,' and cannot be enjoyed at all in the absence of some minimal support from society; this topic is discussed at length in Chapter 5. Of course, the difficulties of operating such a society are obvious; people have no more idea of what to do with the 'sturdy beggar' in the time of Elizabeth II than they had under Elizabeth I. Why should a man 'on welfare' live in comparative poverty, just because society can produce all the goods and services it needs without his aid? Against this, why should a lower-paid worker put in a full working-week and receive little more than he would get if he himself joined the unemployed; why should the better-paid workers have their 'differential' eroded to remedy this problem, either? Apart from the problems of those who continue to work, how should the non-employed, but state-supported, fill out their days? One supposes that they could engage in ritual warfare (as in Northern Ireland and Vietnam?), paint masterprices, blow their mind on hallucogens—or perhaps do something else? The point is that if one is right in suspecting that the Protestant Ethic has died, no-one seems to have many ideas about what should take the place of economically productive labour as the only reasonable occupation of the able-bodied adult.

Galbraith has suggested that economic science has very little to say to the affluent society, because its tools belong to that age of economic scarcity which has now passed away. Therefore, the second thesis of this book is that none of the 'social sciences' has all that much to tell us either, because none of the others have any real tools at all, at least in the sense that they could be used to *manage* society. Economic scarcity is an insistent claimant for attention, so naturally only economic affairs were deemed to require practical management in a pre-affluent era. At the present time, central and local authorities are turning more and more of their attention to the provision of social services, but, they have no real certainty of success in what they do. The reasons are discussed in Chapter 6; there is a need to extend the science of accounting to cover other societal phenomena besides the economic ones. Unfortunately, this is not a thing which can be done simply by extending the scope of the existing techniques, because our taxonomy for analysing social problems is fragmented and contradictory. As a result we cannot measure the trade-off of economic profit against other social benefits with any degree of accuracy. This book asserts that nothing but a radical reform of accounting theory can bring about even the first step towards solving the problems of affluence, or rather of a limited affluence which has no further physical frontiers to exploit. Social engineering requires this, just as mechanical engineering required a minimal level of expertise in physics and mathematics for its development.

What is needed, then, is a coherent and comprehensive taxonomy for the human condition. If something cannot be the subject of accounting, and hence amenable to objective comparison of the results of dealing with it in various ways, it cannot be manipulated. (This is probably what Sombart meant in the well-known quotation which opens the first chapter of the book.) Human society is an intricate feed-back system, about whose workings very few overarching, general theories exist, although it is well known that it is dangerous to tinker with feedback systems without some convincing (although perhaps less than infallible) theory of how the whole system operates. To the extent that societies do indulge in theories, they seem more disposed to treat matters of faith, rather than bases for accounting taxonomies. Thus we may *believe* that some of our troubles proceed from excessive population, and so institute a programme of family limitation, but if we do not have a model of how society works this really cannot be more than an act of *faith*. A change in the age distribution of the population may have many unexpected results. What appear to be the continual blows of a perverse Fate may be the natural and inevitable outcome of blind struggles with a system that we do not begin to understand, because of a lack of tools for measuring and analysing its workings.

The book attempts to describe a possible machinery for a system of 'societal accounting,' both at macro- and micro-levels. It may be thought that it does not go into great detail for so ambitious an enterprise, but it will be seen that since the system of values proceeds from the social culture, the various taxonomies need to be tailored to whatever general theory is held regarding the operation of that society. It follows that societal accounting is non-political; indeed it is probably the most non-political concept in the history of thought. As we have seen, political theories have always involved acts of faith, and the intensity of feeling needed to inculcate essentially irrational convictions has militated against the development of rigorous models of human society. No doubt the suggestion of an audit of the results of an act of faith is always rank heresy in the eyes of the faithful—as if one was to propose taking electroencephalograms of the Church's confirmation candidates.

I should like to assure my readers that I am aware that other men have written upon these topics; indeed it seems to have been a principal source of employment for the human race, as can be seen, for example, from the astounding bibliographies attached to two Committee Reports of the American Accounting Association. These are those of the 'Committee on Non-Financial Measures of Effectiveness' [2] and the 'Committee on Measures of Effectiveness for Social programs' [3], who clock up, respectively, 230 and 242 references on these topics—and there are surely many more, including a few referred to in this work. Clearly there is plenty of opportunity for academic gamesmanship here ('Have you read *X*'s paper in the *World Bank Staff Papers* for 1970?'); it would be pleasant to be able to claim to have read them all. In part one can only plead *Ars longa, vita brevis*; but the reading of a fair number of them will leave one a little less humble, because while many can tell you about the problems few can offer much more than obviously *ad hoc* solutions to any of them. This is only to be expected; the theme of this book is the social scientists' failure to see the wood for the trees. One could conclude that it is as dangerous to write about (let alone administer) social problems without a fairly rigorous *Weltanschauung*, as it would be to discuss topics in the physical sciences without a background of Newtonian physics (or some equally comprehensive alternative). The alchemists were prolific authors.

Some parts of this material have already appeared in *Accountancy*, *The International Journal of Accounting* and in some discussion papers issued by the Faculty of Commerce and Social Science at the University of Birmingham, England.

In conclusion, I hope that practising accountants will read the book as well as academic colleagues; it has as much of a message for the former as for the latter. Also, I hope that all readers will have as much fun reading it as the author found in writing it!

Birmingham, England, January 1973

1 Classical Micro-Accounting

1.1 Historical development of accounting

The theme of this book is that accounting is not so much closely connected with the societies which it serves, but rather an integral part of the fabric of every society. Consider these well-worn quotations:

> 'Capitalism without double-entry book-keeping is simply inconceivable. They hold together as form and matter' [Sombart, 109, pp 118–19].

and

> 'Accounting and control—that is the main thing required for the smooth working, the correct functioning of the first phase of a Communist society' [Lenin, 74, p 71].

Clearly the societies with which accounting relates can be very different and, especially if one accepted Sombart's statement as being correct, one might wonder how Lenin found the system of accounting so well-suited to his purposes. Other historians, notably Yamey [126], have in any case disputed Sombart's view; if book-keeping means no more than the preparation of formal records of debtors, creditors and cash, then the technique antedates anything which could be described as 'capitalism' by several centuries. Nevertheless, it seems possible to see in the development of *double-entry* book-keeping, at the end of the thirteenth century, a very necessary change of approach to business. Double-entry book-keeping was a product of its time; the medieval merchant carried on his business without very much understanding of those business methods which we would call collectively 'a system of control.' Quite apart from its book-keeping system, a modern business is organised in such a way that similar transactions are always handled in the same fashion; in part this means that employees do not have to be all that clever to carry out their duties, because they can just follow the rules. However, the greater part of the reason for insisting on a systematic treatment of transactions is that it enables us to practise one form of 'management by exception,' because unusual items, especially frauds and mistakes, will not be fitted so easily into the normal procedures. For example, creditors are only paid when they have submitted invoices and the invoices have been 'passed for payment.' This means that someone checks whether the goods referred to have been properly ordered, properly priced, properly delivered and so on.

The medieval merchant, however grasping an individual he may have been, would scarcely be able to comprehend what we mean by 'organisation and method'; he relied on personal supervision and the rigorous enforcement of legal rights as evidenced by formal legal documents such as promissory notes, bills of sale, and the like. Once the business got too large for personal control, or family control, he was as much at the mercy of his employees' standards of honesty as was the biblical employer of the 'unjust steward' who was given his notice, and in return for a share of the proceeds, he gave his employer's debtors their promissory notes back, so that they could forge them for lower amounts. In the absence of any system of control these notes were all that the employer could rely upon to enforce payment, so no doubt this fraud was a great success in its time. Before double-entry bookkeeping was developed, ledger accounts had been kept for many years, back into the Silver Latin period. However, these accounts were kept in so-called single entry, rather like a bookie's ledger; so that the entry in the book and the race ticket (or its commercial equivalent) were all that there was to show for the transaction. This approach to accounting made fraud still relatively easy, because it was no straightforward matter to reconcile the outstanding debtors and creditors with the cash in hand. It was to remedy this that double-entry book-keeping was developed. The idea was to link debtors, creditors, cash, and inventory in a balancing system of transactions in which, once something was entered it could not be overlooked or mishandled without a fair exercise of ingenuity. In short, double-entry bookkeeping was a system of control, and one might note that it was as such that it was at first used; the idea of profit and loss accounts, balance sheets, and costings came along much later—in the late-seventeenth century.

In part it may be supposed that the late appearance of the 'final accounts' was because before that time investments by several capitalists in ventures with indefinite lives and recurring opportunities of distributing dividends were rare. So long as traders operated alone, or as family groups, or alternatively only collaborated with others for limited-life ventures, there was little danger of any one person acting unfairly by drawing more than his 'fair share' from the enterprise—and hence no immediate pressure for the preparation of statements designed to show the divisible profit.

Technological development itself would in any event have necessitated the income statement even for the sole trader, as time went by. In general, the capital equipment of early capitalists was of robust construction, with very few moving parts of any complexity; technological development was in any case very slow. This meant that the use of plant for long periods produced a need for overhaul and repair, but not for replacement; it would follow that equipment of this sort did not require any depreciation charges to be made in respect of its use, and thus most of the difficulties over the calculation of divisible profit were avoided. This argument is persuasive, but one might still wonder whether early traders may nevertheless have felt some need to safeguard themselves against overdistribution following a reduction in inventories. It may be that this discussion is taking altogether too modern a view of these early traders and manufacturers. At several points in the following chapters consideration will be given to the concept of a 'production boundary,' the point at which a society conventionally chooses to measure its economic activity, and hence arrive at its income. This concept implies that there are some activities which the society sees as 'production' while others are described as 'consumption.' A plant or an animal does not make this distinction, which is quite artificial; neither did man until comparatively recently, it would seem. Whatever the early writers of accounting textbooks may have advised, the merchants who used the technique seem to have felt few qualms about passing 'private items' through their books. As sole traders, or perhaps as 'extended family' traders, there was nothing illegal in mixing public and private affairs. This might lead one to speculate whether early traders thought of their business policy as a separate thing from their private concerns; probably they viewed their whole situation as a need to keep their heads above water. It would follow that their need to maintain inventories would be more akin to the parallel need for a peasant farmer to hold back from eating his seed-corn and breeding stock. Only an absentee proprietor can remain unaware of these needs.[1]

1.2 Uses of accountancy

It was probably the 'control' aspect of book-keeping which appealed to Lenin; a guard against the petty dishonesty and by no means petty incompetence commonly displayed by people undergoing their first experience of organised commerce and industry. No doubt he was right in laying such emphasis on the introduction of this skill in any scheme to accelerate the industrialisation of his country. However, the control aspect of book-keeping is not the sole reason for its central place in the development of a collectivist society. Marx and Engels also referred to this enhanced need for accounting activities wherever market-activities are to be superseded. This places emphasis on the accumulation of costs—physical costs, at least in theory. The prices of most major commodities in the USSR are fixed by law, and are supposed to reflect the 'socially necessary costs of production,' i.e. standard labour costs. The theoretical difficulties of achieving this essentially circular activity are obvious; the bureaucratic apparatus which in practice carries out the operation (as opposed to the elegant theories which are advanced from time to time for its solution) is mercifully obscure. However, it is apparent that once some more or less satisfactory 'prices' have been arrived at for various key commodities, the remainder of the price-system must be arrived at through accounting techniques.[2]

The difference between Sombart's view and that taken by Lenin is central to much of this book; book-keeping is a very useful discipline for controlling the handling of cash and credit within a system of complex trading relationships, but its extension to encompass the extraction of some economic significance beyond the control and calculation of costs from the analysis of the corresponding entries in the nominal ledgers is optional—and more debatable. To the accountant in the Soviet Union, and to his counterpart in many developing countries therefore, his professional activities involve the application of a fairly rigid technique, aimed mainly at security and stewardship matters, plus cost-accumulation. It follows that the job itself tends to confer less status than it does in the West (since no 'Financial Wizards' are likely to be found—at least on the right side of legality). Accounting is essentially seen as a middle-management function, on the lines of production-scheduling, or inventory control, where the criteria for success are likely to be a combination of honesty, accuracy and that subtle mixture of respect for regulations and facility to manipulate them which is the mark of an efficient bureaucrat throughout the world. It is worth noting that in the Soviet Union the planning aspects of industrial accounting are commonly dealt with by what are called 'engineering-economists,' so that the 'accountant' is much more closely confined to financial accounting matters than is the case in Western countries.

To such people, the concept of 'accounting theory' has little meaning. In the Soviet Union, until recently, ideas about 'profit' and 'value' were very much subordinated to those of plan fulfilment, largely in physical terms. Dissatisfaction with the general infantilism which this approach induced in management led to the introduction of a limited profit motive into Soviet industrial and commercial affairs, in the shape of a profit-based bonus system [61] together with the levy of a tax based upon the assets employed by the enterprise. Even now there is no indication from the technical literature of that country of any awareness that there might be more than one interpretation of what the profit of an enterprise or the value of its assets might be. Instead it seems that a number of alternative methods are in use, and the various industrial ministries adopt and enforce whichever method seems best to them. Probably, the Soviet business accountant does not agonise over replacement cost versus historical cost and the like, but follows and interprets fairly detailed instructions and regulations without giving thought to the existence of an underlying theory. From time to time those adversely affected by these interpretations complain of the unfairness of the regulations and alterations may be made in the code, but one probably looks in vain for any suggestion that some over-arching theory should be established for dealing with such matters.

1.3 Sources of accounting theories

As will be observed more than once in the coming chapters, it is never an easy matter to generalise about other societies. It is probably true to say that *accountants* in the USSR are not exposed to anything that Englishmen or Americans would call 'accounting theory' (notwithstanding the fact that so many elementary textbooks bear the title *Teoriya Bukhgalterskogo ucheta*, which means that it talks about double-entry in general rather than how to fill in specific records, etc). However, it has been pointed out to the author that this was not always so; in earlier times *Bukhgalterskii uchet* (accounting) was rarely mentioned apart from *ekonomicheskaya analiz* (economic analysis). It now seems that work in economic analysis has been transferred from the colleges where the accountants are trained to the economics faculties of the universities, where it covers very similar ground to Western 'industrial economics.'

It is not possible to say that pure 'accounting theory' is a product of Western capitalism; probably the concept can be even more narrowly confined to the Anglo-Saxon section thereof! An interesting paper by Scott [99] points out that the Dutch have developed a comprehensive accounting philosophy which does not concern itself with 'generally accepted accounting principles' but bases its claims on what may be a rather tendentious interpretation of managerial economics. This development was largely the work of one man, the late Theodore Limperg, whose particular concern was the integration of accounting, auditing and management consultancy in a fashion which seems odd to the Anglo-American accountant.[3]

Social statistics and accounting are not sciences in their own right, but techniques of measurement and control, and so they can hardly produce theories at all. However, since they have not taken coherent taxonomies from social science, it is clear that the practitioners of accounting in the Anglo-Saxon world have devised their own system of analysis of socio-economic phenomena—and one based on the ready availability of certain sorts of data within an enterprise rather than the needs of any particular theory of social science. This development is in contrast to that described in the Netherlands, or elsewhere in Europe.

Since the other taxonomies only represent partial truth, it does not follow that the accountants' theories are likely to be worse than any others. The adoption of a taxonomy for accounting may depend on social organisation. British and American auditors make a special point of remaining totally independent of their clients. It seems that Dutch firms follow a contrary philosophy, so that they become deeply involved in the management of client enterprises, and indeed they seem to take a degree of personal responsibility for the accounts which goes some way beyond the professional negligence concept of Anglo-American firms. Clearly they would justify this loss of strict independence by claiming that unless one was closely involved in the management processes of the enterprise, it is not possible to make sensible assessments of the various business economic criteria used in the compilation of Dutch accounts. The price of professional independence is often professional ignorance; the price of professional knowledgability may sometimes be professional complicity.

Something similar can be observed in Eastern Europe and the USSR, where accounting theory also seems to be equated with business economics. Apart from the reasons discussed previously, an additional cause may be that there are no regular independent audits or professional auditors. Thus, there is no one who would be likely to construct a purely accounting-based theory. A good deal of the audit-function in the Soviet Union is carried out by the chief accountants of the enterprises, who hold joint appointments from the Ministry of Finance to give them the necessary independence. In addition, other audits are carried out from time to time by special staffs from the industrial ministries themselves, but these are more in the nature of *ad hoc* inspections of particular aspects of the enterprises' operations, and in no sense regular, general audits of their affairs.

The content of these economics-based theories does not concern the argument at this point. It is interesting to observe that they have had virtually no effect on Anglo-American accounting thought, although they represent a substantial literature elsewhere.[4]

1.4 'Budget-financing' and 'self-financing' organisations

There are organisations engaging in involved financial transactions which do not find themselves in any difficulties over the interpretation to be placed on their accounting records. This is where the enterprise is financed by means of an external budget, when it spends, over-spends or under-spends previously approved amounts on previously approved objects, using funds which have been made available centrally for those purposes. This has the effect of reducing the problems of financial control to the same level as the physical budgets of the older Soviet industrial plans, where money is just another resource to be accounted for.[5]

Most enterprises engaged in the supply of goods and services to the public, or for eventual consumption by the public, are organised on a quite contrary basis, even in socialist countries. In the Soviet Union this principle is known as '*khozraschet*' or 'self-financing' and has applied to industrial enterprises since very shortly after the Revolutionary period. In any society this system requires that, given an original input of capital, the enterprise should arrange its affairs so that the sales of its products or services cover the full costs of their manufacture and provision, including the eventual replacement of the plant, governmental taxation and, in the capitalist countries at least, adequate rewards to the suppliers of the original capital. Thus instead of concerning itself with negotiations over the size of its budget with some higher authority, the organisation has to plan internally for its own survival. To the extent that the future is uncertain, and plant and machinery and other assets have to be bought now in the confidence that they can be employed in recovering their costs in a future period, it will always be problematical whether any enterprise is truly succeeding in covering its costs, until it is finally wound up.

Once an enterprise has been made financially self-reliant in this way even a socialist administration is compelled to give the management a fair degree of financial autonomy; it is not possible to require such an organisation to undertake operations which will put it out of business, and directors are likely to be in a dominant position when it comes to negotiations over what is and is not possible within their plant. It is well known that local optimisation is likely to secure sub-optimal benefits for society at large; in theory, therefore, the principle of 'self-financing' must be counterproductive.[6]

Several further difficulties arise, or more correctly become apparent, in these solutions. Many authors have drawn attention to the difficulties of formulating socio-economic problems in a meaningful way, since the data, the constraints and even the objectives which the organisation is *really* trying to achieve are highly elusive. The result, in East and West is: (a) to restrict 'planning' very much to economic, i.e. monetary, transactions and leave the more subtle externalities of the situation to political and legal controls which have the object of preventing positively harmful decisions being enforced; (b) similarly, the complexities of pricing (even in terms of this limited economic formulation of the problem) are delegated to, admittedly imperfect, market mechanisms, or bureaucratic controls, while the need for self-finance of the enterprises is looked to as a control over the long-term matching of costs and sales.

It can be seen that the solution of these difficulties has produced the same mechanism under capitalism and socialism—the independent/*khozraschet* enterprise. One might wonder then why accounting theory has become a matter of interest to capitalists but not to socialists. Probably the heart of the reason is that while *khozraschet* enterprises are expected to finance themselves, they are not specifically required to grow or even to perpetuate themselves. In the West a company retains its own depreciation provisions and accumulated profits; in the Soviet Union these items are actually paid over to the State Bank. If the Soviet enterprise wants to replace an asset it has to get the proposal written into the plan before it can get the necessary finance, since this needs an allocation of funds from the Bank just as if the proposal was for an extension of the activity. This means that the Soviet accountant and his director have no need to worry over whether the depreciation provisions are adequate or the work-in-progress is properly valued, in case this may lead to an excessive distribution of dividends which will endanger future growth and solvency. If they can meet the *current* demands of the State, the provision of future finance is someone else's problem.

In section 1.1 it was observed that historically the technique of book-keeping developed as a control system (and perhaps a system for the accumulation of costs), rather than as a device for making some sort of 'model' of the economic activity of the enterprises that used it. Moreover, the last paragraph goes on to suggest that in systems where individual enterprises are not required to use their own judgement about their future financial viability, there is much less need for concern over precise definitions of 'profit' and 'value' as they appear in the accounting records. As a result their managers do not concern themselves with any variation of accounting theory. It should be pointed out that this concern with future viability is not to be found at all levels within the capitalist organisation; departments *within* such enterprises[7] are financed entirely by budget. Even where 'divisionalisation' confers a large degree of commercial autonomy on large sections of a single enterprise, the very largest expenditures, usually on plant, are still financed in this way, although the division's trading activities are likely to be self-financed. It follows that classical accounting theory can apply only at those levels of aggregation of organisation at which total self-finance is practised.

1.5 Classical accounting theory (basic assumptions)

It may be helpful at this point to attempt a very brief summary of 'Anglo-American accounting theory.' This is not easy, since the problems are always discussed against an existing body of *practice* which largely antedates and certainly totally ignores the work of the theorists. The more usual approach[8] is an attempt to find a series of postulates and axioms, akin to those underlying Euclidean geometry, which would justify current practice and at the same time provide some basis for identifying aberrant interpretations. By definition, 'axioms' are incapable of proof: moreover, they do not have to produce results which accord *in all respects* with observed fact to be useful devices for developing scientific theory. As such they take on many of the attributes of cultural belief, as will be demonstrated in Chapter 4. Also, the axiomatic approach is essentially 'formalistic' (in the sense discussed in Chapter 3), in that it proceeds by deduction from first principles, rather than adopt the 'substantivist' methods of induction from observation. As Hendriksen[8] observes, the theories are usually somewhat eclectic, in that they are prepared to modify the product of pure reasoning to accommodate practice, but the basis seems to lie in axiomatic formalism.

One of the most comprehensive schemata of axioms has been provided by Mattessich. This list of nineteen axioms is divided by that author into ten 'basic assumptions' and a further nine 'secondary' assumptions which provide surrogates for various specific empirical hypotheses which can be entertained as seems most fitting to the matter in hand [79, pp 32–45]:

Basic Assumptions

> 1 Monetary values. There exists *a set of additive values*, expressed in a monetary unit . . .

Mattessich clearly confines 'accounting' to monetary values. The reason for restricting the subject in this way is to provide additive values; in turn, this implies an attempt to maximise some one, single, goal. This is a very strong assumption, which is present in macro-accounting (National Income Accounting) as well as in micro-accounting. One may suppose that all human systems of value are multi-dimensional and multi-goal (see Chapter 4), but it may be that (basically irrational) selection of a single dimension and a single goal (whatever it may be) is a powerful incentive towards the *manipulation* of one's environment.

> 2 Time intervals. There exists *a set of elementary* (*or minimal*), *additive time intervals* . . .

Again, this division of time is quite artificial. As Mattessich points out in the course of a footnote, '*It has the advantage of emphasising from the very outset the discreteness* (*or discontinuity*) *of the time function with which accountants operate.*' Differential calculus plays no part in the accountant's work, which of course antedates its development. The sense of time is very much a part of the cultural pattern of any people, and many cross-cultural problems arise from this: this assumption also may be very strong, for some cultures.

> 3 Structure. There exists a structured set of classes . . . reflecting significant categories of an entity (for the latter see Basic Assumption 9).

The 'classes' are of course the account-heads, and the 'structured set' is therefore the *chart of accounts*. It is important to realise that the construction of these sets is an exercise in taxonomy; both the selection of the phenomena to be recorded and the aspect of them which is to be measured is a matter of deliberate *choice*. We shall see that this choice is likely to be influenced by the 'model' that is held about how the system as a whole operates. A complex model will encompass many more variables (and so need many more classes) than a simple one; a complex (but imperfect) model is not necessarily more reliable than a more simple version of no greater authenticity.

> 4 Duality. For all *accounting transactions* it is true that a value is assigned to a three-dimensional concept . . . consisting of two accounts and a time instance (date).

This is probably the most limiting of the assumptions made about accounting. The only aspects of a transaction that are to be recorded are the direct flows from (say) creditor to goods supplied or from cash to creditor. The inevitability of second-order effects, or externalities, flowing from almost any direct transaction is ignored. The decision to make or not to make the original flow occur is in the hands of the manager or proprietor, but once set in motion, the secondary effects follow; this means that accounting is limited to providing a listing of decisions taken rather than of the results achieved.

It might also be noted that the *khozraschet* self-financing enterprise, by definition, is restricted to a particularly narrow approach to duality, and can take no account of second-order effects, that do not find expression in physical flows of cash.

> 5 Aggregation. Every *balance* assigns a (monetary) value . . . to . . . the pertinent account and the above-stated period which starts with the accounting period.

All aggregation invites the user to consider as homogeneous a number of items which are probably in fact disparate in several respects. Thus, if one says a particular machine shop has a capacity for 10 000 hours of work, and some particular item takes fifteen minutes to machine, the implication is that an output of 40 000 of these items could be achieved. In reality, some of the machine-capacity may be unsuited to the job. On the other hand, too low a level of disaggregation may disguise the fact that some jobs could be carried out by a wide range of machine-tools. . . .

Also, the device of a 'balance' assumes that the final net position is the only one of importance; perhaps this follows naturally from the assumption of duality, and the decision to ignore secondary externality effects. Clearly, the primary flows may often be netted in this way without doing violence to common-sense, but this will rarely be the case for *all* the second-order results. A very important example of this problem will be discussed in the next chapter, on macro-accounting, where it will be demonstrated that the relative sizes of the factor-payments involved in the production of a similar final product is not likely to be a neutral matter.

> 6 Economic objects. There exists *a set of economic objects*, whose values and physical properties are subject to change. . . . Economic objects may be either real or financial objects.

These comprise commodities (including services), claims (to property and money) and ownership rights. Accounting is seen as the process of valuing these objects and recording their changes in value over time. In the very general terms in which this axiom is phrased, it is probably unexceptionable. However, it does make the assumption that value is in some way attached to objects (including claims), rather than to income-bearing 'projects.' This means that it is contrary to the spirit of discounted cash flow methods of capital appraisal, for example. In fact, the human mind seems very resistant to the concept of wealth divorced from objects.[9]

Another problem would arise if one *were* to read into the axiom any suggestion that the 'commodities,' 'the claims' and the 'ownership rights' should in some way represent a 'balanced' system where all the commodites not subject to outside claims were necessarily the object of some ownership right. This would exclude from consideration objects that were for common enjoyment by the community at large; one might create an artificial *entity* (see Assumption 9) for this purpose, but this would be a travesty of reality in most cases.

> 7 Inequity of monetary claims. There exists a custom to enter *debts* with the understanding to *redeem them in legal tender at face value*. . . .

Mattessich himself points out that this assumption could equally well be included in the later 'surrogate' assumptions, since it hypothesises a certain pattern of debtor-behaviour, which is pretty general, but probably did not always exist and might cease to exist. Perhaps it earns its place in the first basic series, because it leads automatically to a concept of a necessity of meeting one's debts as they fall due—or *solvency*. This has been shown to be the *basic* duty laid upon the self-financing enterprise.

> 8 Economic agents. There exists *a set of economic agents* who set specific goals to an accounting system, command resources, and make plans and decisions with regard to economic actions.
> (a) Economic agents (shortly: agents) are natural persons engaged in the economic activities (actions) of producing, owning, managing, storing, transferring, lending, borrowing, and consuming economic objects. An economic agent cannot be owned.
> (b) Agents may be classified (into different groups such as owners, managers, employees, customers, suppliers, etc). . . .

This axiom, as defined, seems unexceptionable, since it clearly covers all the 'collaborators' that the 'Behavioural Theory of the Firm' sees as cooperating to make up an enterprise. Perhaps one should also include certain 'involuntary' collaborators, whose plight will be discussed in Chapter 5; those who have to suffer the negative outputs of the firm—its pollution, the accidents caused by its products, the waste materials, etc.

> 9 Entities. There exists *a set of entities* setting the frame for economic actions.

The entity is seen as some social institution or unit from whose point of view accounts can be prepared. This is an essentially 'Protestant' concept (in Tawney's sense); firstly because the entity is seen as being required to order its own affairs to its best advantage as against the world outside. As is pointed out in note 8, and when discussing Assumption 4 (duality), it may be that this concept follows on from the traditional concentration of attention on first-order effects only.[10] Secondly, it assumes that there will be little difficulty in identifying the dominant entity whose point of view must prevail. Many devices permit people to trade with themselves in various guises.[11] Clearly, 'economic agents' can come together in some very tenuous circumstances, and require accounts to be prepared (for control purposes and to show divisions of profit) where no question of a dominant entity can be said to exist.

Finally, it may be that many entities seem reasonable subdivisions of agents provided that the assumption of duality is also observed, and only direct transactions are taken into account. In Chapter 5, and subsequently, it will become apparent that the inclusion of externalities can often strain the credibility of the conventional entity structure.

> 10 Economic transactions. There exists *a set of empirical phenomena* called *economic transactions*. . . .
> (a) Economic transactions are relations arising out of the actions of producing, holding, transferring, lending, and consuming economic objects. . . .

Again, provided that one overlooks the emphasis on *economic* matters and otherwise defines the phenomena to include externalities this assumption seems unexceptionable.

1.6 Classical accounting theory (surrogate assumptions)

> 11 Valuation. There exists a set of hypotheses determining the value assigned to an accounting transaction.

Mattessich now turns to the surrogate assumptions, which enable the accountant to employ one of a number of hypotheses, as seems most appropriate to the circumstances. As for valuation, Chambers has summarised [27, p 43] the main techniques employed as follows:

> *Original cost accounting* (OCA): the general basis of asset valuation is the initial purchase price of each asset in possession at balance date.
>
> *Price level accounting* (PLA): the general basis is the original cost modified by application of a general index of changes in prices.

Because of its link with original cost, this system has many of the characteristics of OCA.

Discounted value accounting (DVA): the general basis is the discounted expected net product of each asset. In essence all such values are based on sets of hypotheses about the future, including the primary hypothesis that the firm's operations will remain substantially the same.[12]

Replacement cost accounting (RCA): the general basis is the replacement cost of assets. This entails that replacement is intended and feasible, and is thus akin to DVA in the assumption that the firm's operations will remain substantially the same.

Continuously contemporary accounting (CCA): the general basis is the measure given by prices of assets held as they are evidenced, at balance dates, in the resale markets of those assets.

The traditional preference has been for original cost, with some concessions to price level and replacement cost accounting in extreme circumstances. Professor Chambers' preference is for continuously contemporary accounting; it can be seen that the system which approaches nearest to the theoretical economic concept of profit and value is described here as discounted value accounting.

In Chapter 4 it will be argued that in practice the 'choice' of hypothesis will largely be dictated by the 'values' (in the widest sense) entertained by the society in which the accounts are prepared, reinforced by its peculiar institutions.

12 Realisation. There exists a set of hypotheses, specifying which of the following three mutually exclusive effects are exercised by *a change* (in quantity, value, legal status, etc) *of an entity's economic object(s)*. Such a change either: (1) affects the value assigned to the current income of the entity; or (2) does not affect the owner's equity of this entity (within the specified period); or (3) affects the owner's equity without affecting the current income of the entity.

It will be apparent that although the more traditional approaches to valuation achieve a high degree of isomorphism, they immediately involve themselves in some debatable issues as to the correct allocation of income and expenditure to specific trading periods; for example is a sale 'made' when the order is received, when the goods are sent, or delivered, when the invoice is issued, or when it is paid? Again, one can see that different circumstances and courses of dealing might produce a variety of answers.[13]

> 13 Classification. There exists a set of hypotheses required to establish a chart of accounts.

From this it can be seen that while the *existence* of some *Structure* (Assumption 3) and *Aggregation* (Assumption 5) is basic to any form of accounting, the precise *taxonomy* to be adopted is not unique. . . .

> 14 Data input. There exists a set of hypotheses required to determine the form of data input and the level of aggregation. . . .

> 15 Duration. There exists a set of hypotheses about the expected life of the entity (or entities) under consideration, and the duration of individual accounting periods . . . .

Both these Assumptions refer to matters which will be dictated largely by cultural considerations.

> 16 Extension. There exists a series of hypotheses specifying the empirical conditions under which two or more accounting systems can be consolidated . . . .

Clearly, these hypotheses provide criteria for judging the validity of the various entities or super-entities of the types discussed in note 11 on Assumption 9.

> 17 Materiality. There exists a set of hypotheses (criteria) determining *if and when* an economic transaction of related event is *to be reflected by an accounting transaction.*

Here too, cultural norms of discipline and self-discipline will have an effect over and above the cultural influences which already govern realisation.

> 18 Allocation. There exists a set of hypotheses (determining the

allocation of an entity's economic objects or flows of services *to subentities* and similar categories.

This assumption covers the possibility that the principal set of accounts may be divided *internally* so as to show sectional or sectoral results for purposes of management. The comments on Assumption 9 suggest that the recognition of such subentities is not likely to be uniform across cultural boundaries.

The Report of the Committee on Foundations of Accounting Measurement refers to an additional Assumption which Mattessich has added in the German edition of his book [1, p 44]:

19 ... there is given a specific purpose or need for information which a specific accounting system is to fulfil and the accounting rules to be chosen depend on this purpose or need.

At first glance this seems a useful and practical statement; no accounting can or should exist in a vacuum. On the other hand, Chapter 4 will examine the thesis that an accounting system is just a formal attempt at committing a sort of group consensus to paper. The whole of the content of the accounting system was originally 'in the mind'; it may be that any rules are dictated by the culture of which those minds are a part, rather than any deliberate choice.

It can be seen that these assumptions will accommodate a more sociological (or societal) approach than that traditionally adopted by the users of accounting theory, *provided that the terms are interpreted broadly*. It will be seen in Chapter 3 that the dispute between the 'Formalist' and 'Substantivist' approaches can be resolved similarly, but at a cost of making the basis of economics seem to lie in the blandest of platitudes! The heart of the problem in both areas is probably that we are discussing terms and concepts that are undefined and uninterpreted, and tend to remain so because they lie close to the mainspring of human motivation.[14] Another problem is simply that much of what are usually termed 'accounting principles' and (so enshrined in the official statements of professional bodies) are really attempts to secure a standardised and uniform 'best practice.' This introduces concepts of conservatism and verifiability, which may well be justified as necessary preventatives of fraud and speculation but receive little support from axiomatic theory. Society is saying 'We'd rather be safe than right.'

1.7 Governmental accounting and accounting for funds

It has been suggested in section 1.4 that the device of self-financing enterprises enables trading organisations to be controlled in a semi-automatic fashion; if they can keep solvent they can be assumed to be fulfilling their function. The task of managing such an organisation is comparatively simple where management is not required to plan for its own perpetuation, but more complex when it is necessary to retain funds for depreciation internally. Moreover, this system of self-finance can only work where a transferable benefit is being conferred on individual consumers, who can be charged a price for it that is adequate to secure perpetuation of its supply. There are many benefits that cannot be conferred upon individuals to hold as their private property, and for which they cannot therefore be expected to pay for on an individual contract basis. Public health and security are typical examples.

Perhaps the main feature of capitalist society, certainly of Western capitalist society, has been to multiply the amount and value of benefits which an individual can acquire and hence own or transfer. This may make the essentially non-transferable collective benefits which he obtains as a member of his society much less apparent to him than in less materially affluent societies. In fact, these collective benefits are basic to his enjoyment of the private wealth he is able to acquire. Personal health is difficult to maintain where plague is endemic, as is a comfortable home in a civil war: indeed, the expense and the nature of the precautions needed to maintain them under such circumstances will almost certainly detract from their utility. Nevertheless, the mainspring of the system is supposed to be an urge to maximise one's own collection of transferable benefits. Of course, transferability and ownability are the essential features of the type of values that result in 'prices' and so are capable of being recorded in accounting records; collectively enjoyed benefits have 'utilities' that can only be measured in subjective and debatable terms.

It follows that the provision of collectively enjoyed benefits cannot readily be made the object of a self-financing enterprise, either under capitalism or under socialism. The objectives of self-financed enterprises cannot be more complex than to survive, and perhaps to grow [33, 105]. The provision of collective benefits is a more complex objective, involving political decisions that cannot be controlled by a simple directive to stay solvent. For this reason, the provision of benefits of this type has traditionally been handed over to the 'state,' as a central or local authority, even in countries which otherwise are devoted to the pursuit of private capitalism; occasionally the tasks have devolved on other bodies such as churches or charities, but in every case the provider has been a 'non-profit-making' body, at least in the sense that it is budget-financed.[15]

Because of the impossibility of pricing the services they give, and hence an absence of market mechanism, it makes no sense to require an organism supplying a collective benefit to conduct its affairs in such a way as to generate the funds for its own survival.[16] Its income is in the form of levies rather than sales, so the extraction of this income and its division amongst the various collective service agencies is a matter of politics rather than marketing. The absence of a market means that the limits to the demand for these services are indefinite, so the limit to their provision can only be the amount of the levy which the community is minded to submit to for these purposes. Sometimes the levy will be for some specific purpose such as a 'water rate,' when the community could see this as the collective price it pays for its water supply. More usually however, the levy will be raised for a variety of purposes, and even where the demand notices set out the proposed division of the sums demanded, the community will tend to view this as a levy rather than any sort of price.

Not unnaturally, since the size of the levies depends on the proposed expenditure rather than on a demand, these services will be budget-financed. Budget-finance implies the use of a particular form of accounting record—the fund account; this type of account gives rise to a very different theory of accounting to that normally associated with the self-financing organism. Mikesell and Hays [82, p 713] define a fund as follows:

> An independent fiscal and accounting entity with a self-balancing set of accounts recording cash and/or other resources together with all related liabilities, obligations, reserves, and equities which are

segregated for the purpose of carrying on specific activities or attaining certain objectives in accordance with special regulations restrictions or limitations.

This text also sets out [*op cit*, p 4] the recommendations of the (American) National Committee on Governmental Accounting as to the various types of funds which should be maintained by governmental units:

1 General funds. This category covers the whole range of supporting services which the agency has to supply for its citizens. In here will be found the basic services of the community, such as security and public health, as well as the general administration of the agency. Clearly, the police, the sanitary department and so on will have separate budgets and hence separate funding.

It is worth drawing attention to the parallel problems in the ordinary, self-financing enterprise. The purpose of depreciation is to set up some sort of provision for the maintenance of the plant and other equipment, and this it achieves by artificially restricting the profits available for dividend; in the same way LIFO and base-stock methods of inventory valuation seek to maintain the basic investment of the enterprise. Nevertheless, it is most unusual for the resources accumulated in this way to be set aside within the business, and such funds are commonly used generally for financing the enterprise. This course of dealing can be justified by the fact that plant rarely falls to be replaced all at once, so that funds are continually becoming available in this way for current needs; moreover, the plant is not often specifically replaced by an identical item, so that the provision of the equipment needed to service a different and more technically complex project could very reasonably demand finance beyond any available internal resources.[17]

2 Special funds. Where revenue is designated by law for some specific purpose, it would not be proper to merge the accounting for such items with other items.

3 Capital projects funds. As has been said, there is no implied objective to survive under budget finance; moreover, legislative bodies are only given power to levy taxes for one year at a time, for the most part, and the general funds are not normally considered to be available for the finance of *substantial* capital expenditure. In any case, the rates of levy, by convention, do not vary by large amounts from year to year, and the carrying forward of large balances from year to year is unusual. As a result, major capital works tend to be financed from special funds, which are usually financed by means of loans.

4 Debt service funds. It follows that separate fund accounts will also be created to handle the various loan accounts created in this way. In general, it will be the interest charges, capital repayments and/or sinking-fund contributions necessary to finance the debt service funds, which will be debited to the general funds, rather than any sort of depreciation charge.

5, 6, 7 Trust and agency funds; intragovernmental service funds; special assessment funds. The nature of these funds is largely self-explanatory. Their common feature is that for one reason or another it would not be appropriate to merge them with the other categories.

8 Enterprise funds. These are operated where the public body supplies gas, water, electricity and so on to the public at commercial, which is to say self-financing, rates. Once they have been set up and financed, they will not normally receive any further funds but will be expected to 'survive,' using the same techniques as any other self-financing enterprise.

Groups of accounts. In addition to these eight categories of fund accounts, the NCGA also recognises two types of self-balancing groups of accounts, whose operation is very similar to that of a fund, but which lack some of the essential qualifications of a true 'fund.' These are called the 'general fixed asset group' and the 'general long-term debt group'; they differ in that they do not represent resources to be used for specific purposes. Their use often enables an authority to offer a better spread of securities to the market, and so obtain, overall, a lower cost of capital.

The peculiarities of fund accounting can be summarised in this way:

1 A total dedication to the use of specific resources for specific purposes only. The primary purpose of the accounts is to demonstrate how the resources have been levied and disbursed; in short 'stewardship accounting.'

2 The specification of the resources tends to be as to time as well as to objective; resources are levied and spent in the same year. It follows that considerable importance is attached to the formal budget, which is usually entered into the books of account, contrary to commercial practice, and shows the amounts 'appropriated' to various headings. Actual expenditure is then debited against the budgeted amounts, thus showing a balance of over or underspending to date.

3 In fact, the importance of keeping within the budgets leads to the creating of an intermediate stage of expenditure between 'budget' and 'actual'—the 'encumbrance.' Encumbrances are [82, p 710] 'Obligations in the form of purchase orders, contracts, or salary commitments which are chargeable to an appropriation and for which part of the appropriation is reserved. They cease to be encumbrances when paid or when the actual liability is set up.' The intention is to avoid an impression that a crude surplus of resources over expenditure represents free resources available for additional expenditure.

Fund accounting contains several features that are not readily reconciled with the purposes of a self-financing enterprise, either in a collectivist or capitalistic society. Primarily, the emphasis placed upon the budget implies a rigidity of approach that would make it extremely difficult to take advantage of changed commercial circumstances. It might also seem that the budget makes a virtue out of expenditure up to the limit; when dealing with intangible, non-transferable services, it may be that the only concrete statement that can be made as to the outcome is whether the service was provided as planned. Questions as to whether the service was performed adequately, or whether the service was the optimal means of providing the overall objectives of the community, have a high subjectivity content. However, it should not be assumed that governmental accounting is the sole sufferer from the lack of objectivity. In Chapter 8 it will be argued that the difficulty is due to the lack of accepted models of how society (including commerce and industry) works as a whole; this makes it impossible to be sure of the real significance of any data about social or economic affairs. It follows that one can make very few incontestable statements about the social effects of a firm's operations, for the same reason. To the extent that one accepted the firm's *commercial* objectives as valid, it is probable that meaningful budget revisions could be expected to be made more frequently in a commercial enterprise, and one would also look for greater justification of items of expenditure than the mere fact of its inclusion in a budget.

It might be argued that the need to limit activity to the objectives specified by a Memorandum of Association and the use of budgets, together with a record of orders outstanding, is also a feature of the management of many self-financing enterprises. In part this could be answered by reference to the point made a little earlier—that such enterprises are also budget-financed *internally*, and it is in their internal management where fixed, periodic budgets are used as a means of control. On the other hand, in a rather unjustly neglected book *The Fund Theory of Accounting and its Implications for Financial Reports* [118], Professor Vatter has argued that the ideal theory of accounting for any type of organisation would be to consider it as a fund which had to account for the resources entrusted to it; in his view both the 'entity' and the 'proprietorship' approaches are defective, since the concepts of liabilities as claims against assets import ideas of 'ownership' which inevitably lead on to basically insoluble problems of valuation. He says [*op cit*, p 43]:

> One of the distinctive features of fund accounting is the absence of emphasis upon 'net income' and related notions of 'profit,' 'operating margins' and the like.

Perhaps Professor Vatter is right in not differentiating between budget-financing and self-financing. Attempts to extract values and profit margins from accounting data probably do require assumptions about the future to be made that should not really be made at all without very explicit qualifications. Unfortunately the users of accounts are unwilling to accept these restrictions, but continue to look to their accounts for guidance as to what should be retained in a self-financing enterprise to maintain its capital investment, hence they look for an accounting theory that claims to prevent overdistribution of dividend.[18]

It will be useful to consider an example where a type fund accounting has been used for entirely capitalistic enterprises—the 'double account' system of the early railway and canal companies. Here 'fixed' capital was carefully separated from 'circulating' capital, and depreciation, as opposed to repairs equalisation was not employed. Clearly the major investment, at least in the early days of such enterprises was in the track or canal itself; this type of asset is not replaced in any real sense, but has to be maintained at a reasonably efficient level at all times. Moreover, the financial problems of extending the tracks and so on were clearly of a different order from those of maintaining and perhaps extending the circulating capital.[19]

It may be that the approach to enterprise finance used by collectivist societies could be explained by means of a 'fund theory of accounting.' This would explain why some years' experience of a limited use of the concept of 'profit' had not in fact aroused any noticeable interest in accounting theory; presumably a convinced fund-theorist can look upon profit as a financial phenomenon of limited significance, without importing any of the broader concepts of welfare which Western theorists seem unable to ignore. The lack of emphasis on net income and valuation has been remarked on, and no doubt this is more easily acceptable in the Soviet Union, where fixed prices and the planned usage of the full capacity of plant are the norm.

In conclusion it is necessary to establish how this 'fund theory' relates to the 'Assumptions' of the classical theory. Most of the 'Basic Assumptions' seem to be present in a fairly strong form but clearly 8 (Economic agents) and 9 (Entities) are much modified. The accounts do not attempt to show how any group's interests have been served as against the world outside; its purpose (Surrogate Assumption 19) is purely to demonstrate the receipt and disbursement of funds. As regards the other 'Surrogate Assumptions,' 'Fund Accounting' has a purely neutral approach to valuation (Assumption 11) and concerns itself only with legal disbursement. Of course, the incorporation of budget appropriations and encumbrances represent a more carefully documented approach to realisation (Assumption 12) than is customary in commercial usage.

1.8 Notes

1 Winjum [125], in a paper that provides very ample references and quotations to much of the material being discussed in this section, confirms this view:

> 'Early merchants still had household accounts in their ledgers because it was difficult to separate business and personal activities. Their apprentices lived with them and received a major portion of remuneration in lodgings and board. Thus the business of trading and the business of living were closely associated . . .' [*op cit*, p 349].

In Chapter 4 it will be possible to consider some present-day examples of societies whose assessment of 'welfare' is very direct, and little concerned with distinguishing 'capital' from 'revenue' or even 'business' from 'personal.'

2 In two illuminating footnotes Ijiri [62, pp 41 and 64] points out that the Marxist-Leninist 'labour theory of value' is therefore in complete accord with Western procedures. It takes a 'cost' or 'sacrifice' approach to valuation, rather than a 'benefit' or 'future income' assessment.

3 The societal nature of differences between Dutch and American theory is well illustrated in the following quotation from Scott's paper:

> 'Dutch accounting is likely to remain something of an enigma to American accountants. Yet a coherent picture is beginning to emerge, and there is reason to believe that the replacement value accounting which many think to be the only distinctive characteristic of Dutch accounting is but one manifestation of an impressively different organisation of accounting. The Dutch, by using business economics as a foundation, appear to have developed a cohesive and completely integrated accounting philosophy and structure which is entirely at ease in its business and social environment . . .' [p 316].

The fact that a philosophy is at ease does not guarantee that it is right, but it is probably the case that Dutch accountants benefit from the identification of their theory with at least one of the 'social sciences.' A recent paper by Kosiol (a German writer) also states:

> '(My theory) uses the scientific language of business economics' [69].

Social scientists call themselves 'economists,' social psychologists 'sociologists' and so on, and tend to develop idiosyncratic analyses of the same basic problems according to their own intellectual inclinations. The result is that there is no uniquely accepted taxonomy for the analysis of any social problem. This point is developed further in Chapter 8.

4 Thanks to the reputation of Limperg, and the fame of Phillips NV and its excursion into accounting for changing price levels, something is known of Dutch accounting thought in the Anglo-Saxon world. In fact there are at least two other major sources of independent accounting theory, France and Germany. Their respective influences are probably on these lines:

ANGLO-AMERICAN—*Commonwealth and colonies—ex-colonies*

FRENCH—*Italy—Spain*

DUTCH—*Colonies*

GERMAN { —*Imperial Russia—USSR—East Europe*
—*Turkey*
—*Japan* }

Like most diagrams, this schema is debatable; for example Turkey and Japan certainly exhibit some signs of Anglo-American influence as well. The point is that the German theory is very influential, although its authors' works, e.g. Schmalenbach, Gutenberg, Heinen, Mellerowicz and Kosiol, go virtually unknown in the English speaking world. Schmalenbach has in fact been translated and a recent paper by Kosiol has appeared in the *International Journal of Accounting* [69]. See also the paper by Clapp [69] in the same journal.

5 Even if the budget-financed organisation charges for its services, there is no requirement that these charges should cover the costs of providing them, or equate their value to the recipients. The activities of budget-financed organisations are therefore almost always by way of a subsidy (or tax) on the community at large. Since the security and welfare services of most states are financed largely in this fashion, it is apparent that all societies can countenance situations where the value of the service rendered is not put to the test in the market-place. However, the surpluses and deficits arising from budget-financing have to be met from some source, basically the National Budget; the budget is financed from taxation of various kinds unless it too is allowed to run into unbalance. This book does not propose to deal with monetary economics, so suffice it to say that both surpluses and deficits on national budgets are thought to affect the economic prosperity of the nation in a variety of ways which are not always beneficial. Moreover, because public demand is not being tested for the services rendered (at least in the sense of establishing preferences amongst them), there is a real danger that people will not be given the mixture of benefits that would please them best. Finally, it can be seen that budget finance must involve a substantial and continuing bureaucratic effort in preparing and agreeing the budgets and in the subsequent reporting and auditing of their implementation.

6 Unfortunately, mankind is faced by comparatively few vast, open-ended, dynamic, stochastic and non-linear problems—with only the equipment necessary to resolve self-contained, single period, deterministic and linear problems, because of the large size of the problems encountered in the economic and social fields. Considerable effort has been put into devising schemes to overcome these limitations, both in communist countries and elsewhere. What is needed is a method of pricing that would ensure that by seeking their own interests, i.e. solvency or super-solvency, the individual firms would nevertheless arrive at a decision that would optimise the common interest. The general form of these schemes is that of the decomposition programming problem; a series of sub-problems, plus an overarching master-problem. (See the more general discussion in Chapter 8.)

7 The internal collectivism of the capitalist enterprise suggests that socialist experience in management may throw some light on a variety of problems over the internal management of large-scale enterprises under any political system. Conversely, it can be seen that the problems of the exact significance of the data produced by the accounting systems of socialist enterprises have merely been thrown forward to whatever aggregate organisational level at which financial viability has to be faced. There is no evidence to suggest that aggregation in any way lessens the difficulties inherent in the interpretation of accounting data. These phenomena will be discussed further in section 7.2.

8 An interesting summary of the various (and largely contradictory) approaches to accounting is given by Hendriksen [57].

> '(1) The deductive reasoning and the axiomatic approaches, (2) the inductive approaches, (3) the ethical approach, (4) the use of communication theory, (5) the application of behavioral relationships, (6) emphasis on sociological factors, (7) a macro-economic approach, (8) the pragmatic approach, (9) non-theoretical approaches and (10) a theory of accounts approach. These approaches however are not independent of each other. Generally more than one must be used either explicitly or implicitly in the development

> of accounting principles. The theories developed and discussed in the following chapters (Hendriksen's) are eclectic in nature . . .' [p 3].

Obviously, *this* book proposes to give more weight to the sociological and macro-economic approaches than is usually accorded to them in Anglo-American writing. Hendriksen's comments on those approaches are:

> 'The sociological approach is similar to the behavioral approach in that accounting principles are judged by the resulting effects. But the goal is the broader sociological effect rather than the decisions of the immediate users of the accounting data. It is more of a welfare approach. . . . Examples of a direct application of a sociological approach are difficult to find' [p 12].

He seems to imply that these approaches involve the coercion of the managers to act contrary to their own best interests. Probably it would be more correct to say that the sociological approach is a welfare approach which insists on defining welfare in broader terms than purely economic ones. It can be seen that 'the immediate users of accounting data' are themselves members of society, and so in some danger of kicking themselves when they think they are merely kicking the other fellow. In short, Hendriksen (like other writers on accounting theory) concerns himself with direct flows of cash only, and ignores resulting externalities. Thus he continues:

> 'A macro-economic approach is similar to the behavioral and sociological approaches in that one of the objectives of accounting is to direct the behavior of firms and individuals. However, the objective is directed toward the implementation of specific national economic policies' [p 12].

Clearly this book adopts a macro-approach, rather than an exclusively macro-*economic* one; perhaps one could argue that the approach does not imply 'direction' to any greater extent than the others, unless making obvious the infelicity of a purely micro-economic approach has this effect. It might be noted that Professor Hendriksen finds his examples of these approaches in the United Kingdom and Sweden. The Swedish attempts to smooth trade cycle effects through accounting and taxation regulations are described in detail in a paper by Ameiss [7].

9 The principal objection is simply that the future is uncertain and that the distribution of given events in particular portions of the future is even more so. This implies that the expectation of future benefit (if it exists at all) may be of a much more general and subjective nature than a DCF calculation.

The secondary objections follow from the latter observation. People expect the accounts of an enterprise 'to give a comprehensive history of the relationships and transactions of the firm' [27, p. 44], in other words to achieve a *form* of isomorphism, or one-for-one-correspondence. This means that they are looking for a statement of the value of the enterprise which can be identified with specific assets and liabilities, and a revenue statement which shows profit as the net difference between some clearly defined transactions which can be identified as the 'income' and the 'expenditure' for the period. It follows that some sort of transfers will be needed to transform the assets and liabilities of earlier periods into income and expenditure of later periods, and these transformations are required to be related to some tangible event, such as wear and tear, use in production or sale.

Perhaps the reason for this preference for some isomorphic form of statement lies deeper than a mere dislike of data based upon assessments of an uncertain future; part of this uncertainty lies in the behaviour of those making the forecasts. The achievement of the forecasted results depend on the relevant managers, etc, doing what they currently propose that they will do, as well as on external events beyond their control. As a result, the users of accounts seem to be seeking measures of profit and wealth that are neutral as regards future actions.

10 This limitation of concern lies at the heart of the controversy over the question of the 'entity' and the 'proprietorship' approach to accounting. At first sight this problem appears to be a particularly arid exercise in logic-chopping; should the basic equation of a balance sheet be stated as:

$$\text{Assets} = \text{liabilities} + \text{proprietorship}$$

or as:

$$\text{Proprietorship} = \text{assets} - \text{liabilities?}$$

The former equation suggests that the enterprise is a totally separate entity from its owners. It is seen as a slave who has to account to his master for the assets entrusted to him; it is of no significance to the slave whether his master or his master's creditors have claims on the assets. The second form of the equation identifies the proprietorship with the enterprise, so that increases in assets and liabilities are seen as respectively increasing or decreasing the 'net worth' of the proprietors. One supposes that the entity concept might be more appropriate to the corporate enterprise, while the proprietorship would be better suited to the unincorporated firm. Against this Goldberg [48] for example has pointed out that accounting is in any event concerned with only a fraction of the influences that impinge on a proprietor with respect to his business activities. If this view is accepted, one could say that from a purely economic viewpoint even an unincorporated firm could be indebted to its proprietor just as to anybody else; anything that could adequately be described as 'the proprietorship' would need to be a much more complex concept than the simple, economic net worth of the enterprise. It would seem that the entity approach would accord better with the principle of self-finance or *khozraschet*. Enterprises that operate in this fashion are only required to maintain themselves financially, and no stipulations are included about the maintenance of any other values (say ethical or cultural) except in so far as they are converted into legal claims and liabilities expressed in monetary terms.

It follows that traditional accounting theory concerned itself entirely with the economic aspects of the enterprise, and dealt in historical, or at least in history-based terms. It may be a useful extension to the terminology in this area to refer to 'economic (entity) accounting,' as opposed to '(whole) proprietorship accounting'; the former term being confined to accounting for economic affairs only, while the latter is reserved for such attempts as are made or will be made to include other values.

11 Thus Mueller writes [90, p 80]:

> '. . . the traditional US-based notions of an accounting entity may not be applicable in other countries and may be useless or even misleading in cases of multinational companies of the host-company-oriented type (polycentric) or globally-oriented type (geocentric). Let me cite an example. I am aware of a case where a Japanese company approached a US company with a proposition for a business combination. Investigating the situation, accountants for the US company found that there was virtually no owners' equity outstanding for the company, since nearly all of its financing was in the form of ninety-day demand notes issued by several banks. . . .
>
> 'Now did the banks control the Japanese company, or did the stockholders on the basis of a very minor investment? Similar riddles exist with respect to international petroleum consortiums, German inter-company groups known as "organschaften." . . '

12 It would not be difficult to make a more convincing defence of discounted value accounting than this. Chambers seems to think that it involves discounting back the expected future cash flows which can be attributed directly to the existing plant. In fact, flows cannot be attributed to individual items, but only to investment projects as a whole, including the necessary working capital. Any attempt to allocate these values to tangible assets would be unavoidably based on most dubious premises. The result of using DVA would be a single 'value' of the undertaking which cannot be subdivided, and so would be particularly unsatisfactory from the point of view of 'isomorphism.' In fact, this value would have to include not only the present projects, but also the present value of projects which have not yet commenced. In any case, a project would cut across 'normal' accounting practice in other ways. The replacement of a fixed asset does not necessarily imply the commencement of a new project; a project might well cover more than one life-cycle of its constituent plant, so that the replacement of capital equipment will simply be a negative cash flow, like any other item of 'repairs and renewals.'

13 In turn this has led to the initially rather surprising definition of (accounting) 'objectivity' as being measured by the closeness with which any accountant (of repute?) would assign the same value to the item under discussion, rather than to any inherent rectitude in the data itself. To the extent that this implies that 'a true and fair view' of such matters cannot be more than a modal view for the culture as a whole, the concept accords well enough with the discussion of the place of accounting theory in culture to be found in Chapter 4 of this book.

14 Mattessich himself discusses this problem in another place [80, p 471]:

> 'In accounting, unfortunately, the distinction between interpreted and uninterpreted concepts is even more neglected than that between defined and undefined terms. *Concepts like income, wealth, value and measure are treated as though they were well interpreted concepts*, but at best an interpretation is merely implied, and in the case of scholarly controversies the two opponents often imply different interpretations, usually without realising it.'

15 Governmental control does not guarantee that the service being provided is a collective benefit; the whole of Soviet industry and the 'nationalised industries' of capitalist states provide ordinary transferable benefits, and so run on a self-financing basis. Again, there are activities like medical care, education and communications which may be organised as collective benefits, or made the subject of individual payments in different countries. Finally, there are facilities like public utility services and transport which are the subject of individual metering or fares almost everywhere, but which conceivably *could* be provided as a free good. The real point however, is that whatever may be made the subject of pricing, and hence of a self-financed enterprise, there will always remain some *residue* of security or public health that remains to be serviced on a collective basis.

16 An apparently contrary view is expressed in an interesting paper by Mead [81, p 55] where *he* claims:

> 'Fund accounting is not an irreducible principle of governmental accounting.'

However, Mead is by no means advocating the adoption of self-finance in these areas, but rather the use of common-sense to prevent instances where the mechanics of fund accounting could prevent the pursuit of entirely legitimate objectives. Clearly, it is much easier to associate funds with means than with ends; to talk of 'parks' and 'police,' rather than 'recreation' and 'security.' This must not be taken as a good reason for letting the public baths fall apart while the parks superintendent looks about for something to spend his money on.

17 In any case, it is often felt that the financing of capital equipment should be arranged by means of loan capital, so that the appropriation of cash from depreciation is in fact (more or less) taken care of in servicing the loan repayments. Another aspect of this lack of specificity in the internal funding of enterprises is often encountered in the operation of groups of companies, where the group management simply manipulates inter-group loans between the constituent companies as the need arises; indeed, this is the name of the game. Here is another example of the parallels that Horwitz draws between a Soviet enterprise and a subsidiary in a Western group of companies, since depreciation and even accrued profit are not permitted to remain within the enterprise but are immediately put to use elsewhere. The point seems to be that if there is no *legal* reason for segregating funds to specific purposes, the convenience of using a much larger sum as a resource for numerous small budgets usually decides people against segregation. What is necessary is that (a) there should *be* budgets and they should be adhered to and (b) that the total fund should be adequate to service them. The big difference between the 'general fund' of governmental accounting and the financing arrangements of an enterprise is that the income is less certain for the latter, and the enterprise also has to consider demands in the foreseeable future, without being able to work from year to year as in true fund accounting. Again, if debt-financing is employed, the resemblance between the two types of organisation is strengthened.

18 Boulding provides a further argument in favour of 'keeping it simple' and not interposing too many of the *accountant's* assumptions between the statement and its user:

> 'If accounts are bound to be untruths anyhow, as I have argued, there is much to be said for the simple untruth as against a complicated untruth, for if the untruth is simple, it seems to me that we have a fair chance of knowing what kind of untruth it is. A known untruth is much better than a lie, and provided the accounting rituals are well-known and understood, accounting may be untrue but it is not lies. . . .
>
> 'At present one suspects that a great deal of information is collected and processed which actually is irrelevant to the making of decisions or the taking of any kind of action. . . .
>
> 'Nobody, to my mind, has yet developed an adequate theory of information collection and processing from the point of view of the decision-making process. When this is done, we may find that both accounting and economics may each lose their life in a larger science and a larger process' [21, p 55].

It will be seen in the next chapter that Boulding's approach is the one invariably used towards macro-accounting.

19 The influence of the growth of the railway system upon accounting theory is also remarked by Hendriksen [57, p 40 footnote omitted]:

> 'Until the latter part of the 19th century a wide variety of methods intended to provide for the maintenance of capital was in use both in England and in the United States. Toward the end of this period, the most commonly accepted method among railroad firms in the United States and England was the "replacement" or "renewal" method whereby all replacement expenditures were charged to expense at the date of replacement or renewal; the original cost of the asset was not depreciated.'

It was not until 1923 that the American Interstate Commerce Commission endeavoured to enforce the provision of depreciation, and opposition to the proposal delayed effective implementation as late as 1943. The more recent history of the American railroads has not given grounds for belief that reform of accounting methods can ensure commercial viability. Of course, it may be that considerations of social cost (see Chapters 6 and 7) might have disclosed railroads to be more profitable investments than their stockholders or government were led to believe.

2 Classical Macro-Accounting

2.1 Outline of a system of national accounts

The previous chapter has attempted to say something about classical accounting theory, with especial reference to those aspects of Western social organisation that may have influenced its development. Discussion has so far been limited to enterprise accounting (or micro-accounting), because the theory of accounting has traditionally been discussed exclusively in these terms. This limitation is artificial and unhelpful, and it is probable that a truly defined 'accounting theory' would be equally significant in its influence on so-called 'National (Income) Accounts,' or macro-accounting. Later chapters will be devoted to consideration of these theories as they affect an individual; if one accepts the 'behavioural theory of the firm,' the enterprise is simply a consortium of individuals who are induced to collaborate in certain ways. Since the national accounts are, in effect, the consolidated accounts of all the enterprises (in the widest sense) which are comprised in the nation, it follows that the enterprises are subsets of a larger set which is the nation, whose basic elements are a number of individuals. One might suppose that the accounting theories of the individual, the enterprise and the nation would need to be interdependent, even though the influence of 'group dynamics' prevented them from being a straightforward aggregation.

National income accounting is a large subject, on which a number of excellent texts exist at varying levels of sophistication, e.g. Abraham [4], Powelson [94] and more general works by Beckerman, Edey, Peacock and Cooper. The author would not wish to add to the weight of this material, but the present book is aimed largely at accountants and perhaps sociologists and anthropologists as well, whose training will not often have covered the topic of macro-accounting. National income accounting has not been developed by accountants, nor is it normally taught as part of an accounting course.[1]

The treatment of macro-accounting in this section will therefore be confined to a brief résumé of the topic. Moreover, it will attempt to emphasise the role of accounting theory, and to the latter end, it will be assumed that the national accounts really are drawn up as a consolidation of the micro-accounts of individual enterprises and other organisms. The reason that they are *not* built up in this fashion is that in practice micro-accounts are too numerous, made up to differing dates, inadequately analysed or even not prepared at all, so that the effort of collecting them, analysing them and reconciling them would be too great for the value of the information eventually obtained. Even in the Soviet Union and other countries where standardised accounts are prepared for identical accounting periods, it would seem that the national accounts are still built up in a fairly indirect fashion.[2]

	£	£
SALES		200 000
Less Manufacturing expenses	100 000	
Selling and administrative expenses	40 000	
		140 000
		60 000
Less Taxation		20 000
		40 000
Less Dividends		10 000
Transfer to retained earnings		£30 000

Table 2.1 Company A

Consider then, the summarised profit-and-loss account shown in Table 2.1. The numerous transactions comprised in this summary have been analysed according to their 'function' in the activities of the organisation, or perhaps by their 'nature' only, if a costing system has not been employed. However, the same transactions could be analysed in a third fashion, by reference to the 'status' of the other party involved. The headings for this type of analysis are usually of a fairly broad nature and are called 'sectors'; the 'Producing sector,' the 'Household sector,' the 'Government sector,' plus two more general accounts—'The rest of the world' and 'Savings and investments.' A number of conventions need to be observed here.

1 One of the objectives of the social accounts is to arrive at a figure of National Income, representing the creation of 'wealth' by the community as a whole. This means that the producing sector may not be confined to what is generally recognised as manufacturing and service industry, but may include the wages and salaries of the armed and civil services, the receipt of rents and dividends by private individuals from overseas, while corresponding debits and credits are included as 'sales' or 'wages' to balance the account. This means that the cost of Vietnam was part of the National Income of citizens of the USA, and the cost of military activities in Northern Ireland is added to the income of the United Kingdom in the same way.

Although the matter will be developed at length in the following chapters, it is worthwhile observing that 'wealth' and 'income' can mean different things to different people, as this illustration shows. It is important that not only the National Income accounts but also the underlying micro-accounts should measure what the people concerned are in fact interested in controlling. Thus there have been, in the past, communities that have derived very genuine satisfaction from waging wars, building pyramids and similar costly and *prima facie* unrewarding activity. In the West it is convenient to construct macro-accounts in terms of sales, wages, profits, and the like, because it is assumed that our main interest lies in the consumption of transferable goods although this is not likely to be a universally correct assumption.

2 Because the wealth-producing activities of both the state and private citizens are all included in the producing sectors, it follows that the household and government sectors merely show how the income of particular sectors were under- or overabsorbed in the purchase of consumer goods. The difference represents positive or negative 'savings.'

3 Since the household and government sectors cover only current consumption of 'consumer' goods, the 'capital' transactions are dealt with in the savings and investment account, which therefore shows the current capital investment being made by the nation as a whole. Sometimes these items appear in a 'below the line' section of the appropriate sector account.

4 All dealings with people and organisations who cannot be included in the producing, household or government sectors are put into the rest-of-the-world account, which then shows the overall balance of payment of this particular society as against other societies.

		£		£
Current purchases from other producers		45 000	*Sales*	
			Other producers for current consumption	25 000
'Factor payments' to households	£		Household consumption	50 000
Wages and salaries	40 000		Government consumption	5 000
Rent and interest	10 000		Capital goods	80 000
Dividends	10 000		Exports	40 000
		60 000		
Taxation		20 000		
Corporate savings	£			
Depreciation	14 000			
Retained earnings	30 000			
Changes in inventory	1 000			
		45 000		
Imports		30 000		
		£200 000		£200 000

Table 2.2 Company A

The profit and loss account might look like that shown in Table 2.2 if it were restated in a sectorised form. The next step is to consolidate all these accounts for the whole country. Let us assume that this is a very small nation indeed with only one additional enterprise,

	£		£	£
Current purchases from industrial enterprises	85 000	*Direct taxation*		
		Companies	32 000	
'Factor payments' to households		Individuals	70 000	
				102 000
Wages and salaries	20 000	*Revenue deficit*		3 000
	£105 000			£105 000

Table 2.3 Government Accounts

	£		£
Consumption of goods	100 000	*Factor payments received*	
Taxation	70 000	Wages and salaries	140 000
Savings	10 000	Dividends	20 000
		Rent and interest	
		Home	19 000
		Foreign	1 000
	£180 000		£180 000

Table 2.4 Household Accounts

Sales	*A* £	*B* £	*Govern-ment* £	*House-hold* £	*Total* £
Other producers (including the government) for current consumption	30 000	125 000	—	—	155 000
Household consumption	50 000	50 000	—	—	100 000
Public consumption	—	—	105 000	—	105 000
Capital goods	80 000	10 000	—	—	90 000
Exports	40 000	22 000	—	—	62 000
Net property income from abroad	—	—	—	1 000	1 000
	£200 000	£207 000	£105 000	£1 000	£513 000
Current purchases from other producers	45 000	25 000	85 000	—	155 000
Factor payments					
Wages and salaries	40 000	80 000	20 000	—	140 000
Rent and interest	10 000	9 000	—	—	19 000
Dividends	10 000	10 000	—	—	20 000
Net property income from abroad	—	—	—	1 000	1 000
Taxation of companies	20 000	12 000	—	—	32 000
Corporate savings					
Depreciation	14 000	5 000	—	—	19 000
Retained earnings	30 000	12 000	—	—	42 000
Changes in inventory	+1 000	−6 000	—	—	−5 000
Imports	30 000	60 000	—	—	90 000
	£200 000	£207 000	£105 000	£1 000	£513 000

Table 2.5 Producing Sector Accounts

Company *B*; also the 'government' accounts are very straightforward, and can be summarised in a 'general fund account' as shown in Table 2.3.

If the 'households' did prepare a collective statement of their activities, it would be on the lines of that shown in Table 2.4. The resulting production section would then be as shown in Table 2.5, which also includes some data for Company *B*. The final accounts are then as shown in Table 2.6.

It would be possible to devote considerable time to discussion of the economic analysis which might proceed from this statement, but it need not be pursued here in full, since we are concerned solely with the accounting implications of the system. It is apparent that the activities of the individual company can affect the National Income and other aspects of a nation's economy in a variety of ways:

1 As has been mentioned above, the balance of payments would be a fairly obvious interface between a firm's own accounts and the social accounts. In this example, Company *A* is a net earner of £10 000 in foreign currency, while Company *B* is a net spender of £38 000, the effect is that the rest of the world has increased its holding by £27 000 (after paying dividends to householders of £1000), which is in effect a forced investment in the country.[3]

2 Since the intercompany elements in the transactions are cancelled out, it can be seen that the National Income of this particular country is substantially the factors payments, plus taxation and the corporate savings. To the extent that firms declare dividends, negotiate wages with their employees and sign agreements for the payment of rent and interest, they are able to influence the division of this domestic product not only between savings (and taxation) and factor payments, but also between the different classes of factor payment recipient. The spending patterns of the various recipients are likely to differ; it is a matter of some importance whether any additional money paid to some class of recipient is invested, spent on locally made consumer goods, used as a deposit for a hire-purchase agreement, spent on imported goods, sent home to Ireland, or put in a sock under the bed.

An extreme example of this sort of distinction is commonly met in the developing countries, where expatriate employees from overseas have a different economic behaviour from the indigenous inhabitants;

	Producing sector		*Household sector*		*Government sector*		*Savings and investments*		*Rest of the world*	
	Dr £'000	*Cr* £'000	*Dr* £'000	*Cr* £'000	*Dr* £'000	*Cr* £'000	*Dr* £'000	*Cr* £'000	*Dr* £'000	*Cr* £'000
Wages and Salaries	140			140						
Rent and interest (19+1)	20			20						
Dividends	20			20						
Company taxation	32					32				
Individual taxation			70			70				
Depreciation	19							19		
Retained earnings	42							42		
Changes in inventory	−5						5			
Imports		−90								90
Household consumption		100	100							
Public consumption		105			105					
Capital goods		90					90			
Exports (62+1)		63							63	
Savings by households			10					10		
Dis-savings by government						3		−3		
Deficit on foreign trade								27	27	
	£268	£268	£180	£180	£105	£105	£95	£95	£90	£90

Table 2.6 Final Accounts

in such countries the two classes are usually treated separately in the social accounts, as will be discussed in Chapter 3.

3 These factor payments are also of importance, since they provide the funds with which the household sector is able to consume the goods made available for it. If the factor payments are not adequate for the purpose, either (a) prices fall so that losses are experienced, (b) the household sector has to borrow to pay for them or (c) the producing sector has to make a forced investment in inventory.

4 It follows that firms have some discretion as to whether they increase the *Real* National Income, or merely inflate its monetary value, and the argument can be summarised like this: a firm has to choose between two investment opportunities of identical life and capital cost and *net* annual cash flow. However, the relative cash flows are made up as shown in Table 2.7. If the statement about the capital cost is literally true, and the flows cannot be distinguished on the grounds of the relative risk involved, should the firm be indifferent to which project is chosen?

	Project A	*Project B*
Income		
	£	£
Income	4 000	100 000
Expenditure	2 000	98 000
	£2 000	£2 000

Table 2.7

If the 'expenditure' consists largely of factor payments it is apparent that the affect of the two projects is likely to be very different from a National Income viewpoint.[4] Notice how the savings and investment account received the balancing figures from the household sector, the government sector and the rest of the world account, and how savings therefore equals investment, at least in the Keynesian sense. The national investment of £95 000 [£90 000 in capital goods and £5000 in (net) increases in inventory] is made good by the difference between the corporate saving plus the forced investment from the rest of the world and the deficits on the household and government sectors. Of course, as regards any one enterprise, its 'investments' can be made directly, or indirectly through the banking system.

2.2 Towards a theory of macro-accounting

Is it possible to make any statement of a 'theory of accounting' to cover macro-accounting? The national income accounts do not in practice include a balance sheet, and thus much of the material commonly discussed in micro-theory might seem difficult to apply. In part, the absence of a 'national balance sheet' must be attributable to the fact that if it were drawn up it would have to be inferred indirectly in much the same way as the income account itself; moreover the problems experienced over valuing industrial plant and inventories would be considerably more acute in respect of housing, public works and defence installations. Nevertheless, since the accounts are theoretically built up from commercial accounts and governmental fund accounts, as shown in the previous sections, this must be taken to imply the existence of theoretical balance sheets and supporting asset accounts as well.

The existence of balance-sheet-style material is also inferred by the preparation in some countries of flow-of-funds accounts to support the national income accounts.[5]

Since the national income accounts are in effect consolidated group accounts, they are composed of micro-accounting statements about which people will already have held some sort of theory. Indeed, because the national accounts are a mixture of business accounts, governmental accounts and the household accounts of individual citizens, it is obvious that at a micro-level a variety of different and not necessarily compatible theories may have been entertained regarding their component parts. This suggests that accounting theory is not immutable, but resides in the user rather than being something inherent in the data itself, or even in the form in which the data is presented. It has been observed already that a self-financing enterprise will operate internally as a budget-financed organism; this is the basis for the earlier assertion that yet another theory might apply to the same data at the macro-level.

It is implausible to apply the fund theory directly to the national income accounts, even with the addition of a flow-of-funds account and a putative balance sheet. The national funds are entrusted to a variety of organisations (even in a socialist economy), on a self-financing basis, so it cannot be appropriate to try to visualise these collective accounts as being a record of stewardship. Similarly, the concept of an entity divorced from its owners, *and* the concepts of a proprietorship which is identical with them, seem equally inappropriate.[6]

A more fruitful approach might be to look more carefully at the form in which the accounts themselves are produced. The provisions for depreciation are not appropriations of profit, at least in enterprise accounting; these charges have to be made even if there is not enough income to cover them. However, in the national accounts, 'depreciation' and 'retained earnings' are described as 'corporate savings,' and transferred to the 'savings and investment' section of the accounts. This sector shows how the actual capital formation has been financed by the net savings (including provisions for depreciation) in the various sectors of the national economy. (This is on all four with the 'sources and application' approach to micro-accounting.)

And yet depreciation charges are not neglected in macro-accounting. The various figures required to show the activity of the economy are linked as follows (using data from the previous illustration):

		£
a	Gross domestic product at market prices	267 000
	All net property income from abroad	1 000
b	Gross national product at market prices	268 000
	Less indirect taxes (here nil)	—
c	Gross national product at factor cost	268 000
	Less depreciation	19 000
d	The national income	£249 000

What the national income consists of is said to be the 'value added' to some existing stock by trading and industrial activity of its people; the figure can be re-analysed as follows:

			£
a	Factor payments:	Wages and salaries	140 000
		Rent and interest	20 000
		Dividends	20 000
b	Corporate taxation		32 000
c	Corporate savings: retained earnings		42 000
d	Changes in inventory		−5 000
e	The national income		£249 000

If the National Income figure is taken, rather than one of the gross product figures, is it necessary to assume that the depreciation charges do represent a correct assessment of the cost of using the plant in their manufacture? Perhaps the really notable difference between macro-accounting and micro-accounting lies in this; the mechanics and the underlying assumptions are always made plain in macro-accounting. Also, and probably consequent upon the open construction of the items, macro-accounting attaches none of the implied secondary meanings which tend to complicate micro-accounting. For example, micro-accounting produces figures of 'profit' or 'loss,' which are supposed to be the amount that could be distributed without reduction of capital, or that has been lost from capital. In turn this introduces all the problems of 'valuation.' Even if the fund theory is used, at least for a self-financing enterprise, it is necessary to assume some method of allocation of cost over time which guarantees the future viability of the enterprise.

Perhaps it might be helpful to see *any* micro-accounting theory as consisting of two distinct parts:

1 The ideal of solvency, which in the case of straightforward fund accounting would be simply the provision of adequate resources for the agreed budget(s). The situation is more complicated for the self-financing enterprise, which will either be responsible for the indefinite maintenance of the whole of its capital (which is the usual case), or solely for the maintenance of its working capital (as with the Soviet *khozraschet* enterprise, or a subsidiary of a centrally financed group in the West). In such enterprises, the management will pursue the ideal of solvency by preventing loss of excess cash through the provision of depreciation and the proper valuation of accruals, inventories and so on.

2 This pursuit of solvency is virtually universal, but it must be contrasted with another ideal, that of establishing the success or failure of the enterprise in the pursuit of its other goals. The ideal of solvency is laid upon enterprises by the nature of their organisation, and is invariant, but the ideal of the true measure of achievement will vary according to the values of the people who comprise it, and hence of the society in which the enterprise operates. It is unfortunate that the development of accounting theory lay in Western societies where the measurement of achievement is a monetary profit, which means that the two parts of the theory largely coincide—for us.

It is now necessary to ask whether either of the ideals are present in macro-accounting. It has been shown that national accounts are not greatly concerned with solvency; this is because, traditionally, it has not been necessary to accept a nation's currency at its face value unless its units had some international value of their own, such as gold. Thus currencies can depreciate or appreciate in their external values, so that a nation can always 'meet its liabilities as they fall due,' by depreciating its own currency if need be.

Neither is the need for a generally accepted measure of achievement so pressing at the macro-accounting level. It would seem that although Basic Assumption 7 (Inequality of monetary claims) can be applied to the National Income Accounts, it can only do so in a strictly Pickwickian sense.

One talks of such concepts as 'Gross national product at market prices'; any ambiguities in the figures used represent concrete (and reasonably well-known) problems of defining 'gross national product' or 'market price,' and not at all more abstract questions of whether, if one used the figure in a certain way, one could be sure that the economy would continue in a viable state. Thus 'the National Income' is just 'the gross national product at factor cost, less depreciation provisions' and not a synonym for 'the National *Profit*.' No dividend is paid to citizens on the strength of the National Income Accounts; in fact they have already evaluated their services to the national economy and drawn the benefit thereof, whether as wages and salaries or as rents, dividends or even retained earnings in definitions comprising quite concrete terms. It seems to be possible to describe this as a truly 'neutral theory of accounting.' It should not be imagined that this 'neutrality' implies that macro-accounting cannot be reconciled with the various 'Assumptions' described in Chapter 1.[7]

Reference has just been made to the applicability of Assumption 7; this was said to be 'Pickwickian' because while it is certainly true that 'there exists a customer to enter *debts* with the understanding to *redeem them at their face value*,' national economies have some influence over the real values of debts expressed in their own currencies.

Probably the most elusive assumption is number 9 (Entities) as will be shown; this was also noted with respect to fund accounting in general. Since Vatter has drawn attention to the absence of concern over 'profit' and 'valuation' in the fund theory, it may be that the neutrality consists essentially in the total absence of expectation that accounts mean anything more than they say. It is up to the user to provide his own *interpretation*. An econometrician confirms this, as regards national income data:

> As a constant user of the data contained in the *Survey*, I have learned that I can use them fairly effectively even when I disagree with the definitions procedures and even when the data is quite rough due to inherent difficulties of measurement and source materials, provided that I clearly understand their nature [8, p 2].

It might be asked whether this neutral theory could ever be applied to non-governmental micro-accounts. In one sense this might be done for *any* set of consolidated accounts, even for a holding company and its subsidiaries, since the legal requirements for solvency lies with the individual companies and not with the group as a whole. It could be argued that the group accounts simply report how the holding company and its subsidiaries have severally resolved this problem. The heart of the matter is that it is a legal requirement that the management of the self-financing enterprise is trying to satisfy. The law requires 'reasonability' rather than absolute accuracy when it comes to forecasting the future. If a company is finally unable to pay its creditors in a liquidation, after it has paid out anything at all in dividends to its shareholders during its life it could always be said that, in the event, those dividends should not have been paid.

But companies have indefinite lives and it is hard to make worthwhile forecasts of future activity for as much as two or three years ahead. Thus all that a Western board of directors can do at any point in time is to make reasonable provisions for expected losses and the replacement of fixed and current assets as they see the position at that moment in time. Micro-accounts for self-financing enterprises always carry the implication that reasonable provisions have been made.

2.3 Some conceptual problems of macro-accounting

Reference was made in the previous section to the existence of concrete problems over the ascertainment of the national product, factor prices and so on. Since they arise largely from the need to infer data indirectly, while the theoretical analysis used here implies their direct compilation from micro-accounts, it is not necessary to discuss them except in so far as they would still occur even if the micro-accounts actually existed. Readers are referred to the work of Stuvel [110], Beckerman [*op cit*] and the United Nations [115] for detailed discussions of the practical difficulties. Those which need specific examination in this chapter are:

1 Productive activity. The sectorisation of the national accounts seems to imply that it is possible to distinguish productive activity from simple transfers of wealth from one person or organisation to another, or 'transfer payments.' Payment to an old-age pensioner is simply a transfer of spending power from the working population to a retired member, and does not increase the national income in any way. On the other hand, payment for service, say to a waiter, or for that matter to a ballet dancer, is rather more debatable. Do their services really represent an increase in the national wealth, or are they just redistributions of incomes which have arisen from the creation of more tangible items?

Some countries do one thing and some others; in many cases the decision is largely dictated by whether the figures for payments to the particular activity are available. Again, the expenditure of non-profit making bodies such as trade unions and charitable trusts, is commonly treated as a transfer payment.

2 Production boundary. Similar problems arise over whether various items are additions to the national income or just intermediate purchases by other productive units; if they are correctly classified in the latter category, it would be 'double-counting' some part of the national income to include them as finished products in their own right as well. Physical raw materials and components and services purchased by factories are no problem (at least in the West), but some countries argue that things like the services of the police force and the transport industry are really intermediate inputs into final products, since these things are necessary to provide the conditions in which production is possible and materials and workers can be brought to the locations where they are needed. In general, the countries which want to do this will be those who prefer to treat personal services and entertainment as transfers of income, and confine the national income to material outputs as far as they can. One can see that the drawing of the 'boundary' at which goods and services are deemed to be available for personal consumption is a matter of taste, and is likely in the end to be an arbitrary decision. It has been pointed out that a case could be made for confining the national income to exports and capital formation only, since all food, consumer durables, entertainment and everything else consumed by the residents of the country itself are just the necessary inputs to keep them directly or indirectly on the job of making capital goods and services for foreigners. One particular problem might be noted: some countries prefer to include major overhaul of plant and equipment as part of the national income. Although it is the Scandanavian countries rather than the Soviet Union who adopt this treatment, the logic behind it is the point already discussed with respect to Soviet depreciation charges.

Major overhauls could be said to be substitutes for the replacement of the plant, and hence a real contribution to the national wealth.

3 Second-hand goods. Another danger of double-counting the national income arises over the sale of second-hand goods and claims to existing goods such as shares; these items can be bought and sold many times over without directly adding to the national welfare at all. Because these things were counted as income when they were made originally, they cannot be included again, and their sale simply represents a transfer between their old and new owners. Here too a number of exceptions and provisos need to be added, which underline the essential arbitrariness of any definition of 'national income.' It is often recommended that large sales of 'government surplus stores' ought to be added to the national income, notwithstanding that the items have already figured as 'public consumption' in previous years. The reasoning behind this seems to be that this material could be said to have achieved its original, very different and usually much more expensive purpose, and its sale as 'surplus' means that it has been given quite a new use. In any case, additional labour and materials put into the renovation of second-hand materials are additions to the national income, as are any profits made on selling them; this treatment can be justified because these items presumably result in something that was unwanted being put into a condition and position where it is wanted.

4 Residents. One can also have debates over who are the 'nationals' to whom the national income relates. It has been shown how the gross product differs from the domestic product by the inclusion of the net income received or paid abroad; the distinction is between the total produced within the country and the total benefits received by its residents. 'Residence' and 'domicile' are important technical points in the taxation regulations of most countries of the world, and clearly there are many people in any country who are earning money there and even spending some of it there, but are not in fact technically residents in the country.

Again a fairly arbitrary approach is generally employed; usually only cash actually transferred overseas will count as income paid abroad, whatever the legal residence of the recipient may be. Foreign diplomats, international civil servants and occupying forces are interesting and sometimes substantial exceptions.

5 Consumer durables and dwellings. With one exception, the things bought by households are deemed to be consumed immediately. Clearly, this is not in fact the case with motor-vehicles, furniture and the like, but the task of calculating believable depreciation rates for these items is too great to make any other treatment possible. Because of their importance and comparative durability, dwelling-houses are capitalised, whether they are purchased by owner-occupiers or landlords.

6 Imputed income. In the case of tenanted properties the return on these investments appears in future years as the rentals received, so to ensure comparability the *imputed* rents of owner-occupied property are also put through the accounts. Other imputed incomes are sometimes included in the national accounts, for example the domestic services of housewives, or the home-brewing of beer, etc.

7 Pricing. The need for comparability will give rise to a host of difficulties over pricing. Hire-purchase trading, co-operative store dividends, discount trading and trading stamps, in the end require various 'judgements of Solomon' as to whether the sum in question is a rebate on a nominal price (which should be deducted) or a finance charge, or a dividend or an advertising charge (which should be treated separately but not adjusted on the stated price).

8 Recognition of income. The problems of allocating income to time periods and matching expenditure against it, which are encountered in micro-accounting, have their counterparts in macro-accounting. Generally, income is recognised when the ownership changes, but problems can still arise; the real value of an existing item can change without any change of ownership, and these changes can correctly be included in the national income, it seems.

2.4 Micro-treatment of problem areas in macro-accounting

This brief résumé of the main headings of difficulty in applying quantification to the national income accounts has been included to emphasise the essentially arbitrary nature of many of the rules which are applied in practice. This situation can be contrasted, to some extent, with the way in which parallel problems in micro-accounting are usually resolved. The particular (micro)-accounting theory adopted by the accountant would suggest fairly definite answers to most of these dilemmata. Thus:

1 Problems of defining productive activity receive a clear-cut, if also arbitrary, solution in micro-accounting. Horngren [60, p 24, 2nd edn] says 'If costs can be looked upon as "attaching" or "clinging" to units produced, they are classified as *inventoriable costs*, also commonly called *product costs*. . . . In general the costs of operating the factory—the manufacturing costs—are classified as product costs.' The remaining items (selling expenses and administrative expenses) are treated separately as deductions from the gross profit on the productive activity, so it would seem that conventional cost accounting seeks to draw a line at 'the factory,' and looks on the other overhead expenditure as in some way absorbing the income created therein. This matter will be discussed more than once again in the next chapter, since collectivist societies not only use a similar convention in their micro-accounting, but persist with the distinction, in varying degrees, in the national accounts.

Here it suffices to point out that in the West the micro-treatment differs from the macro-treatment of items of this type, since not only the selling and administration expenses of enterprises, but also the costs of purely administrative agencies are treated as though they created income in their own right.

2 The theoretical treatment of ballet companies and the transport industry is unambiguous, at least in the West, where the concept of a 'service industry' is acceptable. Presumably the distinction referred to in the quotation from Horngren's book continues to apply in such industries, so that the labours of the dancers, dressers and directors are 'product costs,' while the costs of the box-office, publicity and general administration are treated as deductions from an 'operating income.' The distinction between the 'productive activity problem' discussed above, and that of the 'production boundary' is simply that the former is over whether an activity ought to be treated as part of the productive effort of the society (whether it is taken up as an addition to the National Income or not) or merely treated as a transfer of wealth between private householders. The latter distinction accepts 'productive activity' as given, but considers whether to include it as 'income,' or to treat it as an inter-*industry* transfer.

3 Micro-accounting theory would be insensitive to the question of the recycling of second-hand goods. This is primarily because it normally takes no account of the source of the inputs into the production process, so that it does not concern itself with sectorisation either. The treatment of *internal* recycling in micro-accounting is ambivalent; in general normal spoilage is allowed for in the departmental overhead rates, or perhaps allowed for in setting standard usages [60, Chapter XX 2nd edn], so that the re-working of spoiled units and the re-using of scrap will not be grossed up as the sale and repurchase of materials. However, any abnormal waste should, it seems, ideally be treated separately from the product costs altogether.

Moreover, problems can arise where the internal recycle occurs over more than one process, especially where bought-in *and* internally produced scrap are used. From the point of view of the individual process accounts the scrap cannot be taken as an item to be netted against output, and the need for comparability might prevent this from occurring even in the overall manufacturing account.

4 Problems of the identity of collaborators in a particular enterprise do not seem to arise very often in practical micro-accounting. In general it is clear enough who are the shareholders, directors and employees of the firm, and for which activities they are liable to account to it. Perhaps the answer is that if problems arise in this area for an individual firm, it is usually a matter of legal action for restitution, rather than of definition of concepts. From time to time questions do arise over 'private' work carried out by employees, even in their spare time, or the ownership of patents for their inventions. In many cases it is felt that quite apart from the question of whether official time, supplies and so on may be used on such work, the employee could only obtain both his contacts, ideas and expertise through his association with the firm. Ideally, his contract of service (or employment) should make the lines of decision clear. Of course this 'clarity' may be more apparent to the collaborators than to outside observers, as the discussions in note 11 to Chapter 1 points out.[8]

5 The treatment of consumer durables as current consumption will give a curious distortion to the national income, unless one is prepared to accept it implicitly 'as defined.'[9] For the current treatment to be theoretically 'correct,' it would be necessary for the inventory of such items to remain constant in size and composition.

6 Imputed income is a topic that needs to be discussed in the following chapter; by definition, the calculation will be of an arbitrary nature, and yet in some places it can be a large proportion of the total economic income of the people. The nearest micro-accounting controversy would be that over whether nominal charges for rent and interest ought to be included even where the buildings are owned and the capital is supplied through equity. Here also, the difficulty of obtaining really convincing rates for what is usually an hypothetical situation probably leads most accountants to omit such charges in practice, while applauding their inclusion in theory.

7 Similarly, the problems of pricing have attracted occasional interest from accounting theoreticians. The treatment of hire-purchase accounts and credit sales of all kinds can in theory take account of a financing element that should be treated separately from the normal (cash) trading-element. Once again, the extreme difficulty of ascertaining the appropriate rates (especially since the stated 'cash prices' are often inflated to make the 'interest charges' seem more reasonable) usually prevents the more refined solutions being put to much practical use.

8 It must be obvious that none of the approaches to income recognition as listed by Chambers (and quoted in Chapter 1) are likely to be followed by macro-accountants in entirety. Essentially the value will be based on original cost, but considerable efforts are made to take account of price level changes in their interpretation, as will be shown in Chapter 3. What is entirely absent, however, is any element of discounted value accounting or replacement value accounting. The accounts are therefore aggressively isomorphic, as might be expected in any statement that relies for its meaning on the definitions used to construct it.

The fact that very few of these micro-solutions seem to be adopted by the macro-accountants, may give some support to the contention made at the end of the previous section, to the effect that macro-accounting employs a purely neutral accounting theory. The national income accounts can only be used and interpreted and compared by continuous reference to the conventions and regulations used in drawing them up; these regulations are likely to have been dictated by the availability of data in a particular form, or at best by some particular political viewpoint on the value or significance of the item. The fact that macro-accounts rely so heavily upon definitions provides interesting grounds for debate over the desirability or even the possibility of uniformity of treatment. Obviously the United Nations believes this to be necessary [115], but the following chapter will suggest that even if outward conformity were achieved the comparison of inter-temporal and inter-cultural wealth and income remains strictly impossible. This is simply because the significance of an item will vary from culture to culture. This argument can also be applied with good effect to the problems of micro-accounting for an enterprise whose activities are multi-national. The search for uniform accounting standards is almost certainly in vain; a more fruitful approach would be to establish international standards of accounting disclosure, so that a user could see how such a company's affairs might appear under the accounting conventions of its various host-countries.

2.5 Some statistical problems of macro-accounting

A good deal of work, much of it by Morgenstern [88] and also Kuznets [71] has considered the problem of the accuracy of the social accounts. This is not high, even in those countries which are best equipped to handle the statistical operations involved. In fact, the accounts are revised several times, as more satisfactory data become available for the period, but the changes appearing in the revisions do not seem to suggest that they are continually 'homing in' on more and more accurate pictures of the national income. Nor do they suggest any pattern of bias in the various components, so that one could begin to estimate what the final figure might be.[10]

In some ways this should cause no surprise; as we have seen the accounts are prepared indirectly from the national economic statistics, and not from the accounts of the enterprises. It is as if an attempt was made to reconstruct the accounts of, say, Unilever from retail stock-audit service reports, the accounts of their major suppliers and so on. Of course, one would not necessarily be right in assuming that accounts prepared indirectly will be less accurate but rather that the level of reliability will be different. To the extent one suspected that the formal accounts of the constituent enterprises were biased, either because of fraud or incompetence in their preparation, or because some convention used in pricing or recognising the income and expenditure was not acceptable for the macro-accounting purposes, one might prefer an indirect approach, through physical quantities collected elsewhere in the statistical system. Unfortunately, there is no evidence that the physical statistics are particularly accurate.

Morgenstern himself [*op cit*] draws particular attention to some remarkable discrepancies in the statistics for gold shipments, even between major European countries and the USA.[11] This is an alarming error, since the price of gold is controlled, and its purchase, sale and production are the subject of rigorous governmental control almost everywhere; moreover, it is rarely destroyed or scrapped. Similar errors can be observed in mining and oil-production figures and import-export figures in general, all being outwardly unambiguous matters which are subject to considerable governmental surveillance for excise purposes.

However, there is one further aspect of the problem of accuracy in macro-accounting which arises from the inevitability of including some material that is 'imputed' from estimate. Items of this sort are not subject to statistical deviations; these estimates are 'authoritative statements,' which have to be accepted by the system as they stand. They are one of a large number of figures that have to be taken up into both macro-accounting and micro-accounting whose statistical accuracy is absolute, but whose 'reliability,' in the sense of the confidence one feels in their correctness, is not very great. At least, in my view, this concept of reliability differs essentially from that of Bayesian probability, because these authorative statements are of a 'go/no-go' nature. If I say that the value of a year's hunting to a tribesman is say £5, I doubt if the statement is really extendable to saying 'I'm 65 per cent certain it's worth more than £4.50 but only give it a 20 per cent chance of exceeding £5.50,' which might enable the construction of a probability distribution. Similarly, it is hard to conceive any ex-ante or ex-post probability in these figures, since the proceeds of the hunting are never actually sold, if for no other reason that the menu provided is not very attractive to the sort of people who would actually 'be in the market' for their food.

It is assumed that if anything is worth having it must be possible to estimate a price at which it could be sold, which in turn represents the 'worth' which it must hold for the man who retains it. It seems likely that this assumption does not hold true even for quite material goods which are capable of transfer and private ownership, quite apart from aesthetic or spiritual 'benefits,' or communal property which cannot be the subject of private ownership or transfer. It is the value of the goods obtainable in exchange which determines the value of the money, and not vice versa; a man could starve to death with a pocket full of bank-notes if he is marooned amongst a community which has no use for them. It will be necessary to return to this matter at a later stage in the book. Morgenstern [*op cit*] speculates upon why the people seem to feel so great a need to prepare macro-accounting data, whose essential inaccuracy and inadequacy is so obvious. Perhaps Mattessich had the answer when he likened the confidence which people feel in any form of accounts, to the confidence felt by the Russians of 1812 in the blatantly inefficient activity of General Kutuzov;[12] people need some repository of confidence.

The world had a bad fright in 1929–34 from which it has not yet recovered, and Keynesian economics offer an analysis which could, or at least might, give some measure of control over economic affairs. Even if statesmen would admit to it, one suspects that few citizens would care to face the fact that economic affairs are not much more 'under control' than they were under Gladstone, because of the impossibility of obtaining data of sufficient accuracy to judge the trend of economic events.

2.6 Aggregation and accounting theory

This suggests another area in which an image of some situation has an importance of its own which is only very indirectly linked with the reality that underlies it. It has been pointed out that a variety of accounting theories can be applied to the same accounting data at different levels of aggregation, and later chapters will seek to explain this phenomenon in sociological, or rather anthropological terms, as a means whereby the material-value system of individual personalities are linked (and to some degree transformed) by group dynamics. Before turning to this aspect of the problem, it may be useful to attempt a summary of what has been said of 'aggregation' in 'accounting.' A good deal of this material has already been dealt with in Chapter 1, where the topic was the subject of Assumption 5 in Mattessich's schema; there the concern was over the results of adding (and netting) otherwise dissimilar transactions because of the existence of one or two points of similarity.

Another aspect of aggregation is discussed by Ijiri in his *Foundation of Accounting Measurement* [62, p 117]; he points out that:

'The most important and the most basic characteristic of the accounting valuation methods that currently exist is that they are a linear aggregation of quantities—a weighted sum of quantities where the weights are prices.'

In Ijiri's view, the quantities are factual, while the prices, or values, are debatable and may vary with the purpose for which the aggregate is required; in practice we are likely to be left with a 'surrogate,' by which he signifies an approximation of the thing we really want to measure (the principal).

It follows that another difficulty of aggregation is that of finding measures of the probability of the sum of several probabilistic products. Ijiri arrives at what he calls the *linear aggregation coefficients*.[13] This distinction between surrogate and principal is of great importance for macro-accounting, since the Gross National Product is arrived at in currency terms, which rightly or wrongly are compared from year to year and from country to country. The techniques used for estimating 'real income' will be described in Chapter 3; no attempt seems to have been made to calculate linear aggregation coefficients in these cases, no doubt because the variables used are rather obviously interdependent—which makes the exercise remarkably difficult.

Finally one might look at what 'traditional' accounting literature has said about the problems of 'aggregating entities and sub-entities and super-entities.' In part, this was considered by Mattessich under Assumption 18 (Allocation); by and large the conclusion seems to be that it involves no great problem at all, notwithstanding the well-known difficulties and controversies which have always been associated with the preparation of consolidated accounts.

2.7 Notes

1 In fact it was developed by the economists, who very reasonably have always been interested in the measurement of national income, growth and so on; it follows that it is traditionally taught as part of the basic macro-economics course, where it forms a useful introduction to Keynesian and post-Keynesian analysis. This detachment of macro-accounting from the main body of micro-accounting is reinforced by the fact that national accounts are prepared from a variety of national sources of statistics, and not directly from accounting sources. Although the national accounts are prepared in this fashion, it is apparent that the underlying data must have come from accounting records in the first instance, in whatever form they may have been compiled by the governmental statistical services.

2 Even if adequate micro-accounting data did exist, it is unlikely that direct consolidation would, of itself, produce more timely or more accurate national income accounts. It will be seen that only some of the items in a set of micro-accounts are taken up into the national accounts—primarily sales to ultimate consumers, wages, rents and profits. (Purchasing of raw materials, partly finished goods, public utilities and professional services all 'contra-out' against the sales incomes of the organisations that supply them.)

If national accounts were to be prepared by direct means, not only would it be necessary to analyse sales by ultimate consumers, but it is all too likely that the remaining items would fail to cancel out. This discrepancy would be due to a variety of clerical errors, the existence of goods in transit and so on; one might hope that they would prove of a random nature, and hence of no great significance. However, one would either have to find the differences or ignore them; if they were ignored, one could have arrived at some sort of totals for the items without going through the labour of attempting a consolidation, which is what is done at present.

3 One should not be naïve over this; a banana wholesaler is not likely to be a net earner of foreign currency and there would be no point in trying to make him export a few machine-tools as well just to balance his own account. Moreover, there is not necessarily any great virtue in being in exact balance in this respect as a nation, although the ins and outs of this matter would lie in macro-economic theory and hence outside this discussion. Nevertheless, to the extent that there is some desired situation at any one time, its achievement will require that all firms, whether net earners or spenders of foreign currency, must arrive at the appropriate net balance or deficit on average overall.

4 The firm's differentiation between them will depend in turn on the degree of importance it attaches to matters of this sort. The point to notice is that one cannot say that Project *B* must be the 'better' thing to do because it is bound to bring about bigger increases in the Domestic Product. This would be true to the extent that it brought into production some 'factors' which were hitherto unemployed, or displaced other projects which could only produce smaller returns from the same factors. If little more than £2000-worth of unemployed factors of production exist so that other projects have to be displaced, Project *B* can only come about through bidding up the price to be paid for the factors by all projects, maybe without increasing the real income significantly.

5 These accounts are examined at length in Powelson [94]. The flow-of-funds version of the foregoing example is shown in the table (*U* and *S* signify uses and sources):

	PRODUCING		REST OF THE WORLD		HOUSE-HOLDERS		GOVERNMENT	
	U	*S*	*U*	*S*	*U*	*S*	*U*	*S*
A *Items from the 'savings' and 'investment' sector of the National Income Account*								
	£'000	£'000	£'000	£'000	£'000	£'000	£'000	£'000
Corporate savings		61						
Domestic investment:								
Inventories	5							
Capital goods	90							
Personal savings						10		
Government saving								−3
Foreigner's saving				27				

B *Balancing* items needed to articulate and balance the statement*

	£'000	£'000	£'000	£'000	£'000	£'000	£'000	£'000
Government securities					3			3
Currency and deposits			7		−7			
Corporate securities		34	20		14			
	£95	£95	£27	£27	£10	£10	£–	£–

* Although this is not apparent from the National Income Account itself, it is now being assumed that the producing sector financed its investments solely by issue of securities, and the government sector financed its deficit in the same way. £14 000 and £20 000 of the producers' securities were taken up by households and foreigners, respectively. This leaves foreigners holding additional currency, etc, of £7000 while households have reduced their holdings by a similar amount.

These items represent changes in a generally non-existent National Balance Sheet. A recent paper by Most [89] advocates the preparation of such a statement, but wisely draws attention to the difficulties encountered by Goldsmith and Lipsey in this exercise. Of course, the first steps are already being taken; Nancy and Richard Ruggles outline 'The Proposed National Accounts for the United States 1966' in their recent book, mainly in Chapter 7 and in Appendix *C*.

6 This is because the national 'society' comprises a very large number of proprietorships which are all fiercely independent; there is usually no question of the deficits on one man's proprietorship being made good out of the surplus of another, except as may be laid down by law, in bankruptcy or otherwise. In this, the national accounts are much the same as the consolidated accounts of a group of companies. At the same time, it seems very fanciful to think of the national economy as an entity which is reporting to its owners about something that it is legally liable to hand over to them; clearly the proprietors are also the employees and rentiers, who all collaborate in the economic activity in so intimate a way as to make nonsense of the entity approach. However, if one takes the point referred to in the last chapter, that 'proprietorship' (but not 'entity') embraces a much wider scale of values than the purely economic ones, it might seem at first as if national income accounting must be closer to the Entity Theory than to the Proprietorship Theory. Again, however, it must be emphasised that this is not necessarily true of all societies. By and large it may be the case with Western capitalist, developed countries, and these have been the principal producers of macro-accounts. However, to the extent that macro-accounts are used to measure something else than domestic consumption and investment, this cannot be so, and it will be shown that other societies do in fact measure other things. Even so, they will probably fall short of the multi-dimensional idea and they will display only a single (albeit different) dimension of 'wealth.' Possibly some societies could consider all other objectives to be subordinate to one main criterion, at least for a limited period of time.

7 The only work known to the author that specifically deals with the accounting theory of National Accounts is unfortunately in Norwegian. However, its author, Odd Aukrust, has appended an English summary to his book [10], which confirms a general coincidence with the Mattessich Assumptions:

> 'The basic premise upon which the present work is founded is that important aspects of a country's economic activity can be studied by observing those objects which are at the centre of economic activity. Such objects we shall here call economic objects. They can be of two kinds, either real objects (goods and services) or financial objects (claims of all kinds, including money). We assume that a definite value can be assigned to economic objects, so that such objects can be measured. Associated with the objects

are economic transformations (events, processes) of various kinds, which the objects may be subject to. We think of these transformations as being distinguishing characteristics (properties) of the objects, which—together with other characteristics—form a basis for classifying the objects. . . . Among all different types of transformations which economic objects can be subject to, there are only a few that will be of interest to us in what follows. We shall call these types of transformations economic transactions. Transactions can be real transactions or financial transactions. By real transaction we understand the emergence of a real object as the result of a production process, or its cancellation through being put into a production process or go into a final consumption, or the change of ownership of a real object. By financial transaction we understand the emergence of a financial object (claim), or its cancellation, or change of debtor or creditor in respect of it.

'We assume that a date can be given for every transaction, so that we can select for special study those transactions that have taken place in the course of a definite period of time, e.g. one year. Further, all transactions are characterized by their concerning one particular or two particular transactors or economic sectors, and on this basis can be described as intra-sectoral or inter-sectoral respectively. Inter-sectoral transactions are those where there is change of ownership of a real object, or change of debtor or creditor in respect of a financial object. Other transactions are intra-sectoral. Moreover, for the inter-sectoral transactions the distinction between requited and unrequited transactions ("bilateral" and "unilateral" transactions) is of some significance' [10, pp 20–1].

It is then pointed out in the text that one can distinguish between four main types of problems encountered, when attempts are made to draw up national accounts on these lines. These are problems of classification, evaluation, observation and presentation. Chapters III and IV of Aukrust's book contain a more detailed discussion of these four problems taken in turn.

8 A parallel point arises over the treatment of 'associated companies'; these are concerns in which another company holds a very substantial interest (say 20 to 30 per cent) which nevertheless does not give legal control. In fact, a holding of this size will almost always give effective control, while even 10 per cent commonly gives the holding company a very great deal of influence over the associated company's affairs. Best practice suggests that relationships of this sort are not very different from those of a holding company and its subsidiaries.

9 Like most people in Western countries, the writer has spent a large proportion of his income over the years on purchasing and maintaining automobiles. Had the laws relating to motor finance, and the confidence of finance houses in his future earning capacity permitted it (which they did not), it could well be that he would have done better to have purchased one of the less pretentious Rolls Royce vehicles at the outset—and run it to this day. The average durability of consumer durables would very much affect the significance of the national income that contains them.

10 The general state of affairs can be judged from the following extracts from newspapers:

'Revisions to economic statistics are never long out of the news. This is not surprising as economic statistics are, by their nature, subject to frequent revision. It is the price to be paid for getting out first estimates as quickly as possible and for seeking to improve their accuracy as soon as more information becomes available.

'Normally, this does not seriously affect the overall pattern of the figures, but just occasionally circumstances combine to produce a really large revision which may change the economic picture. This inevitably leads to comment—sometimes hostile—about the revision, and although such comment may sometimes be justified, it quite often springs from an incomplete understanding of the nature of statistical estimates.

'Statisticians are as sensitive to criticism as anyone else, and mildly resent suggestions that they can't get their sums right first time. The problem of revision is far more complex than this, and I want to try to clear up some misconceptions and to indicate our current thinking on the subject.

'Most people who follow economic developments are aware that statistics are subject to revision. But occasionally one still comes across someone who directly, or in a letter to the Press, expresses genuine surprise that, for example, our current balance of payments surplus or deficit for a particular year is no longer exactly £549 million, as he had read in a reputable journal only six months before. Indeed political legerdemain might be implied. That may be thought to represent a very unsophisticated level of understanding but it does exist and it provides the natural starting point for a discussion about revision.

'Very few economic statistics can be said to represent the "fact" of the situation in terms of accounting accuracy. We do not have and would not want to have at our disposal a complete record of the transactions of every company in the country or of those of our 55 million fellow citizens. Nor do we necessarily have good sample surveys covering every important aspect of economic activity, though the coverage of our data is being constantly improved. What are produced are the statisticians' best possible estimates of what is happening, or has happened, based upon the information that is available to them at the time.'

An article *Economic statistics: the problems of revision* by C A Moser (Director of the Central Statistical Office), *The Financial Times* (15 October 1971).

An extract from *Labour Weekly* of the same day (under the headline *Scandal of the missing exports*) gives a possible reason for the appearance of the first quotation at that time.

'HM Customs and Excise introduced a new system of recording export shipments this month. To those with short memories this may not seem much to write home about. But in fact it is an event full of significance for the Labour Party, and its lessons deserve to be learnt and remembered.

'Victory for Labour in the last General Election seemed assured until, as George Brown said afterwards, it "slipped through our fingers" in the closing stages of the campaign.

'And if one was asked to pinpoint the moment when Labour's popularity started to crumble, one might well say the Monday of election week—three days before polling day—when the Board of Trade published a surprisingly bad set of trade figures for May, which the Tories seized on to predict another devaluation and a "ten bob pound" if Labour remained in office for another five years.

'The fact which did not emerge till November 1970 is that the trade figures for April and May—which went a long way towards losing Labour the election—were wrong. The Board of Trade was "underrecording" exports and making the balance of payment figures seem worse than they were.

'This was not the first time: through most of the six years of the Labour government there was persistent underrecording of exports by the Board of Trade, and this was an important factor in every sterling crisis in the Labour years.

'Incredibly, the Board of Trade system of recording exports—which was the cause of all this trouble—was only introduced by the Conservatives in 1963, a year before Labour came to power, and soon after the Conservatives came back to power in 1970, they scrapped the system and replaced it with a system similar to that used before 1963.'

The article also included a table setting out the data in question, reproduced below.

THE FIGURES—RIGHT AND WRONG

Month-by-month trade figures in the months running up to the 1970 General Election did not look at all good:

January	+£36M
February	−£8M
March	+£4M
April	−£11M
May	−£31M

But when you allow for the 'under-recording' of exports and spread the costs of Jumbo jets through the year you get:

January	+£49M
February	+£5M
March	+£17M
April	+£2M
May	−£2M

Roy Jenkins's target was a £500 million balance of payments surplus in 1970 (the final figure was £579 million) but the month-by-month forecasts were predicting a much lower surplus because they were based on incorrect information (column 1): on the correct information the forecast would have been over £500 million (column 2).

	Incorrect forecast		*Correct forecast*
January	£960M	January	£1116M
February	£432M	February	£588M
March	£576M	March	£732M
April	£396M	April	£552M
May	£156M	May	£504M

The 'bombshell' trade figures of May 1970, showing a £31 million deficit for the month and forecasting a surplus of only £156 million for the year, were wildly wrong.

11 Here are Morgernstern's data:

STATISTICS OF GOLD MOVEMENT

Test of quarterly gold Statistics (1900, 1907, 1928, 1935)

		Algebraic differences between pairs of countries and a test of their significance*			*Standard deviation of sample mean, σ/√n*
Pairs of countries		*Average differences†* (1)	*Standard deviation‡§* (2)	*n* (3)	(4)
United Kingdom and	I	1 741.7	3 466	12	1 000.55
United States	II	168.5	600	10	189.74
United Kingdom and	I	1 696.6	5 230	12	1 509.77
France	II	727.0	2 302	8	813.88
United Kingdom and	I	−171.5	652	8	230.52
Germany	II	81.6	94	16	23.50
Germany and France	I	−45.1	109	8	38.54
Germany and United States	I	−67.5	83	4	41.50
United States and	I	38.4	2 458	5	1 099.37
France	II	832.4	2 326	7	876.85
United States and	I	97.7	272	13	75.43
Canada	II	303.4	912	14	243.75
Silver					
United Kingdom and	I	−13 810.3	27 959	14	7 556.48
United States	II	−6 426.8	4 854.1	12	1 402.92

* For each pair of countries there are four possible differences for each year of every series. There are four countries and six possible pairs of differences between them. In

addition, the differences between Canada and the United States is introduced; and for silver the difference between the United Kingdom and the United States is examined.

† The series of differences in observations between each pair of countries is divided into two parts:

I The difference between the observations of *A* and *B* with regard to the gold flow from *A* to *B*, i.e. the exports of *A* minus the imports of *B*.

II The difference between the observations of *A* and *B* with regard to the gold flow from *B* to *A*, i.e. the imports of *A* minus the exports of *B*.

‡ Statistics of first country minus those of second. These algebraic differences are then summed and divided by their total number. In some pairs of countries, data are not reported for all years. This diminishes the number of differences to less than 16 (quarterly figures taken for four years) since years for which no data are reported are excluded.

§ The computation of the standard deviation of the sample means is sometimes conventionally restricted to $n \geq 10$. We nevertheless include the values for smaller n since the tendency of the different computations appear to agree in all relevant aspects.

He adds: 'The result of the computations is clearly this: the statistics are so bad that a finer list is not warranted. The standard demonstration of the sample means show this directly. A reasonable interpretation of the situation is that it is impossible to determine what bias exists, which is to say that the reliable and the faulty statistics cannot be identified' [88, p 158].

12 This is the author's favourite quotation from the literature of accounting:

> 'Therefore accounting and its effectiveness can be understood much better from a psychological than from a logical point of view. It may be far-fetched to compare its main function to that which Tolstoy assigned to General Kutuzov in his *War and Peace*, but a certain analogy undoubtedly exists. There, an institution (the Commanding General of the Russian Army) was painted as one whose importance lay in the representation of a stable (but perhaps purely fictitious) authority in the midst of chaos. It would be too dangerous to carry this analogy further but it is notable that this commander, whose actions were not backed by any systematic strategy and whose actions usually defied logical analysis, ultimately carried the victory over the precisely logical and highly strategical war machinery of Napoleon. . . . Napoleon might have won, had it not been for the *belief* of the Russian people in an undefeated—though constantly retreating—army. Likewise the effectiveness of traditional accounting lies not in the preciseness of information to management for maximizing profits or any other entrepreneurial goal, but in its authoritative character' [79, pp 413–14].

13 He adds:

> 'This linear aggregation coefficient is mathematically the same expression as the linear correlation coefficient widely used in statistics. The difference is that the former is defined in a "function space," while the latter is defined in a "data space," the two spaces being the dual of each other' [62, pp 130–1].

3 Macro-Accounting in Non-Capitalist Societies

3.1 National income accounts of developing countries

One might argue that developing countries are not essentially non-capitalist societies. However, it seems fair to assert that any developing country will differ profoundly from a Western industrialised capitalist society, and is unlikely to be able to develop itself without some substantial intervention from its central government. Moreover, there has been a good deal of material published [e.g. 117] about the national accounts of such countries, which refer to special problems over the compilation of such records in areas where statistical skills are scarce and resources limited; it might be wondered whether the problems experienced in this area are any more than aggravated examples of the difficulties experienced elsewhere.

The discussion in the previous chapter has attempted to examine macro-accounting with a view to discovering its underlying accounting theory, if any, and largely overlooked the practical problems of their compilation. To this end, it was assumed that the component micro-accounts in fact existed, so that the macro-accounts were discussed as if they had been built up by techniques akin to the familiar consolidation of groups of micro-accounts. It remains to discuss those problems peculiar to developing countries and would remain even under these conditions.

One such difficulty has already been discussed at some length—'imputed income' will be a large and more than proportionately important part of the total income.[1] Another problem is closely related to this. The reason for the imputed income is the fact that a large part of the population engages in various forms of subsistence activity; this means either that such people engage in very little trade, or such trade as occurs is mostly between a quite limited number of people of a similar type. The excellent monograph on the Hausa economy by Smith [108] describes such activity. In short, the population's economic life is not nearly as closely interconnected as is the case in fully developed economies. It follows that the population will not, from an economic viewpoint, be very homogeneous. Developed societies, even socialist ones, may contain rich and poor citizens, but in developing countries this economic disconnection can produce groups of citizens whose wealth is of quite different orders of magnitude. In section 3.4 something will be said of the difficulties of making meaningful international or intertemporal comparisons of national income. However, where the citizens of a single country at one time are operating in largely separate economic systems, these difficulties of comparison will be found internally.

Often enough these economically super-wealthy inhabitants will be indigenous members of the community, who have been urbanised to a greater or less extent. Another peculiar problem of developing countries is that many of the other more prosperous inhabitants will in fact be expatriates, usually from more developed countries. One obvious result of the presence of substantial bodies of expatriates, is that their patterns of spending are likely to be very different from those of the indigenous people, as indeed are their social needs from those of the community at large. It is not part of the purpose of this book to concern itself with the economic analysis for which macro-accounts might be used, but where diverse and identifiable groups can be found in a community, whose economic standards and behaviour are markedly different, separate data relating to them will be useful. This is commonly provided, but it may be that the existence, side by side, of so many distinct 'societies' can make it almost impossible to arrive at satisfactory measures of the 'real income' of any of them.[2]

A related problem is the nature of the economic and trading relations that are likely to exist between developing countries and more developed partners. Primarily the former will be exporters of raw material and perhaps agricultural products, while the latter will return manufactured products. Again, the economic significance of this situation is not of immediate concern, although it is often profound. However, it might be noted that extractive industries of this type are commonly controlled by the overseas companies which originally discovered and exploited the mineral deposits. Moreover, the labour force tends to be substantially expatriate; since these enterprises commonly import most of their supplies and equipment, they are sometimes said to be 'enclave economies,' which would have very little connection with the indigenous economy at all, except to the extent that royalties and taxation are levied upon these enterprises or their employees. Since further economic development will usually involve the importation of capital goods, the transactions with 'the rest of the world' will have a greater than average importance. In view of the sensitive nature of their relations with the indigenous society, and the fact that the solution to the 'transfer pricing' problem lies in political negotiation rather than economic analysis, it is also customary for these international concerns to be less than forthcoming in disclosing detailed information about their activities.[3]

It is also suggested [e.g. 104] that in these countries the public sector will have greater importance than is usual elsewhere, to the extent that transport, power and even heavy industry may be provided by state enterprise. The point of significance is not, one supposes, whether proprietorship is seen as residing with individuals or with the community at large, rather as to whether the enterprises that result are self-financed or budget-financed. It can be seen that there may not be anything that could be called a 'market' for such goods and services in a developing country; they are provided at largely artificial prices very much as a public service in the hope of stimulating economic development in stagnant areas of the economy. Not only will this mean that public consumption will be a much larger part of the total income than in a developed country, but all the highly debatable points over the significance of this part of the income will have especial relevance here. Does rural electrification contribute directly to the 'wealth' of the inhabitants, or is it to be seen merely as an input into a (hopefully improved) peasant subsistence agriculture?

In short, the national income of a developing country is likely to prove an elusive quantity, only partly because of a lack of technical skill in preparing the macro-accounts in these areas. Apart from simple statistical error, the figures are likely to be highly subjective to the extent they contain substantial elements that are not based on any market system or any other rational pricing system. These elements comprise, as we have seen, (a) the imputed values of subsistence agricultural and other traditional manufacturing activity,

(b) the public consumption and (c) the often rather artificial nature of the trading agreements reached over import and export transactions with developed societies. These conceptual problems really extend beyond the problems of pricing and the imputing values to goods and services whose physical quantities are largely unrecorded, since it is possible to dispute whether some goods or services are benefits at all. A matter commonly discussed in this connection is the so-called illegal activities of the inhabitants—especially prostitution and the illegal brewing and distilling of liquor. In a Western, industrial society these activities will be seen as transfer payments within the household sector, which do not affect the national income in any way. And yet it is apparent that in other societies, the harlot has an accepted social role, so that the exclusion of her services is hardly to be justified on logical, as opposed to practical, grounds. . . . Transcultural problems of this type would become very obvious if any attempt were ever made to reconcile the world's international trade. The cultivation of Indian hemp and opium poppy is an inescapable mainstay of agriculture in certain countries and its sale must be a major part of the foreign currency receipts. As such it must appear, albeit anonymously, in the national income statements of its producers. On the other hand, its importation, distribution and consumption (which constitute the largest part of its final cost) are veiled as criminal activity.

Quotations from Van Arkadie and Frank serve to underline the general problem of the reliability and even the significance of national income accounts:

> The easy answer to those who seek to conduct international or intertemporal comparisons of welfare is to point out the dubious foundations which any such project must rest, even in principle. Nevertheless, it may be that the statistician is not a free agent in this matter, in that willy-nilly his figures will be used for such purposes . . . [117, p 189].

The heart of the matter is that the national income accounting of even a single developing country itself involves both international and intertemporal comparisons. Such countries commonly contain three 'nations,' the expatriates, the indigenous urban population and the indigenous rural population. These subgroups have comparatively limited commercial intercourse; the first two are engaged in modern, monetised, industrial and allegedly 'dynamic' economic activity, while the last pursues a traditional, essentially non-monetary, pre-industrial and allegedly 'stagnant' way of life.[4] Since the development of a traditional way of life is likely to be at best a slow business, it is not surprising that economic policy should, in the end, consist of transferring the population as rapidly as possible from 'traditional' to 'modern' methods. Van Arkadie and Frank also write:

> For example, from the existing estimates of subsistence economic activity in East Africa it is not possible to tell whether the increases in African cash output are at the expense of subsistence production or the result of increased supply of effort or of improved productivity. Similarly, it is not possible to tell whether the movement of labour to the town has resulted in any diminution of subsistence output [*op cit*, p 191].

One might wonder whether it might not be as well for those responsible for economic policy in these areas to find out about these points, before undertaking further drastic upheavals in the lives of their countrymen.

An interesting question must be whether the social or political organisation of the country reflects itself in its national income accounts. The mainstream of macro-accounting reflects the traditions of Western society—the industrial, neo-capitalistic society in which it originated. As has been explained, the accounts are not directly concerned with the ownership of the means of production and distribution, any more than a set of group accounts reflects the legal ownership and liability to charge of the assets which appear upon them. However, such a society is likely to be rather hedonistic; it will not distinguish between material production and services of various non-material kinds, and it will not be interested in any activity apart from that which is finally consumed. The culture will be highly monetised, and goods and services which are not exchanged for money will only be regarded to the extent necessary for purposes of comparison with other, monetary, transactions. It might not be fanciful to suggest that there is an underlying assumption of total interconnection between the citizens through the market system; similarly, the population is perhaps assumed to be homogeneous, to the extent that class and regional differences reflect themselves in aesthetic rather than economic behaviour.

It can be seen that even if these assumptions could be substantially true of a Western, industrialist society, it is not reasonable to apply them to developing nations. Apart from the problems of disconnection and a high degree of reliance on non-monetary activity, one may suppose that these may be communities which, as much by inclination as necessity, place rather less emphasis on 'services' or even 'consumption.' Instead, they may be more interested in other benefits which might be provided, such as social support of various sorts, or even the overall economic level of activity. The succeeding chapters will attempt to describe how other values, and indeed values in general, may be enjoyed, and perhaps incorporated into some kinds of formal account-like statements, but this chapter is concerned only with macro-accounts as they are currently prepared.

These problems of national income accounting in countries with substantial subsistence economies invite comparison with the arguments which have occurred over many years between 'anthroplogical economists' over 'formal' as opposed to 'substantive' economic theory.[5] Essentially this is a debate as to whether generally accepted 'economic theory' is applicable to all human cultures, or whether they apply only to Western-type 'marketing' economies while quite different considerations rule in certain primitive non-marketing societies. Moreover, the main theme of this book is an inquiry into whether accounting theory enjoys universal application, or merely reflects the values of the culture in which it happens to exist.

We shall return to this topic in Chapter 8, when it will be argued that many of these apparent difficulties of analysis proceed from the entirely artificial nature of the division of 'social science' into 'the social sciences.' However, these divisions are the accepted parlance at present, and writers such as Polyani, and Dalton, can therefore argue that 'economic' can be equated with 'materialistic,' and see the adoption of a market-oriented economy as implying a formal 'means-end,' or 'economising' relationship, which can be contrasted with what they suppose to have been less tense, more satisfying relationships in earlier pre-marketing societies.[6]

The formalist economist feels that the use of models and concepts from economic analysis in the study of non-market economies is a useful exercise, which in no way implies the inevitable existence of a market structure of any sort. However, at least one of them rather modifies this reasoned approach, by an unequivocal statement of belief in the non-viability of non-market societies:

> To a large extent, the economic anthropology of the future will be focussed on development—the peasantisation of the primitive and the *proletarianisation* of the peasant . . . —change of revolutionary proportions is ubiquitous; norms, attitudes and behaviours of the Western market economy are rapidly being disseminated throughout the world's culture areas by the many institutions of neo-colonialism [31, p 337].

A comparatively recent addition to the substantial literature on this topic strikes a more balanced note. Kaplan [65] feels that the accusation of romanticism levelled at the substantivists is not well-founded, and they are not so much attempting to revive 'the noble savage,' as to point to the vital importance of 'institutionalised behaviour' [p 233]:

> . . . there is a fundamental methodological difference between the substantivists and the adherents of the basic tenets of formal economics . . . —a difference in terms of whether the greater causal weight is to be placed on individual actors or on institutions [*op cit*, p 234].
>
> . . . if one is willing to grant that 'economising' is a special kind of institutionalised behaviour, then there is no compelling reason why we should submissively follow the economists in defining *the economic problem* as exclusively an allocative problem to be solved by individual economising decisions [*op cit*, p 246].

For the purpose of *this* book, Kaplan's paper provides a most interesting sidelight: he observes that the logical connection of macro-economics and micro-economics is by no means direct. This because the latter is based on a deduced theory of logical decision-making; while the former takes much greater note of empirical observation of institutional behaviour. We have seen a parallel dichotomy between macro-accounting and micro-accounting, where the former requires little support from 'theory' and stands justified in terms of its own definitions, while the latter searches after some ideal of correctness.[7]

3.2 National income accounts of socialist countries

Considerable attention has been given to the national accounts of the Communist Bloc, especially those of the Soviet Union itself. The comparatively cryptic macro-accounts issued by the latter country have been extensively supplemented and reconciled by Becker and others [12] with additional material and estimates. Even so, the comparison of any of these versions with their Western counterparts is extremely difficult, because they seem to be prepared on principles that differ markedly from those commonly employed elsewhere. In part these differences can probably be explained by different facilities for collecting the necessary basic statistical data; since the concern of this work is solely with differences that can be attributed to societal reasons, it will be necessary to eliminate these as quickly as possible. In general, one must suppose that since all means of production and distribution of much consequence are vested in the State, and prepare their accounts on broadly similar lines for the same periods, and since accounts and other statistical data are forwarded at regular intervals, it follows that the Soviet Union will prepare its macro-accounts more directly from this material and rely much less upon indirect sources and imputation than is necessary elsewhere. Although doubt has been expressed as to whether the results were nevertheless any the more accurate, it is probably the case that the official macro-accounts of these countries are more fully articulated than in the West. Further they can be fairly readily broken down into analyses that it would be very hard to reproduce in any country that used indirect sources—although Western economists are rarely given much assistance in carrying out the exercise. Similarly, the Soviet Union and its satellites are not 'market economies' to any great extent, but rely upon a system of administered prices for most goods and services. The details of (and exceptions from) this system are involved, technically interesting and significant, but their main concern here is simply that problems about what prices were used, or what was the effect of any price changes that were in fact authorised, are likely to be less troublesome than in the West. Of course, the absence of a fairly free market to provide updated prices means that the significance of the figures produced is rather reduced, at least as a measure of the level of satisfaction these transactions have produced for the citizens. Despite the continuing interest shown in the Soviet national income statistics, and the undoubted existence of a comprehensive body of instructions about their preparation, there is surprisingly little firm information available on the principles underlying their compilation.[8]

The general consensus of what is known about the principles applied in arriving at the national income is as follows. The basic premise that income originates from and is equal to production is common to both East and West, but a special definition of '*social* production' is employed in the Soviet macro-accounts. This is described as 'the aggregate of consumable material goods produced in the branches of national production' [127]. Almost every word of this statement carries a rather special meaning:

1 The social production is 'consumable,' either immediately or in the immediate future. The domestic capital formation is therefore excluded from this item.

2 The 'goods' are 'material'; as has been mentioned previously, a large measure of more intangible 'service' which satisfies human need is therefore omitted.

3 The production has to take place in 'the branches of national production,' essentially in official state-owned enterprises. In fact 'private enterprise' is by no means forbidden in the USSR, provided it does not involve the employment of labour outside the entrepreneur's immediate family. The output of such enterprises may be quite substantial but clearly they will not be taken into the social production figures (except in the case of agriculture, where private farming, usually in spare time from work on state or collective farms, is too large a proportion of the whole to be ignored). Obviously, housework and other imputed items will be ignored also.

Other differences from Western practice can be noted:

4 Social production is related to only one factor of production, the social labour (in official branches of production) of the people, so that the introduction of such concepts as rent and even depreciation can produce ideological problems in this area.

5 Importance is also attached to what is described as 'the gross social product.' This comprises not only the final social products but also the intermediate products, or 'material input' used in making them. From the convention used in Western countries, this clearly involves an element of double counting, but one can see that the overall turnover of industry may not be without some significance, especially for a nation that places especial value on 'labour' and 'social production' as things to be valued for their own sakes rather than simply as means to other ends. Moreover, there is not much vertical disintegration in Soviet industry, so the inflation would probably be less dramatic than it would be if a similar procedure was followed elsewhere.

6 Obviously, government consumption of the normal sort will be excluded from the social product in the USSR. However, it might seem that this might produce some difficulties in a society where all the major productive resources are owned and operated by the State. The Western reconstructions of Soviet macro-accounts use the following device to separate production activities from administration: the former are assumed to be self-financed while the latter are budget-financed. Even so, there are at least two major production activities which are known to be budget-financed in the Soviet Union. The Repair Tractor Stations (at least until their abolition some years ago) were financed in this way, and clearly are an example of the excursion of the state into 'pump-priming' activity to assist in modernisation, which was noted as a feature of developing economies in general. It seems that industrial project design organisations are also budget-financed, at least in their early stages of development. In an economy where prices are related to socially necessary cost, and in any case the activities enterprises are closely controlled under the annual Promfin-plan, one can see that research and development might be something which it would not be easy to undertake as part of the general overhead operations of a normal enterprise. In fact, these project-design organisations also seem to be the path by which entirely new enterprises (as opposed to geographical offshoots of existing ones) are started up in the USSR.

7 Finally, it follows logically enough that Soviet-macro-accountants will use a different scheme of sectorisation from that encountered elsewhere:

a Socialist production enterprises.
b Non-productive sphere, which includes administration, defence and education, as well as most 'service industries.'
c The population; needless to say, this sector is concerned with the population as consumers only, and does not contain the earnings of private enterprise and so on.

Yanovsky [127] and others from time to time exercise some ingenuity in recasting the national accounts of the United Kingdom and other Western nations in the Soviet form. Not only are there many debatable points of statistics involved in this, but one must doubt the basic utility of translated figures. The Russians are interested in a concept of social production, which means that the object of their macro-accounting is to produce a statistic of the labour-content of particular types of industrial and agricultural production. Their social credo states that this type of production has a significance which goes beyond the value of its output to the eventual domestic consumer. This idea is entirely opaque to Western thought, which looks to its macro-accounts for a statistic of the final value of all production and service activity as it reaches the consumer. It is necessary to accept that this approach is neither superior nor inferior to the Russian approach, but simply that if it were to be adopted in the USSR it would not provide the statistic which its inhabitants seem to feel most appropriate for assessing the state of their economy.

This is *my* diagnosis of the social aims of the USSR as exhibited by their national income accounts. Examination of what the Russians and other East Europeans write about themselves may not reveal so clear a statement; indeed, it may suggest that, to the extent that theory is discussed at all, it may not differ greatly from that held in the West. For example, as has been mentioned earlier the 'labour theory of value' is an unexceptionable expression of the 'sacrifice' (as opposed to the 'income') approach to valuation. However, 'labour' to a Russian may not mean exactly what it means elsewhere; labour is usually 'socially necessary labour,' which clearly has overtones of something akin to 'ideal standard.' Moreover, as had been seen, such 'labour' can only mean labour on collective farms and in officially organised factories as opposed to other forms of labour.

3.3 A further aspect of macro-accounting theory

At the end of the last chapter it was suggested that macro-accounts had an entirely neutral accounting theory, in that the significance of the items they contain cannot be assumed, but depend solely upon the definitions attached to them. The truth of this proposition has been demonstrated by the material in the second section of this chapter; the Russians call their macro-accounts 'national income' accounts (*natsional'ny dokhod*) just as the West does, but uses the phrase in a very different context. What then do the accounts of the developing nations seek to show? By and large, they show the monetised, consumer benefits produced by the modern, urbanised indigenous sector of the population and the expatriates, while saying very little of much consequence about the traditional, rural population. To the extent the purpose of the accounting is to further the growth of these benefits in those sections of the nation, this may be fair enough, but if the government sees any value in the traditional culture of their country the use of these accounts will prove misleading.

It has been suggested that most developing countries have 'collectivist' elements in their policies, to the extent that they will have budget-financed governmental agencies providing service which would be provided by normal self-financing methods in a developed state. One could see that they *might* see some advantages in adopting some of the feature of Soviet macro-accounting, which originated in the attempt by the Soviet government in the period following the Revolution to bring about a massive industrialisation of their country, combined with the collectivisation of agriculture. If these were in fact the aims of another developing nation, it too would do well to discount service industry and administration, and production undertaken outside officially organised enterprises. Since the introduction of more and more of the population to factory-work would be an objective in itself, carrying benefits in socialisation and education, it would be quite reasonable to include statistics of material inputs as well as final output of manufactured goods in the domestic product.[9]

3.4 Problems of the comparison of national income

At the outset it is obvious that comparisons of national income should be avoided as far as possible, as Van Arkadie and Frank suggest. It would seem that one could go no further than the statement that I, as a median citizen of present-day *X*, would or would not feel happier as a median citizen of present-day *Y*, or perhaps as a median citizen of my own country of *X*, as it was some earlier point in history. Even if I could have a really adequate knowledge of what it was to live as a citizen of *Y*, I should have to appreciate that there was no reason to suppose that the feelings of a citizen of *Y* about my own state would be the reciprocal of my own views. Frankel [43] and other economists cited by him have even expressed doubt as to the real meaning which could be attached to even such circumspect comparisons as this. They point out that the proposition implies not only that an Englishman could live as an American, a Swede or a Ghanaian, but that he could do so without his standards and values becoming in any way affected by those of the society in which he was claiming to have immersed himself.

The outward evidence of national income statistics supports these claims that conceptual difficulties rather than measurement problems prevent satisfactory comparisons of welfare. Many nations show national incomes of only \$50–60 per head of the population. Obviously the people of these areas have a poor and precarious existence, with a short expectation of life and continual risk of some natural disaster carrying away a large part of the population by famine and disease. Nevertheless, life goes on, although it is certain that even the most hardy and abstemious could not support life on such an income in the major industrial countries. Frankel very rightly points out that our astonishment at the levels of subsistence in, say, Nigeria, is parochial, since a Nigerian would wonder how a private citizen in the West managed to spend as much as \$3000–4000 on personal consumption.

That is not to say that resolute attempts are not made to compare national income statistics. Quite apart from the foregoing philosophical considerations, the arithmetic of such comparisons is itself less than straightforward. For example it is necessary to make calculations of the changing value of money, so as to deflate or inflate the currency value of the national products. If only one commodity had to be considered, this would not cause any computational problem, but in fact it is always necessary to consider two *collections* of commodities. Since the composition of the commodities in the two collections is not constant, several alternative methods of arriving at the real rate of change can be evolved.

Thus, if a country produced only two commodities, X and Y, the fact that in Year 0 it made $500X$ and $500Y$, while in Year 1 it produced $1000X$ and $200Y$ tells one very little about whether the inhabitants of the country can be considered better or worse off. If the prices ruling in Year 0 were, respectively, £2 and £3, one could do rather better:

	Year 0	*Year 1*
Value of X	£1000	£2000
Value of Y	£1500	£ 600
Value of real product	£2500	£2600

Of course, this procedure expresses the quantities produced in the second year multiplied by the prices of the first year so that one can express the growth ratio as

$$\frac{\Sigma p_0 q_1}{\Sigma p_0 q_0} \quad \text{or} \quad \frac{£2600}{£2500} = 1.04$$

(this is called a Laspeyres quantity index).

The effect is simply to weight the quantities by some factors (prices), which can reasonably be assumed to reflect their relative importance to the people who bought them. Obviously this procedure must contain an element of approximation, since the people did not in fact pay Year 0 prices in Year 1; in part the change in the prices reflects the change in the relative desirability of the products and in part the influence of supply and demand in response to the changing outputs. 'The people' concerned may be a slightly different population

—these are illustrations of the points already made in the opening sections. It follows that it would be equally correct, or perhaps no more incorrect to weight the outputs by the current prices in each case (say £3 and £4):

	Year 0	*Year 1*
'Value' of *X*	£1500	£3000
'Value' of *Y*	£2000	£ 800
	£3500	£3800

The ratio then becomes:

$$\frac{\Sigma p_1 q_1}{\Sigma p_1 q_0} \quad \text{or} \quad \frac{£3800}{£3500} = 1.086$$

(this is a Paasche quantity index).

These procedures both presuppose that all the quantities and prices needed for the computation are known. In fact this will not be the case, so the operation will need to be one of inflating or deflating a value series, using a sample price index of some sort. Designating the base-year as Year 0 and assuming that *X* and *Y* form the 'sample,' one might form a further index for this purpose as follows:

$$\frac{\Sigma p_1 q_1}{\Sigma p_0 q_1} \quad \text{or} \quad \frac{£3800}{£2600} = 1.46$$

(this is called a Paasche price index).[10]

To the extent that this book assumes also that national income accounts are in fact aggregations of micro-accounting statements, it is apparent that this will cover price deflation in those cases. In practice, these accounts are derived less directly, and much more difficulty will be encountered in deflating factor income, savings and so on.

Probably the only remaining aspect of price deflation that needs to be described is the deflation of foreign trade transactions. For a country that has a well-balanced foreign trade operation, or where foreign trade is not a major item, it is possible to use straightforward indices of import or export prices. However, where this is not the case, it is necessary to take account of the 'terms of trade' affecting the country; in the long run a country pays for its imports with the foreign exchange it earns from its exports. The real income from foreign trade is dependent on how import prices move as against export prices. This matter is of great importance to developing countries, where a very limited range of export commodities usually of raw materials or semi-manufactured goods is used to pay for the import of capital goods and manufactured items.[11]

Turning to comparisons between nations, one can see that the type of indices discussed above will be equally effective (no more no less) if they are used to 'deflate' the transactions of one country into the currency of another. The technique is to compare outputs either in terms of the currency of Country *A* or that for Country *B*:

$$\frac{\Sigma p_a q_b}{\Sigma p_a q_a} \quad \text{or} \quad \frac{\Sigma p_b q_b}{\Sigma p_b q_a}$$

where 'Country *A*' is 'Year 0' of the earlier illustration and 'Country *B*' is 'Year 1,' i.e.

$$\frac{2600}{2500} = 1.04 \quad \text{or} \quad \frac{3800}{3500} = 1.086.$$

The weakness of all these indices is simply that p and q are not independent; between two periods in the same country, prices are liable to rise or fall *because* the goods become relatively less or more plentiful. The effect is even more significant in the international field, where not only will the things that are plentiful tend to be cheap, but the things that are plentiful will also tend to be those which have particular significance for that particular society. This means that the value of a country's product will always be more valuable when expressed in the prices of another, than in its own.[12]

So much for the mechanics of the comparison of 'real incomes.' Taken together with the dubious nature of the national income and price series data published by many countries, it is obvious that these comparisons can have only a limited reliability. Even if these problems could be overcome, however, and those conceptual difficulties with which this section opened, there would still remain the argument 'that money won't buy everything.' In short, that no amount of restating of the domestic product will derive the 'domestic *welfare*.'

Many economists feel that an attempt to pursue 'welfare' is likely to lead to sloppy and inconclusive thought; Dr Beckerman puts it:

> However there is all the difference in the world between recognising the theoretical assumptions that have to be made in order to derive welfare propositions from comparisons of output in the national income sense, and making comparisons that are not based on any clearly defined theoretical concept of output at all [13, p 10].

The pamphlet from which this quotation is taken is, of course, a literature survey in this area, at least in part; Beckerman lists a number of fairly reliable exercises in deflating national accounts along the lines just described, and some attempts at international price comparison, with the obvious difficulties of reconciling the nature, utility and quality of the 'basket of goods' necessary for this purpose. He then turns to non-monetary indicators:

> In essence the method is as follows: Bennett [16] takes various non-monetary indicators, such as the number of passenger cars, postal traffic, fuel consumption, school enrolments etc. etc. and for each variable he expresses the ranking for all countries concerned in the form of an index with the highest-ranking country taken as equal to 100 . . . [*op cit*, p 21].

Beckerman rightly observes that Bennett does not provide any real arguments for supposing that this arbitrarily selected and combined series of indices is really meaningful, since no verifiable theoretical model seems to underlie it.[13]

Beckerman's own thesis is that estimates of real income have some tangible significance and there is some relationship between the non-monetary indicators and real income—and hence that given some countries whose real income can be estimated with some accuracy, it is then possible to make a further estimate of real income for other countries on the basis of their non-monetary indicators. Non-monetary indicators will be discussed at some length in Chapters 6 and 7; Chapter 8 contains further examination of the essential meaninglessness of statistics which are produced for political argument, and not as input for some comprehensive model of the problem to be solved. Dr Beckerman's model fulfils this requirement, if you care to believe that real income statistics are a reliable measure of welfare. If you do not, it is necessary to overcome these very real objections which he makes.

3.5 Quality of life and national income

Dr Beckerman seems to be very much a 'formalist' in the sense of the discussion which closed section 1 of this chapter. In his pamphlet [*op cit*] he, probably justly, criticises an attempt to minimise the disparity of real income between Thailand and the West, by the omission of expenditure on heating and warm clothing. While it may be true that the Thais do not need these items they most certainly could use air-conditioning; the fact that they don't ask for it merely means they don't have much hope of getting it. Beckerman points out that there is no real empirical evidence to support the view that individual *needs* of human beings are any less keenly felt in poor countries than in rich ones. So far so good. However, he goes on to assume that the paramount economic drive is the aggregation of these individual needs, and thus he takes little account of the effect of the institutions through which these needs have to make themselves felt.

It is suggested that one can only begin to evaluate the 'welfare' obtainable from an 'income' in the context of the society in which it is spent. Indeed, one probably ought to say rather 'the society in which it is earned and spent,' since the idea of separating the two processes is a purely Western capitalist idea. It is said that of all African peoples, the Kalahari bushmen are the most resistant to any change in their traditional way of life. This is curious, since it seems that they exhibit something of the sort of intelligence and general diligence that would seem to promise them a degree of success in an industrial society. In fact they show a total devotion to hunting; like a squire in eighteenth-century Leicestershire, they feel that every moment and every effort not directed to the chase are wasted. Moreover, it seems to be 'the chase' and not the consumption of the quarry that concerns them, so they are real-life examples of the golf-maniac nation whose national accounting system was described in note 9 of section 3.3.[14]

The arbitrary nature of the production boundary has already been discussed. It might be more correct to say that it is artificial, wherever it is drawn. A plant or an animal collects what it needs from its environment, but one would hardly be able to discuss this activity as two components of production and consumption. People also both consume in order to work and work in order to consume; national income is used as a meter to assess the aspect of the circuitous process that the particular community thinks most important and wishes to develop further. It follows that a 'traditional' culture which does not really separate production from consumption at all will tend to be one that has no desire to 'develop' any aspect of its activities and so 'stagnate'—usually at a fairly low level.

At the same time development will also produce some problems. Most of these difficulties are of a social nature and are fairly fully discussed in works of 'development studies.' They are only of interest here to the extent that they illuminate accounting theory. It may be that there is more to be learned from consideration of Western behaviour as consumers than as producers. The increased production of consumer goods has to find a market, which means that developed nations which nevertheless continue to grow have to be organised so that they can consume increasing amounts of such goods. This is in contrast to other societies where the opportunities for consumption are strangely absent; perhaps the situation could be compared to that of a series of central heating boilers, of varying efficiency, which produce more or less heat per unit of fuel consumed. Traditional cultures are very 'dense' in so far that they are an all-embracing range of personal relationships and set, ritualistic activities, which can fill time very effectively, for those who accept the culture in its own terms.

In fact, they achieve this density by giving their members an established place in society, with a full set of rights and duties attached. In such a society, one cannot advance oneself (in theory) any more than a jackal can become a lion; a viscount is 'expected' in both senses, to live like a lord. Again, in theory, one cannot be ruined by purely economic misfortune. Provided one can continue to fulfil the duties implied by one's position (maintenance of order in one's territory, attendance at the ruler's court, or whatever) a shortage of ready money will not greatly affect one's status. Of course, societies of this type will be economically stagnant, although art and even science can flourish; their standards of social justice are at variance with those of an egalitarian society. One can see that there is no logical connection between an inherited aristocracy and an accepted social order, and plenty of societies exist, and have existed, which have claimed to exalt the status of peasants and workers. Neither does the acceptance of social order guarantee economic backwardness, although there seems to be general agreement that fairly naked self-interest is the most effective spur to the initial steps towards improvement in this area.

A Western consumer-based society has a culture, on the other hand, which is decidedly 'thin.' Preordained activity and interpersonal relationships are considerably reduced, so that assistance and support of all sorts, and even recreation, are not often available except on one's own initiative and by purchase. An interesting example is one which often strikes even a European visitor to the United States; hospitality is usually lavish, but it tends to be more formal and less frequent than its European equivalent. Moreover, much of this entertaining seems to occur through memberships of social organisations (of which a good number seem to exist in that country) rather than from family or chance neighbourhood relationships.

Initially, this might lead one to say that there are concepts which could be described as tangible or transferable 'income,' to which is to be added an essentially non-transferable element of welfare which is contributed by society as a whole. Obviously there will be some difficulties over measuring the latter items in terms comparable to the former; perhaps some societies even have a negative contribution to the welfare of their citizens, in so far as they involve them in real-life Caucus-races, where they find themselves running very fast, just to stand still. It may be that this is a logical approach to assessing the relative welfare of different communities none the less, since the impossibility of surviving in some societies on visible incomes which would suffice well enough in others would seem to require an explanation along these lines, rather than, say, a reliance upon diminishing return alone. The traditional explanation of this phenomenon is in terms of 'comparative deprivation,' which suggests that one's feelings of satisfaction with one's lot depends upon the standard of living of other people with whom one believes oneself to be comparable. This dilemma has been discussed for a long time; the parable of the labourers in the vineyard explains the difference between justice and benevolence, but we are not told whether the man who complained was convinced by the explanation. In fact, this is a basic problem of accounting—can accounting take any notice of 'satisfaction'?

It is well known that the 'threshold of pain' varies from individual to individual, so that some people can catch hold of much hotter plates than others. Perhaps it would not be too fanciful to suppose the existence of a similar continuum of socio-economic pleasure-to-pain. In either case, the reason for the difference will be a complex matter of physical and neurological make-up, reinforced by education and experience. In either case, the fact of the existence of the *difference* will be so personal and internal to the recipient that it could hardly give rise to any sort of accounting statement that would have significance to anyone else. This is primarily because it is hard to see what anyone ought to do about the difference; the fact that I can hold hotter plates than the reader does not imply that I ought to take them out of the oven, since the risk of damage to the tissues (as opposed to the sensibilities) probably does not vary at all. Similarly, there is no evidence that the relative strength of individual desire for wealth and status is any indicator of one's ability to acquire it or administer it; indeed many suppose the contrary to be true. The fact that a whole group, or a whole nation, were more or less susceptible to pain/pleasure sensations than others, on the average, might be more interesting, but scarcely more worthy of inclusion in any accounting statement, for much the same reasons.

However, the fact that 'system' itself contributes to such sensations *is* worthy of record, since something can be done about that. It might be possible to set out a taxonomy of the ways in which society as a whole increases or diminishes the sensations of benefit which its citizens feel:

1 The law or custom may permit other individuals to commit acts of nuisance of one sort or another against their neighbours (this is typically 'pollution' and will be discussed further in Chapter 5). This is a loss of benefit which could be corrected by requiring those responsible to make good the damage.

2 Society also provides communal services for its citizens, which make it possible for them to enjoy their economic incomes. These were discussed in the previous chapter; since they are not capable of individual ownership (if they are, they are just a state subsidy), it is not sensible to attempt to value them or add them to the individual's psychic income, although this is commonly enough done in macro-accounting. It is probably not valuable to attempt to formulate some trade-off between the values of these services to the individual, for the same reason. A multi-dimensional approach through statistics that measure 'quality of life' may be the best that can be hoped for. These will form the usual 'profile' of readings, since it is equally futile to trade off, say, population density and the suicide rate. The possibilities and dangers of this operation will be the subject of the closing chapters of this book.

3 Finally, it seems possible to distinguish a third category of societal contribution, which really measures the 'thermal efficiency' of the society, and so has a claim to be included in any statement of individual or national income. This will involve the construction of an index, which attempts to measure the 'Caucus-race' effect of the society in question; obviously, the selection of variables for an index of this type will be debatable. However, it seems that this debate is a common feature of all index numbers, and it is possible to defend its use on similar grounds to those used to justify the use of (say) the Retail Price Index. That is to say, if the index is constructed consistently, it will give a fairly good guide at least to the *direction* of any change, and perhaps some guide as to the comparative rates in different areas.

What this index is intended to measure is the discontent that the average citizen feels about his share of the national income. Following the idea of 'relative deprivation,' one would expect the index to be some function of the spread of income within the recipient's peer-group. Clearly he will only be interested in the incomes of the people with whom he feels he ought to be compared; for example an expatriate in a developing country will be interested in what other expatriates get, but not much affected by the income of the average member of the indigenous people. To the extent there are several identifiable peer-groups in a society, presumably some weighted average of the relevent indices will give a measure of the overall discontent from this cause.[15] This matter will be examined further in section 20 of Chapter 5.

It might be reasonable to add at least one further component to such indices. Discontent with the status quo is likely to be enhanced as the prospect of changing it increases; it follows that it might be appropriate to include some function of the rate of change in the money-incomes within the group. Presumably when money-incomes change one is all the more incensed because other people in one's group are managing to maintain their differentials. This suggests that the change in money-income should be used here, rather than any increase or decrease in real income which may result.

As described in the foregoing paragraph, it seems that this societal 'contribution' to income is negative. The suggestion is that a society where all members of the same group got the same share of a constant money-income, or perhaps where they were indifferent to the spread of incomes, for some reason, their individual and joint economic incomes could be taken at their face values. There are societies and groups which, to a greater extent than others, make a point of inculcating pride in membership; might not this pride enable members to 'get by' on less real income? Perhaps so, but we are merely discussing an index. There may not be much point in trying to measure super-satisfaction of this sort, unless one found that the spread and rate of change in money-incomes in emerging societies was quite as great as elsewhere, so that the index, as described, in no way reduced the gap between what might be called the 'survival income' of those countries and those of the developed nations. It can be seen that the heavy weight of imputed income in the national accounts of most emerging nations will make the ascertainment of such an index very difficult, in practice.

Finally, it should be emphasised that there is no moral judgement implied in the construction of these societal measures of satisfaction. Obviously it is discontent with the status quo that commonly inspires people to improve things; satisfaction with the status quo will frequently be accompanied by a stoic acceptance of poverty, disease and death as 'the Will of Allah.' However, this dynamic assessment of the value of discontent does imply a confidence that in fact 'something can be done'; as it becomes apparent that the resources of the planet are not infinite, this confidence becomes less self-evidently justified. Viewed as a static phenomeon, relative deprivation simply reduces the value of present income.[16]

3.6 Notes

1 For example:

> 'In the Federation of Rhodesia and Nyasaland this value added by rural households is estimated at £38 million in 1959 or 7½ per cent of the gross domestic product. If in ten years time half of this contribution to the domestic product has ceased to be made by rural households, but is then made on a cash basis, is it reasonable to represent that the gross domestic product at constant prices has been increased, on this account alone, by £19 million?' [Billington, 18, p 11].

In short, this part of the national income is only guessable. A Nigerian expert writes:

> 'Our work has, however, shown us how little is really known of the most important sector of the economy . . . and how difficult it is to make meaningful judgments in this branch of activity. Our data on agricultural output are defective . . .' [Okigbo, 91, p 173].

Neither the size of the 'traditionalist' population nor their productivity are susceptible to rigorous investigation. Even the definitions used will be liable to gross misconstruction:

> 'The major problem is that the rural "household" unit is not identical with the biological unit. "Households" are usually larger than the biological unit, either consisting of several biological units together in an undivided family (e.g. the Muslim people of Northern Nigeria) or consisting of blood-kin alone, with existing biological units split between different households (as in the Aken tribes of West Africa). . . . Budgets have to be recorded on behalf of "housewives" and there is constant danger that misunderstandings will characterize both question and answer in such complex households [Ady, 6, p 53].
>
> 'We must conclude therefore, that with the data available, estimates of domestic production in the rural sector are likely to be very "soft" figures. Does this render national accounts valueless in Africa? The usual aggregates are certainly valueless, at present, for certain purposes: welfare comparisons using *per capita* income, for example, are obviously nonsensical when income estimates themselves are in part derived by multiplying up *per capita* averages of doubtful accuracy by population averages equally subject to error' [Ady, *op cit*, p 55].

2 'Much more serious than the inadequacies of the product or population estimates is the absence of any comprehensive or even relevant price series. . . . In addition to the figures of import and export prices there is also a cost of living index for Europeans in the three principal cities. . . . Finally, there exist index numbers of retail prices for the lower-paid Africans.

'In our view none of these price series is adequate, either separately or in combination, to provide a satisfactory deflation of the money domestic product. . . . It is therefore not possible to construct a useful series of *per capita* real incomes' [Kennedy, Ord and Walker, 66, pp 392–3].

3 Thus Okigbo says:

> 'Having chosen to focus on the gross domestic product, we had to make up our minds on how to treat extra-territorial companies. . . .
>
> 'Such questions arise for two reasons. The first is legal—should such companies be treated as resident producers? . . . The second is a practical accounting problem: it is extremely difficult to obtain estimates of the income of such companies in Nigeria' [Okigbo, *op cit*, p 13].

A Western observer adds:

> 'The identification of domestic subsidiaries and associated companies of foreign parent companies is a formidable task . . . it is virtually impossible for any country in the early stages of economic development of a balance of payments and national income accounts to investigate the ownership of domestic concerns' [Billington, *op cit*, pp 6–7].

4 By definition the traditional culture is not capable of being manipulated in the short-run, although, also in the short run, it must supply the material support of a large section of the population, whatever plans, or hopes, may be entertained for the future. Thus:

> 'It is in the context of national accounts data needed for short-period analysis and forecasting as a base for policy decisions that the importance of subsistence incomes is most obvious. . . . Further, in any case, subsistence outlay is always self-financing.
>
> 'In the short-run the chief variable and income-generating component in the tropical economies of Africa is the value of exports. For each major export a separate sector account is required' [Ady, *op cit*, p 64].

Of course, the real problem is that already discussed at length above; nobody really *knows* the true strength or weakness of the subsistence economy. This means that decisions to modernise these sectors have to proceed from a *belief* that the end result will be an increase in real income.

5 Unhappily, this whole topic is one that invites the adoption of extreme positions. Thus an early writer on 'economic sociology' (in 1939) goes so far as to claim:

> 'Actually, once it is baldly stated, the proposition that there should be more than one body of economic thought is absurd. If modern economic analysis, with its instrumental concepts, cannot cope equally with the Aborigine and the Londoner, not only economic theory but the whole of the social sciences may be considerably discredited. For the phenomena of social science are nothing if not universal. The groups, the behaviour, the fundamental social relationships such as those of kinsmen or neighbours, are qualitatively the same the world over. Wherever we look at Mankind we see motives of accumulation, of competitive display, of obligations towards kinfolk, of religious organisation and political activity: these, and such, make up the body of fact with which social science must deal' [Goodfellow, 50, p 4].

(Note the apparently indifferent use of 'social sciences' and 'social science.')

6 'The substantive meaning of economic derives from man's dependence for his livelihood upon nature and his fellows. It refers to the interaction with his natural environment, insofar as this results in supplying him with the means of material want satisfaction.

'The formal meaning of economic derives from the logical character of the means-end relationship, as apparent in such words as "economical" or "economizing." It refers to a definite situation of choice, namely, that between the different uses of means induced by an insufficiency of means. If we call the rules governing the choice of means the logic of rational action, then we may denote this variant of logic, with an improvised term, as formal economics.

'The two root meanings of economic, the substantive and the formal, have nothing in common. The latter derives from logic, the former from fact' [Polyani, 93, p 162].

It is easy enough to have fun with this sort of material. LeClair demonstrates this through a variety of quotations, and concludes from them that:

> 'In short, economists no longer believe, if they ever did, that human wants are confined in market societies, to material wants, nor do they *assume* this to be true of any society.

Nor is the assumption of the materialistic nature of human wants a necessary element in contemporary economic theory' [73, p 1181].

Similarly, Cook seizes upon the rather empurpled prose of the substantivists to observe:

'The present critique is intended to supplement its pedecessors by elaborating the thesis that the substantivists' intransigency concerning the cross-cultural applicability of formal economic theory is a by-product of a romantic ideology rooted in an antipathy toward the "market economy" and an idealization of the "primitive" ' [31, pp 323–4].

7 In the next chapter an attempt is made to explain the accounting function in terms of the systems of values obtaining in the underlying culture. The position to be adopted there seems to have a lot in common with that taken by Kaplan (and perhaps the other substantivists) over economic theory; even micro-accounts only have a real significance in the terms of the institutions amongst which they are drawn. Certainly no romanticism can be imputed to this approach to accounting: a Hausa trader is at least as interested in 'the last penny' as his Leadenhall Street counterpart—and rather more murderous if he suspects theft or default.

8 One might point out that even where very senior officials have written papers on these topics, it is impossible to be sure (so guarded is their language) whether they are describing existing practice, or merely speculating about their own personal preferences in the matter. Moreover, a rather similar doubt surrounds much of the Soviet material on a vexed question of economic planning itself—the 'inter-branch balances'; in fact a Western reader can encounter the same dilemma in almost any Western journal in which industrial operational research specialists discuss 'model-building.' Are the models operational or merely speculative? Even if they operate, how much affect do they have on strategic decisions?

Probably these apparent contradictions can be resolved by a realisation (a) that Russians enjoy a very wide freedom for academic discussion, but (b) that academic thought has only the most limited influence on the bureaucratic procedures of Soviet planning and industrial management. Becker's comment upon one aspect of this dichotomy has already been mentioned. The split between 'official' macro-economic policy and 'official' economic thought is much less noticable; a cynic might wonder if the difference is that the official adoption of a policy in the USSR more certainly implies its practical application than is the case in the West.

9 Alternatively, a nation might have quite other objectives than either consumer-satisfaction or industrialisation, and in such case it would find either principle of national accounting equally misinforming. The 'national income' which should be forthcoming from its macro-accounts should be a measure of a nation's performance in what it conceives to be its central purpose. A fanciful example might serve to illustrate a number of points. Suppose a nation had as its objective the promotion of the game of golf amongst its inhabitants; its 'national income' would then need to be conceived in terms of professionals' salaries, the costs of the manufacture and sale of golf balls, clubs and other equipment, the maintenance of greens and fairways, construction of new courses, the provision of prizes and so on. This particular national income would seem quite useless to non-golfing nations. There would be little point in reconstructing the macro-accounts of the Soviet union or anywhere else on the same lines. No doubt the production of food would be undertaken, perhaps as a public service, on the grounds that a satisfactory diet was an essential prerequisite of good golf. One could argue that it is not in itself a very sensible objective, and that even if it could be achieved, this would only be at the cost of great physical suffering to the population; nevertheless, this is a subjective judgement of the system, and a nation of convinced golf-fiends would claim that the sacrifices were all worth the end to be obtained.

10 It can be seen that the great difference between the Paasche and the Laspeyres indices is that the latter is much easier to compile, since its weights remain unchanged for as long as the original base year is considered to remain relevant. Presumably countries that do not have highly developed statistical services will select as base years those in which major price surveys were conducted. Clearly, the continual updating of the weights might be preferred, but as in other matters of this sort, it is not often thought that the improvement in the performance of these indices as a result would justify the increased costs of the service.

11 The amount lost or gained in this way can be calculated by comparing the deflated export figure using an export index with the same item deflated using an import index:

$$\frac{E}{P_m} - \frac{E}{P_e}$$

where P_m and P_e are the respective import and export indices, and E is the current value of the exports. This can be rewritten to isolate the terms of trade more explicitly:

$$\frac{E}{P_e}\left(\frac{P_e}{P_m} - 1\right)$$

For example, when

$$P_m = 1.05,\ P_e = 1.01 \quad \text{and} \quad E = \text{£2M, then}$$

$$\text{Loss} = 1\,905\,000 - 1\,908\,000 = \text{£}3000$$

or

$$\frac{\text{£2M}}{1.01}\left(\frac{1.01}{1.05} - 1\right) = 1\,908\,000\,(-0.038) = -72\,504$$

12 It should cause no surprise that two distinctly different 'answers' can be provided to questions regarding intertemporal and international comparisons. However, it is sometimes suggested that the two results can be averaged, as follows, by taking the geometric mean of the Laspeyres and Paasche indices, and so arrive at the 'Fisher Ideal Index Number':

$$F = \sqrt{(Q_L Q_P)}\sqrt{(P_L P_P)}.$$

13 His own suggested modification for this is interesting:

'... the essence of the Modified Non-monetary Indicator Method is to find the best statistical relationship, on the basis of inter-country comparisons for such countries for which independent estimates of relative real income or consumption levels exist, between relative real income or consumption and selected non-monetary indicators for which data are readily available in most countries, and use these statistical relationships to predict, from data on the non-monetary indicators, the relative real income levels of all countries for which such data exist' [13, p 27].

14 'Fundamental to the various forms of Bushmen life is a stone-age culture, a highly-developed pictorial art, a poverty of material resources, a highly skilled hunting technique, absence of agriculture and domestic animals and the possession of rudimentary dwellings' [56, p 340].

Other examples could be quoted of societies that never ask 'given these resources, what ought we to do for the best?' They do what they do, within a very limited number of variants, what custom dictates they should do. Clearly such societies are not likely to distinguish the essential nature of 'work' from 'domestic life,' or either from 'religion';

all comprise ritual performances which one observes because one is a member of the society, and persistent non-performance will lead to ostracism. Such societies find it easier to adopt new rituals than a scientific approach to life. A fairly recent study (Miner [83]) considered the bush-clearing which is a feature of life in Northern areas of Nigeria. This was started as an entirely successful public-health measure by the colonial administration in the late 1930's, to eliminate the tsetse-fly which communicated sleeping-sickness to man. The point of the study was to show the resistance of traditional ideas to change, because the Hausa people do not believe that sleeping-sickness is caused by the tsetse-fly at all, even after thirty years as the subjects of an entirely successful campaign to eliminate the disease:

> 'The village headmen were asked why they cleared the streams every year. The common denominator of the reponses was that the slashing was carried out because they were forced to do it. A quarter of the headmen had literally no idea why the work was done. All of the others, however, stated that clearing the bush eliminated tsetse-fly.
>
> 'Half of those who mentioned flies, also stated that they transmitted sleeping-sickness. But . . . they saw this as the British explanation, but held firmly to their old belief that sleeping-sickness was caused by spirits' (*op cit*, p 167.)

However, for our purposes, the important point illustrated by the study is not so much the imperviousness of the Hausa ideas about sleeping-sickness, as the ease with which they seem to have incorporated another ritual into their lives. No-one seems to ask "If it doesn't do anything for sleeping-sickness, and the British have gone—why do other Nigerians make us waste our time?'

15 An unpublished doctoral thesis by Seef [103] makes a real attempt to devise a measure of organisational 'effectiveness,' although it (very reasonably!) contents itself with measuring satisfaction, as opposed to seeking its cause in comparative deprivation and so on. His index combines:

A weighting, supplied by the subjects, of the relative importance to them of various aspects of the performance of an organisation; they are asked to supply this weight which assuming performance of the organisation was entirely satisfactory in regard to this aspect.

The degree of satisfaction which they do in fact find in that aspect of its performance.

The degree of 'involvement' of the subject in the affairs of the organisation.

Since the weights described in (a) and (b) are supplied by the subjects themselves, this index avoids much of the criticism which could be levelled at the work of Bennett [*op cit*] or of Beckerman himself [*op cit*]. At the same time one must query how the 'aspects' to be weighted are selected in the first instance, and how the measure of 'degree of involvement' manages to comprise the managing director and the cleaner, the non-executive director and the stock holder. Once again one is returned to the dilemma to be discussed in the last three chapters—no comprehensive taxonomy of welfare can be devised in the absence of an agreed *comprehensive* model of how the society works.

16 It seems unlikely that this concept of comparative deprivation will represent an accurate picture of what goes on in the mind of a human recipient of both visible and societal income. Frankel seems to justify his claim that any attempt to express 'psychic income' (essentially welfare) in terms of accounting concepts requires the assumption of a form of mental book-keeping which is inherently unlikely. To the extent that accounting income is not a summary of the effects of transactions, it involves calculations of 'depreciation' of durable goods over time, the valuation of inventories and the like. He inquires:

> 'When a person has paid for his education or physical training does he keep a mental capital account showing this investment, and does he credit himself with the "income"

> it yields him in the future? If he does indeed conduct these peculiar operations in his mind, it would be most interesting to know when they occur—hourly, weekly or annually' [43, p 100].

This question is not flippant, since the suggestion that they might occur continually (although omitted by Frankel), seems equally as unlikely as any discrete time period. In short, it may be a useful device to express concepts involving national income and the like in highly aggregated book-keeping terms, but it would be ludicrous to assume that the reality actually *is* appreciated as a series of individual book-keeping transactions relating to individual citizens. Nevertheless, the device is adopted, for illustrative purposes only, in Chapter 7 of this book.

4 Culture, Personality and Accounting Theory

4.1 The anthropologists' look at accounting

Two recent papers in *Human Organisation* have demonstrated how various cultures react towards economic or 'business' activities in ways which are quite contrary to those of Western capitalist, industrial societies. Thus Simpson describes the difficulties encountered in persuading a group of Indians in Arizona to adopt a system of reserve pasturing.[1]

Acheson's more recent paper deals with an alien society's approach to more typical business activities; the way in which a group of Mexican Indians assesses the relative possibilities of the business opportunities offered to them. In general he found that they considered only the 'ganancias' or cash-flow of the various enterprises and completely ignored the more usual Western criterion of 'return on capital invested,' and so esteemed large-scale farming and milling (with returns of only 15.8 and 16 per cent, respectively) over selling furniture and mechanised carpentry (250 and 51 per cent). The contrasting criteria can be designated the Emic (or insiders') and Etic (or outsiders') view, using terminology supplied by linguistic science.

Unfortunately, Acheson concludes:

> It should be made clear that the etic view is not merely an alternative to the local (emic) view of opportunities. Rather it reflects the economic facts of life whether the business men of Cuanajo recognise it or not [5, p 90].

Thus both Simpson and Acheson seem to assume that their subjects' approach to these matters, though natural enough in the light of those cultures, was nevertheless incorrect and inefficient in the light of reality. This assumption can be challenged.

The business methods of the Papago drovers and the Tarascan

villagers seem outlandish to a Westerner; those of the West are equally obscure to the Indians. *They* place little value on future income and concern themselves with communal welfare rather than individual wealth, while *our* approach is quite the contrary. The purpose of this paper is to suggest that 'an accounting theory' is central to any culture. To the extent that cultures differ, ideas of what is 'wealth' will also differ; all such theories find their sole justification in their own systems of values, and cannot appeal to any 'economic facts of life.' Clearly different theories will induce different patterns of behaviour and some cultures will judge certain patterns of behaviour to be more 'beneficial' (by their scales of value), but that is not the same thing at all.[2]

The essentially subjective nature of any accounting theory is illustrated by the following extract from the well-known accounting text by Moonitz and Jordan. In a chapter sub-titled 'Determination of the amount of periodic profit' they say:

> To illustrate the types of practical difficulties that beset us, we shall consider two limiting cases, namely:
>
> 1 All future receipts and outlays of cash are presumed to be completely unknown.
> 2 All future receipts and outlays of cash are presumed to be known.
>
> As a practical matter, we are not interested in these two cases for their own sake—situations in which the future is a complete blank either do not exist or else become so intolerable that we avoid them. On the other hand, the happy state of knowing all there is to know about the financial future of any given project is so rare as to fall outside the realm of reasonable expectations. But there are many situations in which the future is *almost* a blank, for example, the outlook for striking it rich in a mining venture before the exploratory work has been undertaken. Also, many situations exist in which the future is almost an open book; as, for example, the reliability of the promises contained in a US Government bond. Even more important than the existence of situations almost at the limits indicated above, however, is the fact that the cases encountered in the real world fall somewhere between those limits. That is to say, some things about the future we do know; some things we do not. As a consequence,

> the solution arrived at in any given situation will reflect varying degrees of uncertainty and contain elements of the two cases lying at the limits described. After summarising the situation at the limits, we shall then proceed to consider the adaptations accountants have made to a world of uncertainty [87, pp 126–7].[3]

The concept of 'return on capital invested' is therefore much more than a more sophisticated (and *perhaps* more correct) approach to the ascertainment of profit. It requires one to place a 'present value' on 'future income,' and so implies the existence of a market of some sort where claims to future income can be exchanged for claims against current output. In turn, this implies that the community has a surplus of current output available for the support of those whose current activity merely secures future output. Not only does this assume the existence of institutions and levels of affluence which may not be available in all societies, but it requires a willingness to sacrifice present satisfaction for the future which is not equally present in all cultures.[4]

4.2 Culture and accounting theory

These analyses suggest that accounting theory and culture are not very readily separable. One might ask what a 'culture' essentially consists of—what exactly is a 'theory of accounting' or even why does every culture have to have any theory of accounting at all? Kroeber and Kluckhohn [70] define 'culture' as

> . . . that complex whole which includes knowledge, law, morals, custom, and any other capabilities and habits acquired by man as a member of society.

The theory of accounting is concerned with the semantics of welfare —what we *mean* when we say 'income,' 'expenditure,' 'profit,' 'wealth' and so on.[5] (See Mattessich's remarks in note 14 of Chapter 1.) At the outset it will be apparent that our concepts of wealth will define the values and hence the goals that drive us on to action within the 'complex whole' of our culture. It follows that an accounting theory of some sort must be present in any culture, since man is an energy-conserving organism which would not undertake any activity at all except to satisfy some hunger or avoid some penalty. Such a theory is needed to evaluate hungers and the losses of energy needed to satisfy them, prior to deciding on the strategy to be followed.

To use a simile from the writer's own subculture, a culture has much in common with the 'group accounts' prepared for a holding company and its subsidiary, in the sense that it has no separate existence, no underlying substance other than those of the subsets, or rather elements within the subsets which comprise it. This means that the content of a culture is essentially that of an individual personality, since it summarises the contents of the individual personalities of the group. However, like the group accounts, the culture is not a simple summation of the subsets, because they will be transformed to some extent by the group dynamics which link the individual members. The formal accounting theory of a culture therefore finds its origin in the individual personality: however it does not consist solely of those parts of the personality which are concerned with 'values.'

A personality is sometimes described as a 'mazeway'; as were a map which the individual maintains of the mental images which represent the 'real' world to him. Wallace suggests that a normal human mazeway will contain the following types of data [119, pp 17–19].

1 Values (images of situations associated with pleasant or unpleasant feeling-tone):

a Positive organic values (physical hungers of various kinds).

b Positive symbolic values (testimonials of love, etc).

c Altruistic values (images of situations in which the primary and secondary values of others are satisfied).

d Negative values (the reverse of *a*, *b* and *c*).

2 Objects (images, with associations, of animate and inanimate objects):

a Self (of own body, its desires, processes and personality).

b Human environment (persons and classes of persons).

c Non-human environment (plants, animals, tools, natural phenomena).

d Supernatural environment (ghosts, deities, witchcraft).

e Statements of how the entire socio-cultural, self-natural and supernatural system works.

3 Techniques (images of ways of manipulating objects in order to experience desired end-states or values):

a Techniques (what to do when . . .).

b Priority systems among values.

c Priority systems among techniques.

Other writers have suggested rather different structures, which are worthy of mention here, especially since they show that each cultural value is a continuum between a number of dichotomies. This will give some indication of how discussion of these matters may follow a more rigorous, and perhaps even quantitative, pattern:

1 Parson's 'Pattern Variables' [92]:

a Affectivity—affective neutral (immediate gratification or postponement of gratification).

b Self-orientation—collectivity orientation.

c Universalism—particularism (the use of general standards or acting in the light of circumstances).

d Ascription—achievement (whether people are judged by their attributes or upon what they actually do).

e Specificity—diffuseness (whether one's actions towards others are narrowly defined, or otherwise).

2 Kluckhohn's variables [68]:

Man and nature

a Determinate—indeterminate (belief or disbelief in an orderly universe).

b Unitary—pluralistic (viewing as a whole, or division into categories such as 'sacred' and 'profane,' 'mind' and 'body' or 'economic' and 'social').

c Evil—good (belief or disbelief in 'original Sin').

Man and man

d Individual—group

e Self—others

f Autonomy—dependence

g Active—acceptant.

h Discipline—(self) fulfilment.

i Physical—mental (sensual versus intellectual).

j Tense—relaxed.

k Now—then.

Both nature and man

l Quality—quantity.

m Unique—general (concrete versus abstract thought).[6]

These schemata can be compared and possibly reconciled with Mattessich's assumptions. When these assumptions were discussed in Chapter 1, it was pointed out that most of the 'Basic Assumptions' did nevertheless involve one or more cultural attitudes; it is usually obvious that one extreme of each attitude is more conducive to what *is normally described* as accounting and record-keeping than the other. One must consider whether those cultures which exhibit mostly contrary attitudes can be said to have any accounting theory at all. Perhaps it could be said that the key assumption for this purpose is number 1 (as to the existence of a set of monetary values), in the sense it was elaborated in Chapter 1, to include the idea of a single-value objective, and hence of exploitation of the environment. This seems to be the point covered by Kluckhohn's Variable *g* (Active—acceptant); presumably a group that *truly* accepted its environment would find no purpose in any recording activity, save an aesthetic pleasure as in story-telling or picture-painting. However, the slightest interest in the exploitation of the environment *must* set in train some form of each of nineteen Assumptions—and hence an accounting theory of some sort. Different ideas about time, self, categorisation and so on will produce forms of accounting theory that lead to methods of accounting differing quite markedly from the Western model.

A possible reconciliation statement might be:

BASIC ASSUMPTIONS

Mattessich	*Wallace*	*Parsons*	*Kluckhohn*
1 Monetary values (additive . . . single value)	1 Values	*a* Affectivity—affective neutral	*g* Active—acceptant
2 Time intervals (discrete)	?		*k* Now—then
3 Structure (set of account headings)	2 Objects	*c* Universal—particular	*b* Unitary—pluralistic
4 Duality (direct flows only)	2*e* How it works	*e* Specificity—diffuseness	*m* Unique—general
5 Aggregation (loss of detail . . . use of 'balances')	?	*c* Universal—particular	*l* Quality—quantity
6 Economic objects	2*c* Non-human environment		*b* Unitary — pluralistic
7 Inequality of monetary claims (debts)	?	*b* Self—collectivity	*e* Self—others
8 Economic agents	2*b* Human		*d* Individual—group
9 Entities			*f* Autonomy—dependence
10 Transactions	?	*d* Ascription—achievement	?

SURROGATE ASSUMPTIONS

Mattessich	*Wallace*	*Parsons*	*Kluckhohn*
11 Valuation	1 Values 3*b* and 3*c*	?	*i* Physical—mental
12 Realisation	?	*d* Ascription—achievement	?
13 Classification	2 Objects	*c* Universal—particular	*b* Unitary pluralistic
14 Data input	?	?	*a* Determinate—indeterminate
15 Duration	?	?	
16 Extension	2*b* Human objects	*b* Self—collectivity	*e* Self—others
17 Materiality	?	?	*h* Discipline—fulfilment
18 Allocation	2*b* Human objects	*c* Universal—particular	*b* Unitary—pluralistic
19 Purpose	?	?	*g* Active—acceptant

It can be seen that the accountants' 'assumptions' and the anthropologists' variables are *not* 'isomorphic'—there are a number of overlapping categories. This suggests that the assumptions could be restated to advantage; moreover, it is hard to see how Assumptions 1–10 (or perhaps 2–10) are more 'basic' than the remainder. A revised scheme might be:

ACCOUNTANTS' ASSUMPTIONS		ANTHROPOLOGISTS' VARIABLES		
Revision	*Mattessich*	*Wallace*	*Parsons*	*Kluckhohn*
1 There is a system of valuation and a set of values which are ranked in a purposive fashion.	Assumptions 1, 11 and 19	1 Values (also 3*b* and 3*c*)	*a* Affective—affectivity neutral (applies to rows 1 and 2)	*g* Active—acceptant (also *i* Physical—mental)
2 There are data held to be material to these values, which are located in a period of time *and* at some point within it.	Assumptions 2, 14, 15 and 17	?		*a* Determinate—indeterminate *h* Discipline—fulfilment *k* Now—then
3 The data which are seen as relating to the human and non-human environments can be classified so as to demonstrate a significant structure. Data can be aggregated into these classes, and the classes themselves can be grouped and regrouped in a significant fashion.	Assumptions 3, 5, 6 and 13	2*a*–2*d* Objects	*c* Universal—particular	*b* Unitary—pluralistic (also *l* Quality—quantity)

4 The relationships between the objects of agents is seen *either* as a single direct flow at one point in time, *or* as some more complex relationship involving direct or indirect effects over a period of time.	Assumption 4	*2e* How it works	*e* Specificity—diffusion	*m* Unique—general
5 The human environment is distinguished from the non-human environment, in that humans are seen as collaborating in various ways for the purposive pursuit of values. Human collaborators can be grouped and regrouped so as to reflect varying mutual interests.	Assumptions 7, 8, 9 and 16	*2b* Human environment	*b* Self—collectivity	*d* Individual—groups *e* Self—others *f* Autonomy—dependence
6 There are criteria for deciding when material data may be recognised for classification in its appropriate categories.	Assumption 10 and 12	?	*d* Ascription—achievement	?

4.3 Personality and group dynamics

The extension of the individual mazeway to a culture or subculture involves consideration of the changes brought about in the collective outlook by the interaction of a number of human mazeways through the channels provided by a particular social organisation. This type of phenomenon is described as 'group' dynamics. Much that is usually treated under this heading is not very material to the present work—problems of leadership, power, status and so on. However, some work has been done on communication and interaction within the group—'the initiation or transmission of communication stimuli; ... the receipt, understanding or translation of communication stimuli' [30, p 166].

It is not possible to say, from first principles, whether the group mazeway will be of superior or inferior quality to that of any one of its members. Clearly, the more heterogeneous the group, the greater the diversity of its background and sources of information; moreover, one might hope that this diversity might serve to 'contra-out' random misconception of various kinds. On the other hand, it is necessary for the members of the group to communicate with each other and also to communicate in unambiguous terms; here uniformity of background will be of assistance, and homogeneous groups will devote much effort to reinforcing 'consensus' or 'conformity' and so tend to restrict the information content of group below that of the 'sum of the mazeways.' Two peculiarities of group decision-making seem fairly well established:

1 Heterogeneous groups seem to perform better with complex tasks while homogeneous groups do better with simple tasks [59]. The ability to generate alternative strategies and argue their merits extensively are clearly helpful when dealing with the unstructured problem with high elements of uncertainty, but this facility is an actual hindrance in deciding which of a number of well-tried and reliable techniques should be used on a simple problem.

2 Committees seem to be noticeably less risk averse in their decisions than their individual members [120]. It may be that there is some correlation between risk-taking and 'leadership' which produces this effect; on the other hand, it may be, simply, that members feel less keenly their *personal* responsibility for the outcome.[7]

Where do these aspects of group dynamics affect accounting theory? It has been suggested that the information system (accounting system) of an enterprise is an attempt to arrive at a formal, agreed statement of the joint mazeway. Thus at the outset, emphasis is placed on uniformity; the keeping of several sets of conflicting records is not normally assumed to proceed from some unusually democratic, permissive approach to information science. It would follow that unless unusual efforts were made to record dissenting opinions, the contents of such a system are likely to reflect all the strengths and weaknesses of the homogeneous group just described. This would be true even if the group of collaborators were in fact quite heterogeneous, and so not averse to injecting 'information' into the actual decision-making process which is at variance with the agreed story of the 'official' system. Another interpretation is possible. Later in this book it will be suggested that much of the internal cost/usage data of the enterprise contain elements of organisational slack, and so must be considered strictly 'controllable.' Much of the contents of the official information system are simple records of these 'contracts' and the extent to which they are, or are not, observed—the *real* information upon which the various parties negotiate these contracts probably never forms part of the official record. Nevertheless, it would follow that the official record would supply excellent information for the routine, non-controversial decision, but the limitations of this data for more complex, less well-structured situations should be recognised.

4.4 Culture and communication

The purpose of this mazeway is to receive impressions of the situations facing its possessor, and provide him with a pattern to cope with them. However, most anthropologists seem to take the view that other, more complicated elements enter into culture.[8] In particular, these dichotomies, or rather their affects, have to be communicated to society at large in some way. The methods of communication vary profoundly in different societies, and not solely in respect of language. It seems possible to find a continuum of 'honesty—deviousness' or perhaps 'directness—indirectness.' Thus other writers [e.g. 55] have concentrated on the communications aspect of a culture and distinguished a number of interconnected message systems by which members communicate ideas amongst themselves, and also pointed to the existence of loops in the system which are capable of amplifying, damping or otherwise distorting the messages transmitted through them. For example it might be possible to speak of

1 Direct communication (through speech, writing).
2 Indirect influence (through patterns of behaviour).
(However, the attitudes of the cultural groups to a variety of basic concepts make it convenient to think of several channels which receive, filter and transmit particular sorts of data, whether they are communicated directly or otherwise.) Thus:
3 For material on technical matters and affluence. (Some cultures are not only unskilled and backward, but also singularly disinterested in remedying this. Concepts of this type are likely to prove hard to communicate.)
4 Sexual attitudes, for example, regarding the place of women in society. (Where women are expected to be pregnant, hard-working and silent, not only Women's Lib, but also vacuum-cleaner salesmen find it hard even to begin to communicate their various messages.)
5 Spatial attitudes. (How near do I have to stand to you before you are sure that I am really speaking to *you*? How loudly can I address you before you accuse me of shouting? The answer is quite different in London from what it would be in Cairo.)
6 Temporal attitudes. (What does it mean when I say 'I'll fix it for you tomorrow' or 'Drop in for a drink any time'?)
7 Attitude to innovation. (Some very high cultures are essentially conservative, so messages that demonstrate the desirability of change are likely to meet a blockage.)
8 Attitudes to leisure. (This applies especially to subcultures; the black chartered accountant will receive and transmit messages in his professional capacity in quite indistinguishable fashion from his white colleagues, but this is much less likely to be true of their private lives.)
9 Defensive attitudes. (People in different cultures tend to worry about quite different things—loss of money, loss of virility, loss of face and so on.)

10 Attitude to exploitation. (Peoples differ very much as to whom they feel it is 'right' to take advantage of, or even whether it is right to take advantage of anyone at all; this may extend even to the exploitation of natural resources.)

Accountants are normally thought of as implacable and unswerving bearers of bad tidings. However, closer acquaintance suggests that they are at least as prone as anyone else to see and say what society expects them to see or say. Igor Ansoff points out that most investment decisions have to be made under conditions of 'partial ignorance' [9], since reasonable cash forecasts cannot possibly be made to cover the complete lives of most capital projects. And yet discounted cash flow or return on investment calculations are very frequently prepared for periods of many years' duration. Clearly, the decision to invest has already been taken on other grounds and the accountant is merely required to give sacerdotal authenticity to the affair. Seed gives an example of this in his paper [102], together with other cases of 'rational abuse of data.'

The existence of these differing attitudes in the communications systems of cultures does not conflict with the general scheme of a personality set out above; indeed, they can be seen as providing a mechanism which will make a culture remarkably stable. This is because messages which tend to conflict with the basic values held by members are filtered out, while those which support them are amplified. As a result, people will update their ideas about non-basic concepts quite quickly, but any changes in cultural beliefs proceed at an evolutionary pace. Indeed the evidence for the existence of a group or sub-culture in an outwardly homogeneous population is commonly the use of modes of communication that are opaque to non-members.

4.5 The 'firm' as a sub-culture

A business enterprise is a typical sub-culture; the message 'El Cid has been seconded to Millbank, but he can't wait to get back to HOC' is meaningless to anyone except an employee of Imperial Chemical Industries. A business might therefore be expected to possess a mazeway. Cyert and March [33] have defined the Behavioural Theory of the Firm to include all the employees and proprietors as 'collaborators' in the common enterprise. This coincides well with the idea of the firm as a fairly typical group.[9] This group's 'culture' would therefore be the linked mazeways of the various individuals who are currently collaborating to form the enterprise, but most firms (like some other cultures) do make an effort to establish a company-wide, standardised, 'normal' picture of its present situation, history and prospects. I have described a section of a normalised mazeway of this type in a forthcoming book [45]; however, the book does not show the complete system. This is not surprising, since this other work is concerned with accounting systems, and their possible extension to include a sort of technological and environmental data-bank. This meant that the 'taxonomy' adopted for this extended system covered section 2 of Wallace's mazeway scheme ('objects') and perhaps sub-sections 3*a* and 3*c* ('Techniques' and 'priority systems among techniques'), but omitted all mention of section 1 ('Values') and sub-section 3*b* ('Priority systems among values'). The omission is significant; the 'objects' and 'techniques' are readily updated by reference to a feed-back from experience in using them (subject to the distortion introduced by the filter channels described above). The values themselves are largely impervious to any messages from the 'real' world and so the accounting system need not comprehend them, at least in any dynamic form.

However, it would be quite easy to include this material, and complete the enterprise's mazeway, as can be seen from the extended version of the taxonomy [45, Chapter 4] on the following page. The 'flows' of the old taxonomy clearly represent a model of the physical world in which the firm is operating. If the firm is taken to be some sort of economic enterprise, its 'world' consists of a number of opportunities to transfer and/or transform various commodities from one situation or one state to another. The dynamic model of these processes therefore envisages the operation of the firm as the control of the rate at which these transfers or transformations take place. The flows can conveniently be labelled (i) the 'material' which is being sold or worked upon, (ii) the 'orders,' or requests flowing into and out of the firm for materials or supplies, (iii) 'cash,' or the medium of exchange by which external accounts are settled, (iv) 'personnel' or *all* the human collaborators who form the 'firm' and

Flows	*Input-output data*	*Capacity data*	*Prices and rates data*	*Working data*	*Techniques*
Materials	Statement of 'how the whole system works' is 2*e*	Part of non-human environment is 2*c*	The system of values attached to the various flows, and hence the means of evaluating decisions regarding them, i.e. 3*c*	The 'Dynamic,' 'Forecasts,' 'Historical' and 'Housekeeping' data of the original taxonomy, i.e. the raw material for the other data	'What to do when' particular states are observed to exist in the various flows, i.e. 3*a*
Orders		Human environment, i.e. 2*b*			
Cash		Part of non-human environment, i.e. 2*c*			
Personnel		(Collective) 'self,' i.e. 2*a*			
Capital		Part of non-human environment, i.e. 2*c*			

(v) 'capital,' or the physical equipment by which the transfers and transformations are achieved. It might be possible to distinguish a sixth flow, of 'information' regarding the other flows, but clearly neither a firm nor an individual can very readily distinguish between the reality and his conception of that reality.

Flows can only occur between two points; it is convenient to see the system as a 'graph,' a set of points or 'nodes,' with a set of flows or 'arcs' which connect them. This is a *gestalten* system, whose static elements provide the constraints within which it must operate; these seem to coincide with the 'capacity' data of the original taxonomy, and the 'self,' 'human environment' and 'non-human environment' of the 'objects' section of the human mazeway. The dynamic elements show the connection between the static elements, and so comprise the 'input-output data' of the taxonomy or the 'subsection 2*e*' of the mazeway.

The 'prices and rates' section of the taxonomy provides the system of values to be attached to the various flows, and hence the means of evaluating alternative decisions regarding the flows. They correspond to 'subsection 2*c*' of the mazeway, 'Priorities among techniques.' All the foregoing data are seen as 'normal' or 'standard data,' the collective's current beliefs about its present situation. This implies the existence of a substantial body of 'working data,' by means of which new data received into the system are incorporated into the currently accepted 'normal' data.

As we have seen no part of this extended taxonomy corresponds to section 1 or subsection 3*b* of the complete mazeway. The 'values' of the individual or of the firm are not directly concerned with the flows which make up its environment; instead they can be seen as:

1 Providing the filters by which information about the real world is put into a form which is acceptable to the system.
2 Providing filters by which the firm recognises those opportunities for investment which it would be willing to pursue, given available resources. The 'capital' flow in the taxonomy has a much broader meaning than just the plant and equipment itself; the plant, etc, is merely the outward and visible sign of the existence of an underlying 'project,' or opportunity which the enterprise might exploit. The values thus dictate the 'strategy' of the firm.
3 Providing the 'sense of time' of the system. This governs the speed of its reaction to the feedback of discrepancies between the normal, expected position and such messages about the actual state of the world as the system is capable of receiving.
4 Finally, the values of the collaborators in the firm will affect the 'prices and rates' section of the taxonomy, by which the firm will evaluate the techniques (or 'tactics') open to it. The whole system could be visualised as shown in the diagram.

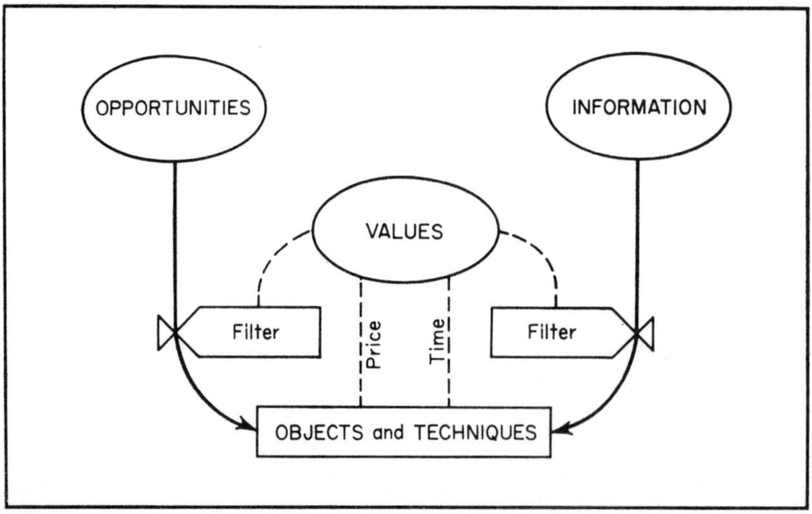

4.6 Perceived nature of the group mazeway

In fact, the reception of new data into this system is likely to be a very complex process; at least three distinct, mutually exclusive assumptions can be made about the nature of the phenomenon facing one:

1. That its behaviour is precisely known and pre-ordained; this assumption proceeds from 'faith'—either in scientific theory or of some other kind and so its behaviour is *accepted.*
2. That the mechanics of its behaviour are unknown, and moreover that its behaviour cannot be controlled by the decision maker; essentially it is a 'black box,' whose behaviour can be *inferred* from its past performance, at least to the extent that it is not totally random.
3. That whether the precise mechanics are, or are not known, the behaviour of the phenomenon is controllable, because it is brought about by the activity of people whom we can influence; it follows that its expected behaviour can be *negotiated.*

Of course, the point about Type 1 assumptions is that they are very firmly built into the personality, so that data contradicting the assumption are either ignored, or 'explained away.' Any changes in such positions probably occur either very slowly, or as the result of some fairly traumatic experience which can be called a 'conversion.' This latter process involves emptying out large areas of the subject's mazeway, and the substitution of what is virtually a new personality. In general the process does not involve logical argument as much as an assault upon the subject's equanimity; he has to be made to lose his bearings, to become 'disoriented,' by physical or mental stress. It is probable that anybody can be converted to do anything, given time; some conversions will be improvements while others will result in less satisfactory states of mind. The trouble is clearly that the decision about what is good or bad rests with the 'evangelist' rather than with his subject. In short, changing fixed ideas has moral overtones.

Type 2 assumptions are those most commonly 'assumed' by academic writers on economics and accounting. This implies solution through some technique involving examination of time-series setting out the history of the phenomenon in terms of one (or more) bases and fitting a line thereto by statistical inference. In practice, the techniques will be confined to instances where the subject believes the phenomenon to proceed from some cyclical trend of events, which are neither the result of some known and inevitable process, nor of some process over which the subject has control, at least to the degree just described. Where data relating to a phenomenon of this type are received, however, the procedure will be simple enough and involve no more than taking up the latest observation into some sort of smoothing operation. One cannot have a smoothing technique which is insensitive to statistical noise while remaining highly sensitive to changes in the trend, so the relative weights given to new data have the effect of damping the sensitivity of the line to either cause.

Many of the phenomena encountered in practical business affairs are likely to be of the controllable/negotiable type. The procedures involved in these negotiations are described elsewhere: the immediate concern is with how data regarding its behaviour are taken up into the mazeway. In general, the current 'contracts' will be the current 'standard costs,' according to which the subject will expect and require the system to perform. It follows that deviations in performance take on the nature of breaches of contract, and imply either a need to ensure that the contract is observed, or some review of the terms in the next round of negotiations.

4.7 'System dynamics' and the mazeway

It is not by chance that the headings of the rows in the taxonomy correspond to the 'flows' described in Forrester's *Industrial Dynamics* [40] (which are now, it seems, to be described as 'system dynamics'). These models visualise any dynamic system as a series of 'levels,' or inventories, linked by flows, whose 'rate of flow' can be controlled. Generally the system is endeavouring to maintain some steady state, or pattern of growth, so the effect is of an interconnected series of feed-back loops. To the extent that it is correct to identify an enterprise as a sub-culture, it is apparent that models of this type must be models of its mazeway; this leads one to suppose that the system dynamics technique could be used successfully to model an individual personality mazeway also.

The suggestion contained in the earlier section, is that the extended information system is continually attempting to update its image of the normal situation of the enterprise, by comparing the expected position forecast by the system with its understanding to the actual position reached at a given point in time. Parallel operations can be observed in system dynamics models, where 'expected values' of various kinds are commonly recalculated, even if some delay is introduced into the reaction.

One might suppose that section 1 and subsection 3*b* will be less susceptible to feedback, except as part of a very long-term evolutionary change. It is possible to equate this part of the mazeway with the 'constants' of the system dynamics model.[10] In fact, the construction dynamic models will be seen to be central to the system of societal accounting outlined in the remainder of this book.

4.8 Accounting theory and culture

Every individual and hence every culture which purposefully exploits its environment possesses some machinery for evaluating the strategies and tactics open to it. This machinery essentially provides its concept of its 'welfare' and so it does not seem unduly fanciful to claim that this individual mazeway or collective culture must possess its 'accounting theory' as was described in section 4.2, plus others procedures making up a meta-theory. This meta-theory will be an amalgam of:

1 The values and some method of measuring the contribution of given situations in terms of such values.
2 The system of priorities among values.
3 The accepted theory about what the whole socio-cultural and economic system consists of and how it is supposed to work, and hence about how various strategies and tactics are to be evaluated. And one could usefully add
4 The various taboos and biases that occur in the transmission of data and the selection of opportunities.

A number of arguments seem to follow from this:

1 Any exploiting society, however (technologically) 'primitive,' needs, and in fact *has*, an accounting theory; they may not be and do not have to be 'verbalised.'[11]

2 These accounting theories will indeed differ profoundly, to the extent that the variables governing the societies differ; the theories will change (very slowly) over time.

3 Just as cultures and subcultures are made up of collectivities of individual personalities, their accounting theories are the collective accounting theories of their individual members, modified by the dynamics of the group.

4 An accounting theory is therefore the 'mode' of the values and other concepts held by the individual members; there is no reason to assume that this theory will coincide with all the values of any one member.

5 It follows that a large variety of individual accounting theories must co-exist in any one society; those which deviate too strongly from the model pattern will be judged 'criminal' or 'insane.' However, to the extent that they are permissible, they will be the 'right' values for the individual who holds them.

6 The more homogeneous the culture, the greater the significance of any comparisons made between 'accounting statements' prepared within it. It follows that the accounts of firms in the same industries and in the same regions are more readily comparable with each other than were others from different industries and regions.

7 The values entertained by a society are certainly not exclusively economic values, and thus this ('societal') accounting meta-theory will include what is normally understood by the term, but go far beyond it. This is entirely reasonable, since the former describes 'total wealth' and the latter merely 'economic wealth'; as Goldberg has pointed out (see Chapter 1), the personal 'proprietorship' must include these wider considerations.

8 Any 'accounting theory' can be said to be 'all in the (collective) mind,' and one can see that 'historical cost, accruals-based accounting' represents a more sophisticated approach to economic wealth and income of a society than one (such as the Tarascan villagers') for which a simple 'receipts and payments account' would suffice for this purpose. To the extent that the concept of 'value' as the present worth of future cash flows is becoming more widely understood in Western society it might now be more appropriate to prepare accounts on this basis, rather than on an historical cost basis. Still more sophisticated concepts may become available in the future, but whatever these may be, their only validity will be for those who entertain them.

9 Although every non-acceptant culture has an accounting theory, in the terms defined here, it is apparent that certain 'developed' nations, not only have equally 'developed' accounting theories of some sort or other, but also, for historical reasons, have passed on their commercial procedures, laws, accounting techniques and theories to less developed societies, which have adopted them rather than evolve their own. Typically this will have arisen through a period of colonial rule, but also such diverse countries as Imperial Russia and Turkey have acquired essentially alien accounting theories.[12]

4.9 Notes

1 He comments that:

> 'Analysis of the structure and function of the Papago and Bureau of Indian Affairs social systems makes it possible to hypothesize about current and potential use patterns of the pastures. A rather startling observation, but one which fits the described cultural patterns, is that although the pastures are considered by the change agents to be complementary in nature, the stockmen act as if they were supplementary. Thus, when an additional pasture is built, herd numbers are increased proportionately and overgrazing continues. Moreover, in addition to the general lack of BIA (Bureau of Indian Affairs) follow-up educational programs and to the broad traditional factors and social constraints already mentioned, there are important economic factors that determine pasture use. Specifically, there is a reluctance to pay cash for grazing which nature provides free. This is known to economists as a lack of regard for "opportunity costs." That is, an individual may readily understand cash flow from his own person; but because he rarely makes an actual cash transfer sort of investment in an animal, he feels no outstanding loss if the animal dies of starvation. Paying a small grazing fee to place the animal on a complementary pasture (as distinct from a supplementary pasture that is indiscriminately available to all) is an alternative now being examined' [106, pp 165–6].

2 Professor Hendriksen [57] also refers to the possibility of cultural differentiation in accounting theory:

> 'While accounting thought has developed over time in response to many changes in economic and sociological environment and because of continued research, it has also developed along geographical lines to meet the different needs of the many national cultures and economic and political systems. Many nations have followed the lead of the more advanced nations of the world, but there is increasing evidence that no single nation or group of nations has a monopoly on the development of accounting thought and accounting research . . .' [p 89].

In the closing section of Chapter 4 some of the dangers of 'following the lead of the more advanced nations' will be examined. There is a radical distinction between adopting an alien technology and adopting alien thought processes.

3 In fact, to 'capitalise' any expenditure is to carry it forward against the future. Assets like land or fairly primitive retail stores can be carried forward in this way readily enough, because they do not wear out in use; once acquired, and provided they are operated with a reasonable intelligence, they continue in general, to produce income. This can be contrasted with 'wasting' assets such as mines, machinery and so on, which have to be replaced if the venture is to continue to operate. When one carries forward any part of the cost of a wasting asset the act always 'implies' confidence that the future will provide an income whose value will *at least* cover whatever valuation be placed upon the 'assets.' Thus 'capitalisation' involves the evaluation of *future* income.

4 The simplest formula for arriving at the present value of a future stream of income (a_n) is:

$$a_{n/i} = A[1-(1+i)^{-n}]/i$$

where i is the required rate of return (expressed as a decimal fraction of 1), n the number of years it is to be received and A the annual amount. Where wasting assets are *not* involved the second term in the formula disappears as n approaches infinity so the value of a perpetual flow is:

$$a_{\infty/i} = A/i.$$

To the extent 'the businessmen of Cuanajo' may be highly disinterested in future income as opposed to 'ganancias,' it is not surprising that they charge and pay very high rates of interest. As i gets larger the value of a approaches A in *both* cases. It would follow that even if they 'wised up' to rate of return calculations, their relative evaluations of a_n would tend to reflect the relative size of A, whatever n might be used. Should they consider the size of a or A relative to the initial investment needed to achieve it? Acheson observes that it is simply not possible to expand the size of the businesses very greatly, so that a mechanised carpenter's shop may be very 'profitable' but not very 'lucrative' while the reverse is true of a large farm. It is obvious that 'return on capital' is a game that cannot be played where expected interest rates for any reason commonly exceed the returns available from new business ventures.

5 It will be recollected that 'valuation' was in fact one of the secondary, 'specific' assumptions, through which various hypotheses can be introduced into the system. This is very much in accord with what is being put forward in this chapter. Obviously valuation is just one aspect of measuring wealth and the other eighteen assumptions are needed to define these concepts of 'wealth' and so on.

Only the specific assumptions are permitted (by Mattessich) to be the vehicle for cultural influences. The *basic* assumptions are supposed to be common to all theories and thus to all cultures. The various comments in Chapter 1 question the claims of most of the first set of assumptions to be 'basic' in this way; this chapter will attempt to identify them with the 'pattern variables' listed by various anthropologists.

6 Returning to the examples cited by Simpson and Acheson, one can see that the (emic) preference for cash-flow accounting as opposed to the (etic) return-on-investments represent systems of values at opposite extremes of almost every one of these continua. Not only does the etic approach involve (a) the postponement of gratification, but also, (b) belief in an orderly universe in which forecasts are feasible, (c) separation of 'economic' from 'other' aspects of transactions, (d) the decision-maker must see himself as autonomous and active and (e) similarly he probably needs to be a self-oriented individualist, to the extent that the technique assumes that his future output can always be converted into current purchasing power without significant effect upon the group as a whole.

7 An interesting suggestion proceeds from the attitude of groups to risk. It is normally assumed that accounting records should be, and by and large are, prepared on a basis of absolute conservatism. And yet 'conservatism' is not normally a feature of group views of anything. Perhaps true conservatism would prevent most collaborators from putting any hard and fast values on a great many of the phenomena which are recorded; the accountant may well be the greatest plunger in the enterprise when he puts a single measure or interpretation on any of them. It would be an interesting research project, were it possible, to discover the extent of the reservations which the various collaborators might hold *privately* about almost all of the material in the official record.

8 Boddewyn summarises the interface of an individual and his culture:

1 *Primary groups* as transmitters of the norms. Such groups constitute the immediate milieu within which the individual operates—for example, the relatives or the co-workers who help the individual perceive his environment and ascribe meaning to it.
2 *Language* as the essential vehicle for such social transmission.
3 *Roles* is prescribed behaviour or socially expected plans of action for individuals in various situations.
4 *Status* as the various positions that constitute the structure of a group—quite apart from the individuals who occupy these positions [19, p 193].

9 Boddewyn also comments:

'Business—as an art and/or a profession—is such a subculture with its own primary groups, roles, status, and language. A large part of the business subculture is indistinguishable from the general culture within which it operates. In other segments, however, conflict or at least disparity with society prevails—to the delight of moralists and novelists.

'This subculture itself is a mosaic of sub-subcultures which take different forms depending on how the "genus" business—like the proverbial bologna—is sliced into "species"' [*op cit*, p 201].

Professor Ladd expresses an interesting (and intimidating) interpretation of current corporate attitudes towards the existence of various classes of collaborator:

'This broad view of the corporation's responsibility is well summarized in this statement (typical of many) of the late Louis D Brown, one-time chairman of the Johns-Manville Corporation:

'"In the evaluation of a complex industrial society the social responsibility of management has broadened correspondingly . . . it increasingly functions on the basis of a trusteeship which endeavours to maintain, between the four basic interlocking groups, a proper balance of equity. Today the executive head of every business is accountable not only to his stockholders but to members of his working organisation, to his customers, and to the public."

'Taken literally, the foregoing suggests for the corporation a most awesome social role. The maintenance of "a proper balance of equity" among virtually all elements of society would seem to require the assumption by corporations of much of the traditional roles of government, of education institutions, of the church. The parallel with feudalism is remarkably close, for that system was characterized by the acceptance by the *seigneur* of the obligation to maintain a balance of equity among the elements of the society' [72, p 12].

Another paper which attempts to link accounting and the theory of the firm is by Schiff [101].

10 A number of people who have been kind enough to read this material in its earlier 'discussion paper' form have complained that this suggestion that values are constants is an intensely reactionary statement. Probably it is, but constancy is relative. Obviously, a society whose values were effectively constant would not develop and this is precisely what we find in the 'traditional' section of a developing country. Even so, one wonders whether our values are as far removed from those of our ancestors as we like to believe. Simon points out in his lecture published as *The Sciences of the Artificial* [105] that a very simple organism which has to respond to a complicated environment can respond in an outwardly very complex fashion. It may be that once a society dedicated to changing its environment begins to succeed in that end, its basic system of values could produce courses of action that imply a quite erroneous sophistication in its objectives.

11 Accounting does not require literacy (as the wooden tallies of our own history will confirm); it does not, *of itself*, require any means of statement in permanent form, although this is usually present, even in quite primitive cultures.

An interesting example (from a bizarre but by no means 'primitive' culture) is provided by Jacobsen:

> 'An accounting device was used by this civilization. In the Quechua language (spoken in the Inca empire) this device is called a *quipu*. . . . The quipu is a series of cotton or woollen twined strings or cords with one end of each string attached to what might be called a rope. When the rope is held in a horizontal position in the hands, the other end of each string hangs free. The rope may vary in length to as much as a yard or more. The strings hanging from the rope may be of different colors. Knots of various kinds and quantities tied at various positions on these strings provide the capacity for record-keeping. Subsidiary cords may be tied to the hanging strings' [63, p 222].

12 In part, these imported theories have grown away from the original models; moreover, the original models also differ from the present-day theories and techniques of the countries which developed them. To this extent, the alien theories may be supposed to have taken on something of the culture into which they have been grafted. On the other hand, it may be supposed that the alien importation has deprived the native culture of some necessary evolutionary steps, for its own development in these directions. It may be that the observer would conclude that these countries were not very creative in their approach to accounting, but tend to view both the technique and its supporting body of commercial law as Coda to be committed to memory and interpreted with Levitical precision.

It follows that formal accounting and business law in these countries may be notably divorced from the main body of their cultures, even though trading and even manufacturing may be a major feature of them. Probably intensive research into indigenous trading sub-cultures would be needed before one could make any really certain statements about this; one could hypothesise that in such countries commercial law and accounting principles will be as it were external forces on a par with the weather, while the management and control of the enterprise itself relied on quite other channels of communication and standards of assessment. It would be interesting to see whether evidence of this 'outsider' view of law and principle could be adduced, and whether, on balance, the importation of a ready-made section of a very important part of a more developed culture helps or hinders the host culture. It is possible that any hindrance would have affected its prospects of economic success, apart from purely 'cultural' considerations. (See also Chapter 1, note 4.)

5 A Theory of Societal[1] Accounting

5.1 Accounting for 'externalities'

A headline in the *Financial Times* of London for 3 November 1970 read 'IATA members' concern at new "sociological costs".' The report continued:

> These include, for example, aircraft noise—involving the airlines in costs for the insulation of buildings—as well as the settlement of legal actions over noise; and the need to ease pollution from jet engines by introducing smoke-reduction and other devices.
>
> It is estimated that in the US alone the airlines are committing about $1000M for improvements to aircraft in response to public reaction to these 'sociological factors,' a sum equal to the entire payroll of the US airlines only ten years ago.

Of course, this reaction by airline operators to demands from those who find themselves aggrieved by their operations is just one part of the current concern for 'ecology' and the general 'quality of life.' However, the accounting problems suggested by these demands would exist quite independently of the current popular interest in these topics. The question of whether the airlines do or do not have to make good these sociological costs may not of itself affect the overall welfare of the countries, since the losses, if airline stockholders do not suffer costs, remain with the sufferers, or perhaps with the community at large.[2] On the other hand, if these costs are not attributed to the operation of the airlines, it is obvious that air transport may appear to have a greater advantage compared with other modes of transport than is justifiable.

One might also suppose that these societal costs will tend to fall for the most part upon those who are least able to order their affairs so as to avoid them. Since the general quality of life in a country is likely to form a larger proportion of the total 'welfare' of such people (because their command of personally possessed goods and services is less), so the 'cost' of compensation or elimination of the nuisance to the average shareholder is likely to be less than the benefit conferred by the expenditure on the victims. It is not the purpose of this book to pursue matters of social policy or natural justice, or even discuss the vexed field of 'welfare economics,' as has already been stated, but it is plain that in the macro-accounting techniques previously described, these costs will go unrecorded, unless the compensation, etc, is actually paid over. This is because the production boundary is drawn so as to show wages, rents and profits as the 'added value,' while taking no account of the fact that the recipients of this value may also be compelled to accept a 'negative income' of dirt, ill-health and general loss of amenity. Societal benefits which cannot be regarded as primary flows will go unmarked for the same reasons.[3]

The point is a special case of the general dilemma of where the production boundary in macro-accounting should be drawn; the argument is the same as that over whether public transport is an addition to the national income—or just part of the cost of getting the labour force to work. The essential artificiality of any boundary can be looked at in another way, if one considers what it is that any productive enterprise really produces. An airline produces transportation as its main product; however it could be said to 'produce' negative by-products like noise, pollution and the risk of accident. Similarly, when one buys a car, one must also accept not only an accident risk but a potential garbage-disposal problem.[4] Any product is so much pollution at the last; it is simply that our environment provides cycles of rust and decay and scavenger organisms which can accommodate limited quantities of pollutants at no cost. When these limits are exceeded, hitherto costless disposal problems become very expensive.

The substitution of the artificial goal of solvency (or super solvency) for the real goals of human activity (although probably inevitable) leads to the following assumptions about the resources acquired by the enterprise:

1 That they can be replaced from an inexhaustible source of identical materials at similar prices.

2 That their usage has no significance except as a contribution towards the stated objective for which they were acquired. This assumption is in part just a particular extension of (1), but it also implies that a firm can acquire supplies and outlets without assuming any sort of responsibility for the suppliers or retailers, and that it can acquire the services of labour without accepting responsibility for much more than the reasonable safety of the people concerned. Moreover, this neutrality of responsibility is mutual, so that provided goods or services are ordered, accepted and paid for within a reasonable time, no action or inaction by the user will have any effect upon future supplies.[5]

3 That to the extent to which the material acquired is not fully incorporated into the goods or services disposed of by sale (or taken up into inventories), the 'waste' material can be freely disposed of by discharge into an inexhaustible sink.

Assumption (2) is of course the subject of the current work on human resource accounting, and proceeds from the increased attention being paid to behavioural aspects of management and organisation. Assumptions (1) and (3) also apply to human resources, but their more obvious implications are for the physical material resources of the enterprise. The destructive nature of these assumptions is not simply that the source and the sink are not inexhaustable; indeed, one could say that they are freely replenished, *over time*; the assumptions overlook the fact that the 'source' and the 'sink' are identical, because solar energy and waste provide the common base for material and energy.... All three assumptions affect the accounting treatment of cost in much the same way—an assumption that resources are fully consumed either in the product (and so become inventoriable) or by the passage of time, as well as the 'duality' assumption that the payments made to the suppliers of those goods or services are the sum total of the effects of the transaction which should be charged to the inventories or periodic overhead accounts.[6]

It is arguable whether when one employs a worker, who thereby gains experience, one is actually making a partial investment in a skilled labour-force. Since the worker has an absolute right to quit his job and enter an enclosed religious order, if he likes, it would be hard to support such an assertion, even on an industry-wide basis. It would not be very sensible therefore to attempt to split the primary flows and capitalise these items to some extent. Of course, dealings with a subsidiary (or an indentured worker!) would be a different matter. In short, these interactions are probably better considered as externality effects, which need to be taken into account in decision-making.[7] The current work on human resource measurement is important as the first conscious attempt to establish criteria and technical procedures for measuring any sort of externality effect. This is how Brummet, Flamholtz and Pyle [23] set out the successive measure to be taken to achieve their aims:

> (i) Specifically, an attempt is being made to measure human resources in terms of their acquisition cost, replacement cost and economic value. *Acquisition cost* refers to the conventional accounting concept of historical cost . . . to acquire its human resources. *Replacement cost* is a measure of the cost to replace the firm's existing human resources . . . *economic value* . . . is the present value of the firm's future earnings attributable to human resources.
> (ii) Periodic measurements are being made of the behaviour of managers and supervisors and their level of technical proficiency, the resulting motivations, loyalties and behaviour of subordinates and the communication, decision-making and control processes of the divisions and profit-centres.

Thus Class (i) measures comprise not only the recruitment, hiring and training costs of the personnel, but also some estimate of the costs (and expected benefits) to the enterprise of sub-standard work while they are learning the job and deliberately induced losses of this type when their work is changed 'to broaden their experience.' Class (ii) measures will contain more eclectic, qualitative and hence debatable material; a variety of measures and rankings devised by the social psychologists for portraying and comparing the behavioural state of the enterprise.[8]

It should not be thought that problems of this sort arise solely from such emotive issues as pollution control or from human resources. Many other activities which a person or organisation can undertake will give rise to effects which will benefit or injure other parties who are not directly involved in the transaction. A typical example was cited some years previously by Hirschleifer [58], when he considered what should be done in a divisionalised firm making automobiles, where the sales under the 'marque' of one division competed to some extent with those of another. The problem was also discussed more recently by Whinston [123]; economists see the solution to such a problem as how to induce independent decision-makers to arrive at strategies that will produce the optimal solution for the system as a whole. However, it is obvious that 'externalities' are indirect effects which happen to reach outside what is considered to be the entity concerned with the matter in hand. The techniques needed to solve such problems in themselves are no different from those needed for a purely internal secondary effect (or 'internal externality'?). It was pointed out in Chapter 1 that the (innately artificial) construction of an entity that can only be justified in terms of *direct* transaction adds further complexity; the self-financing enterprise is automatically committed to a very narrow interpretation of the assumption of duality.

5.2 The concept of societal wealth

The foregoing section has introduced the concept of 'societal cost,' which leads one to enquire whether it might not be possible to speak also of societal income and hence of societal wealth. The idea is not implausable, since the society is a system with a very obvious *gestalt* element; we would not be surprised to find that the whole is greater than the sum of the parts, where the 'parts' are the items normally accounted as 'economic wealth.' The intrinsic difficulty of international and intertemporal comparison of levels of welfare was discussed in Chapter 3, from which it would seem that it will not be easy to measure the effect of this *gestalt* element, because one would be trying to compare the same real income flowing through a system which amplifies its welfare content to some extent with the results achievable with the same real income where the system is absolutely neutral. Since the systems themselves are different, it would not be reasonable to expect the welfare of its members to be any more comparable than those of two distinct national economies.

On the other hand, it may help to make some fairly comprehensive analysis of the nature of such systems, and their basic throughput.

Traditional accounting procedures assume that the whole of the relevant economic activity of any entity is comprised in a listing of its cash and credit transactions. Clearly, the 'sociological costs' of the airlines referred to in the opening paragraph would be only covered by this procedure, to the extent that the costs are in the event recoverable from them. Other externalities might be less readily included; the loss of sales in one division (in the second example) could hardly be 'recoverable' from the division whose own selling activities caused the loss. In short, there may be many events of considerable economic and societal significance which do not involve the transfer of goods or services (or even disservices) from one ownership to another and so occasion liabilities to pay cash in return, either under contract *or* as damages.

Thus it seems reasonable to distinguish 'real' externality transactions, involving transfers of goods, and so on, including disservices *not* under contract from 'true' externality transactions which do not. The real transactions are all flows through the system, while the true externalities provide a multiplier effect. If this is accepted, we can identify the *gestalt* element with the true externalities, which appear as multipliers provided by the system. This distinction between externalities which have the effect of flows from those which have the effect of multipliers, leads on to the need to consider the result as some dynamic system. In general one supposes that the system will operate as a series of feed-back loops, so that an element of control can be exercised by the system over its performance.[9]

It has been seen that traditional accounting makes no overt provision for recording externalities of the multiplier type. Of course one can find some attempt to account the 'internal externalities,' when overhead rates are calculated in an effort to estimate the costs of service centres on the basis of known relationships with activity in production centres. To the extent that an enterprise makes a model for the purpose of sales-forecasting, which relates sales not only to sales-effort and advertising, but also to external influences like (say) car-production, completion of new houses and so on, it makes use of externality multipliers, but they are not looked upon as part of the accounting process. Externalities are also ignored in macro-accounting, although the concept plays an important part in economic analysis of the national income itself. Possibly this is because to the extent that the effect of a true externality is to produce further flows of measurable income in another entity, the national income accounts can comprehend the total effect as direct flows. In fact, Aukrust does refer to a similar concept with respect to macro-accounting:

> The classification of economic objects for the purposes of national accounting can be suitably based upon their following distinguishing characteristics or properties:
>
> (i) the nature of the transactions associated with the objects (e.g. change of ownership), and further—for each individual transaction,
> (ii) the time the transaction takes place,
> (iii) which transactor(s) (one or two) are affected by the transaction,
> (iv) whether the transaction, when two transactors are involved, is requited or unrequited,
> (v) the motives behind the transaction and its typical repercussions.
>
> In contrast with (v), characteristics (i)–(iv) describe technical or economic aspects of the transaction which, in principle, it should be possible to subject to objective observation. It can therefore be tempting to base the classification upon characteristics (i)–(iv) only, as this would yield classes that are relatively sharply defined. It would generally also yield classes that are relatively homogeneous with respect to characteristic (v). This does not always apply, however. Therefore, since transactions which must be assumed to influence differently the behaviour of transactors, should be kept separate, a classification according to characteristic (v) is also needed, even though this, by the very nature of the matter, will of necessity be imprecise [10, pp 107–8].

One must suppose, therefore that Aukrust sees 'motive and repercussions' as another, *singular* basis for taxonomy. In fact, it seems likely that a single, first-order transaction will have a large number of typical repercussions. Nevertheless, his suggestion that one should analyse first-order transactions with respect to their influence on subsequent behaviour is very valuable.

However it might be possible to distinguish a third class of externality; a 'psychic' externality, which affects the *enjoyment* of physical flows. These multiply the *effectiveness* of a flow of real income, rather than the flow itself.[10] It is the mechanics of the concept discussed by Frankel (referred to in Chapter 3).

5.3 Assumption of the transferability of wealth

It seems reasonable to suppose further that some societies will provide more psychic externality/multipliers for their members than others; conceivably some can provide 'multipliers' of less than unity. It may be of significance that the traditional accounting procedures (which largely ignore all types of externalities) were developed for an emergent capitalist society. This limitation presupposes that the multipliers are not important, and proceeds from an assumption that all economic 'welfare' and benefits are freely transferable flows; indeed this is probably the heart of the difference between the capitalist system and what went before. Previously, contracts were personal to the parties who originally contracted them; services, for example, were due to the Lord of the Manor and could only be transferred with the 'Lordship,' which also required the permission of the overlord. Similar formalities governed other contracts.

This assumption of transferability is central to the idea of proprietorship and hence to capitalistic accounting. It enables one to set as a general aim 'the maximisation of the present value of future income streams.' This would be infeasible if the rights to receive streams were not freely transferable, because without current income a man could starve to death, as was discussed in Chapter 4. However, the existence of a 'Stock Exchange' means that future income can be converted into spot cash, in theory, at any time.

In a privately circulated essay [67], Kissack suggests that this gearing of its economic activity to the concept of encashable ownership is the special feature of the capitalist system. Moreover, this differs from all other forms of purposeful human activity (such as science, art or even war), because its execution is governed by a legal convention rather than by logic, aesthetics or even pragmatism. Kissack goes on to make the point that the object of economic activity is to increase welfare rather than to create claims in cash for a proprietorship. He uses this illustration—the objective of a soldier should be to win a battle and not to win a medal; the victory is the goal, but the medal is the reward.

It is not true to say that all welfare is transferable and hence saleable. In a Western capitalist society, however, it may be substantially true, at least to the extent that one *could* conduct one's business and private affairs on that basis, and leave the non-transferable aspect of one's own welfare and one's employees' welfare to 'the public sector.' On the other hand, this approach will mean that any plans made are likely to be sub-optimal and perhaps even strictly infeasible, because incorrect objectives and incorrect data will be used, as was mentioned in Chapter 1. Apart from consideration of the welfare of other collaborators in the enterprise, even the decision maker will find he has not achieved what he might have hoped for.[11]

5.4 Concept of 'cultural income'

This problem is more *acute* in a developing country, where a higher proportion of the total welfare of the populace is made up of this non-transferable welfare. It has been pointed out that a nomadic tribesman might support life adequately, if not exactly luxuriously, on an imputed annual income of about £60, however generously one cared to value the tangible items of food, clothing, etc, he manages to extract from his environment. The same people could be moved into a city; the national income would no doubt be doubled or trebled —but they would starve. All races and nations extract substantial benefit from what one might call their 'culture'; especially in a poor country, these benefits are as important and desirable as any others, and all 'management' and 'planning' should take account of these factors.[12]

One problem would be how these 'externalities' ought to be measured; an even greater difficulty would be to decide how any such measurement could or ought to be taken up in the accounts and planning exercises of an enterprise. The latter aspect of the problem is a particular application of the discussion of the economics of inter-divisional transfer pricing. However, the significant point here is that these cultural benefits are not capable of private ownership, hence not capable of transfer and hence not amenable to any 'net present value' treatment. They can only be enjoyed, pro rata, by the members of the culture at the time when they arise.

'Affluence' means having purchasing power to spare after the provision of necessities, which means that affluence must imply freedom to exercise rather idle choices. The citizen of a developed country will make decisions on whether to buy a dishwasher or a deep-freezer on quite different principles to a peasant deciding whether to buy a new plough or buy more seed-corn. The fact that an affluent developed country is also a collectivist society will not by itself make any difference here, and the proportion of transferable welfare to cultural welfare is probably not different to that in a similar capitalist society.

On the other hand, in a collectivist state the distinction between the industrial sector and the public sector of the national economy will not be a distinction between a number of separate private ownerships and the public domain. It would seem irrational for the activities of a state-owned enterprise to be planned so as to bring about diseconomies in other areas of State activity. And yet the growing affluence of some collectivist societies has meant that centrally-directed and detailed physical planning can no longer provide for the satisfaction of the 'idle whims' of an affluent society. This development lies behind the introduction of the Economic Reforms in the USSR and elsewhere. Once accounting in these countries ceases to be used as a control system, in support of a detailed physical plan, the enterprises start to use their accounts in much the same way as their capitalist counterparts. This will produce similar conflicts in externalities, which will be more obvious in a collectivist society than in the West. As a result, one may expect Communist-bloc countries to concern themselves with accounting theory to an increasing extent, and to become critical of its emphasis on exclusively transferable 'wealth.'

However, the need to include non-transferable welfare considerations in micro-economic planning exercises is not likely to be confined to developing or collectivist societies. The appetite for affluence grows as it is fed, and even now the people of developed countries are showing dissatisfaction with what is probably the acme of material prosperity; they want to have their real and psychic externalities optimised as well. Unfortunately, as the Soviet Union has discovered, imperative planning only works in practice in a subsistence economy, which means that in an affluent society the plan must originate at the enterprise level, even if it is later co-ordinated in some way at the national level.

How can this be achieved? The similarity of this problem to that of the divisionalised firm has been remarked already; Whinston [*op cit*] suggests that such a firm might take account of externalities by *ad hoc* ground-rules which would prevent divisional managers from striking bargains which were contrary to the overall interest. In a sense the Law, and para-legal regulations like Industrial Development Certificates, Selective Employment Tax, Development Grants and the like are attempts to introduce ground rules of this type into the planning of enterprises. Even if these regulations, properly observed, would produce plans which maximised citizens' welfare, they are likely to prove less than successful in practice. Because the enterprise is still using its original incomplete figures of income and expenditure, the governmental regulations are in no way seen as necessary amendments to its planning procedures. Instead, they appear to be interferences in the most profitable operation of the enterprise and considerable ingenuity is commonly devoted to circumventing them so as to approach near to the original, unregulated plan.

A number of rules could be set out which follow naturally on what has been said previously:

1 Any net surplus of cultural income cannot be *taxable*, because it is not transferable. The nomadic tribesman (or the Western farmer referred to in note 11) might be in the surtax bracket if their real and psychic incomes are aggregated, but they could only pay that tax out of their meagre *transferable* income.

2 The surplus cannot be *accumulated*, but will have to be disposed of as it arrives.

3 It is not possible therefore to apply a DCF approach to cultural benefits since the present value of future benefits cannot be sold.

4 Cultural benefits can be enjoyed by communities of participants and hence by individual participants in a 'joint and several' fashion. They cannot be enjoyed by legal entities or by those whose contact with the community is solely through the ownership of rights to transferable wealth.[13]

These rules need to be reconciled with the revised accounting assumptions set out at the end of section 4.2.

1 The existence of cultural income is not inconsistent with the existence of a set of values and their purposive ranking. However the set is enlarged beyond its traditional limitations.
2 Not only the 'data,' but also the 'values' are seen to be 'located' in a period of time *and* at some point within it. It is now apparent that the traditional interpretation of theory locates *transactions*, while assuming the resulting net benefits to be timeless; this seems to be the point at which 'transferability' and hence 'discountability' enters into the traditionalist approach.
3 Classification and structure seem unaffected, save some necessary enlargement of scope.
4 Clearly, the duality assumption is discarded at this point.
5 The inclusion of externality effects is likely to cast doubt on the validity of some 'entities,' whose first-order relationships seem unexceptional.
6 Similarly, consideration of the externality effects may alter the decision as to the materiality of data.

5.5 Society and cost

At various places in this chapter, and in those which precede it, reference has been made to both the possibility that many of costs of an enterprise are externality-effects from outside the entity and so generated by society at large and only indirectly by the enterprise itself, but others arise directly within the firm. The latter provide a direct feedback into the cost-formation and hence into the decision-making processes of the enterprise. That is to say, the former items are uncontrollable by the entity, while the latter can be controlled. If the behavioural theory of the firm is accepted, it seems possible to argue that these controllable costs are *negotiated* between the agents, or 'collaborators' who comprise the firm. Of course, the agents themselves are influenced in their negotiating by a variety of societal influences.

It will be helpful to outline the argument in support of cost negotiation. The organisational theory of the firm suggests the existence of 'organisational slack,' a surplus over the minimum pay-off needed to keep a collaborator within the enterprise. In general it may be thought of as a sort of lubricant needed to make any social organism, but especially a hierarchical organism, work in a harmonious fashion. Clearly the existence of this surplus enables a member of the firm to accept a rebuff or an insult from a fellow-member without walking out. However, the surplus is not solely to be found in the formal remuneration of the collaborators; a most important element exists in the relaxation of strict industrial discipline. It could even be said that some trade-off existed between formal remuneration and more congenial working conditions. Probably this phenomenon is covered by Kluckhohn's 'determinancy—indeterminancy' and 'discipline—fulfilment' variables.

This arises where the standard usages and efficiencies are set at higher levels than those which are 'technologically necessary.' In part this just enables people to take more idle time, lay out work less efficiently or waste indirect supplies, but in addition it permits the building up of so-called secret reserves. These reserves permit workers, supervisors and managers to disguise runs of substandard performance which would otherwise have to be reported and explained to their superiors in the hierarchy.[14]

However, it must be admitted that this hypothesis cuts across much of what many accountants believe to be the ethical basis of their professional activity. Consider what Carl Devine had to say in his review article on Cyert and March's book:

> The implications of this position for the accounting profession are important. Modern cost accounting deals with efficiency, and presumably this portion of the subject is thrown out of the window along with the last vestiges of ethical content. The field then becomes a set of conventions that is said to provide one of the major battlegrounds for a fierce and long-run negotiating process. Perhaps like some statistical techniques, accounting procedures are loose and not obvious to everyone, enabling all bargaining parties to make their positions appear legitimate by citing some convenient esoteric accounting rule or statistical technique. If this hypothesis is true, it seems that bargaining would be almost entirely on other grounds, with flexible accounting 'principles' becoming the rationalizations

> by which the actual outcomes are defended and legitimized. The Cyert-March position is, apparently, that accounting conventions have no more normative content than, say, attendance rules. Thus, favourable accounting treatment becomes a payoff objective in the bargaining process. We cannot debate this position here, but accountants like to believe that their 'principles' have broad application and are too well-accepted to be simple pawns in each individual bargaining session [36, p 216–17].

Probably the answer to this comment is that within a given cultural ambience there may be comparatively little dispute about accounting techniques themselves. Indeed, the author's recollecton is that the negotiations rarely reach as high a stage of complexity as this; rather they concern measurement itself and what normative performance might really be. The general pattern of negotiations within the enterprise may be summarised in this way; usually the budget will be negotiated between the manager or supervisor and his superior. A number of features can be noted with respect to these negotiations:

1 They will bear considerable resemblance to the negotiations over transfer-pricing between autonomous divisions, such as have been discussed and analysed by Hirschleifer [*op cit*], Gordon [51] and others. However, a number of supervisors will be negotiating with the same superior as to their respective shares of the available slack.
2 These negotiations are likely to be just one stage in a cascading series of similar negotiations throughout the whole enterprise—company-wide, divisional, plant-wide, and cost-centre. At each level the subordinate manager will be negotiating in the knowledge that the slack he obtains will have to be adequate to satisfy all the subordinates with whom he has to enter into subsequent negotiations....
3 The negotiation over the budget will be only one of a series of negotiations that any one manager will be conducting; the others will be as to what is the effective, as opposed to the theoretical capacity of the plant and the level of activity to be required of it during the coming period. All these items are clearly interconnected and the budget itself consists of a large number of individual figures; it follows that a philosophy of 'win a few, lose a few' can prevail across the board.

4 The negotiations will be one of a theoretically infinite series over time, as well. This is important, because the negotiations will have the nature of bilateral monopoly, which produces a *range* of feasible prices, where the exact point to be selected depends substantially upon the *status quo ante* from which the negotiations commence. It is this aspect of the situation which might make it an exceedingly difficult one to replicate as any sort of laboratory experiment; in practice end-game strategies cannot usually be employed.

5 Negotiations under bilateral monopoly (including those for inter-divisional transfers) normally involve individual partly finished items whose subsequent external selling price is ascertainable. Cost negotiation will frequently involve multi-product plant that manufactures intermediate products or subassemblies which are only part of any one finally-saleable products, and may contribute to more than one such product. Here the upper and lower bounds of the cost range could best be found by a fairly complex exercise in parametric programming. . . .

Possible equations for arriving at the allocation of organisational slack are discussed in the other book. They follow on from other work in the field of behaviour under bilateral monopoly. The significance of 'organisational slack' for the present book is primarily whether it can be considered as adding to the psychic income of its recipients—or even to their real income. Returning briefly to the material discussed in Chapter 2, it will be realised that the 'National Income' of a Western society could be arrived at (in theory at least) either by securing the factor prices of (final) outputs or by securing the factor payment, taxes and corporate savings. Intermediate outputs were contra-ed out. If it is correct to say that people trade-off industrial discipline against additional remuneration they are effectively converting intermediate products into factor payments (although the conversion goes unrecorded).[15]

5.6 Measurement of externalities

At least five classes of operation have been referred to in this chapter as affecting total welfare:

1 Direct transfers of goods and services which are received voluntarily by consumers such as automobiles and air-flights, which are certainly capable of private ownership even if they are sometimes possessed communally.
2 Real externalities—which are less direct transfers of goods and services (or more often disservices) accepted involuntarily, such as car-smashes and pollution, and which are more usually received by fairly large sections of the community rather than by readily identifiable individuals.

Then there are true externalities, where no goods or services pass at all; for example,

3 Where the establishment of an airport encourages the growth of industry in a remote and underemployed area.
4 Psychic multipliers, which affect enjoyment of real income, are evidenced by all those indicators of 'the quality of life,' such as the suicide rate, which reflect pressures generated by society itself.
5 Finally, one may include the various types of organisational slack.

The measurement of the value of directly transferred goods and services (1) is comparatively straightforward, at least under this analysis. Whatever 'prices' are arrived at by market forces, or the price-fixing apparatus of collectivised societies, can be taken as its 'value,' to the extent that the difficulties (such as the fact that my new car must eventually become *Birmingham*'s garbage-disposal problem) are passed on to the remaining categories of transaction. The involuntary and community-wide nature of the more indirect transfers described under (2) makes it much less easy to attribute values. Churchman has pointed out [28] that the mere selection of a mode of valuation itself determines the outcome of most decision-making problems in this area. He takes the example of a twelfth-century English church threatened with demolition to make way for an airport; if one values the premises at the value placed on them by the church authorities for insurance purposes, the church is a negligible asset as against the airport. On the other hand the discounted present value of the original investment in the twelfth century is enormous, while the perpetuity represented by a quite modest assessment of its aesthetic value to future generations is even greater. Churchman concludes that it is a false premise to suppose that projects can be 'evaluated' by expressing the various considerations involved in money terms and striking a balance. This conclusion is at variance with the conventional interpretation of the classical 'Assumption 5' that transactions can be expressed sufficiently in monetary terms, and further by net aggregations of monetary terms. Human lives and major works of art are strictly irreplaceable, and to that extent any monetary compensation for their loss can only be partial; it follows that although decisions occasionally have to be taken that involve irreparable damage of this type, these must be strictly political decisions (in the wider sense).[16] Moreover, it follows from this that while some conventional money price may properly be placed on the legal (or even the moral) liability arising from affairs of this type,[17] the real accounting for transfers like this will be essentially multi-dimensional. The possibility of 'accounting' encompassing records of this sort has been discussed by Ijiri [62]. It follows further that the decision-making procedures to be followed will consist of discovering the most satisfactory multi-dimensional 'profile' amongst the strategies open; this approach has also been discussed extensively, primarily in connection with investment portfolio selection.

Finally it is necessary to ask what sensible statements can be made about the 'true externalities' and how, if at all, it is possible to 'take account' of them. Many of them will be of type (3) which may be described as of a physical nature, as in the example where the siting of an airport generates desirable industrial development, or where something like the pressure of the population or racial discrimination makes any given real income less satisfactory to the recipient than would otherwise be the case. Also it is necessary to make provision for the type (4) externality, arising from the system of society's culture, as described in the previous section. This can be visualised as a series of weightings which are attached to the multi-dimensional profile of strategies, so that an act, e.g. the slaughter of a human foetus, or of a cow, can assume the significance appropriate to the society in which it is proposed that it should occur.

The indirect externalities are, we have seen, only recognisable to the extent that the society has some model to explain causal relationships of an indirect type. The need for some model-building activity in any exploiting society will be discussed at some length in Chapter 8. For the moment, it suffices that these externalities cannot be 'measured' and cannot therefore be accounted for directly. They can only be 'inferred'; one can record the current value that is entertained for the particular coefficient, as with the overhead rate. What can be recorded are the necessary time-series of the independent variable for one's model, so as to provide some feed-back on its sufficiency.[18] It follows that it is necessary to obtain and record data for these series; *what* data for *which* series depend upon the model selected. The next two chapters will discuss some areas (apart from the normal monetary transaction data) which might provide variables for more comprehensive models at both macro- and micro-levels.

Organisational slack is a somewhat different matter. Reference was made in Chapter 4 to the facility, existing in all cultures, to filter out or transform data that conflict with deeply held prejudices and so produce a distorted vision of 'reality.' However, it can be appreciated that this distortion is socially necessary. The organisational slack discussed here is clearly the micro-version of this necessary cultural distortion—a sort of honourable embezzlement. A macro-version will be described in Chapter 6. Is there much point in trying to measure this 'externality'? In general one supposes that attempts to distinguish 'emic' from 'etic' realities may not be very valuable, since one man's reality is simply another man's illusion. On the other hand, one can produce evidence to support a contention that while the gross amount of the distortion may be unknown (and perhaps unknowable), it is possible that its dimension varies under different conditions. Since the model-building itself depends on feed-back, it is apparent that the coefficients inferred from any data will be internally inconsistent if the degree of distortion in observing them is not constant. Chapters 6 and 7 will examine this problem further.

5.7 Notes

1 The preference of this book to describe its objectives as 'societal' rather than 'sociological' probably lacks validity, save for this: several writers have referred to the possibility of a 'sociological approach'—often rather disparagingly—while discussing aspects of accounting very different from those which are our concern. Hendriksen's assumption that the approach necessarily implied an interventionist attitude by the government was discussed in note 8 of Chapter 1. Again, a paper by Tritschler [113] uses the phrase to describe the diffusion of a (tax-induced) revaluation method of accounting amongst French businessmen. Sociologists themselves seem to find professional accountants a fascinating study as a social group, whose peculiar views and customs vie with those of the Trukese and Trobriand islanders; one calls to mind such gems as a comparative study of the social status of the accountancy profession in various countries (compiled at least in part by asking socially superior young ladies 'Would you marry one?').

Moving a *little* nearer to the interpretation to be used in this book, it is apparent that many people see both the 'behavioural' and the 'sociological' approaches as involving study of the reactions of *users* of accounting statements to their contents. Perhaps this approach could be summarised as the 'emic' reactions (see Acheson [5]) to attempts to introduce introspection and numeration into a group activity. These effects seem well-known to anthropologists and such operations have frequently been a source of superstitious fear, e.g. David's decision to 'number Israel' in II Samuel 24 and I Chronicles 21. However, as was suggested in Chapter 4, this introspection is an essential precondition to any attempt to manipulate the environment and so bring about social change. In fact, the users of accounting statements are not the sole members of society involved in the process. As usual, Mattessich puts the matter very nicely:

> 'Furthermore the question of where to draw the boundaries of behavioural accounting has been left unanswered. There can be no doubt that this sub-area should inquire into the sociological, psychological and economic foundations of accounting, and into the related behavioural traits of *users* of accounting information. But less unanimity exists with regard to the question whether it should also inquire into the behaviour of the *producers* of accounting statements and systems or even into the behaviour of accounting *theorists*' [80, p 477].

2 As was pointed out in the discussion of the basic assumptions of classical accounting theory (in Chapter 1), the assumption of duality is confined to primary flows. There are no reasons to suppose that *external* benefits balance out *external* losses. Some believe that market price does (or ought to) take account of these items. However, there are not so many such believers now!

3 Some attempts have already been made towards developing formal machinery for accounting for externalities within enterprises. The principal example is 'Human Resource Measurement' whose basic concepts are explored in the well-known paper by Brummet, Flamholtz and Pyle [23]. They say:

> 'Human assets are not included in the asset base used to calculate rates of return on investment. Accordingly, human assets are implicitly assumed to be a free good one without cost. But since human as well as physical assets have an opportunity cost associated with their use, this cost should be quantified . . .'

What needs to be added to this statement is the fact that human assets are by no means the only section of the world's stocks of resources which are treated by enterprises as if they were free goods (see also [24], for example). Obviously, the development of the self-financing enterprise ensures this, as has been discussed in Chapter 1.

4 Dr Mishan enjoys a happy turn of phrase; here is what he said about the problems of the validity of classical assumptions about price and value in the affluent growth society:

> 'What is a so-called "merit good" but one which the economist believes ought to elicit social approval? If the economist is permitted to talk of "merit goods," he can hardly be forbidden to talk of "demerit goods," or perhaps—with apologies to Alfred Marshall

—of "quasi-junk." Politicians whose public hearts bleed freely for the poor and who, therefore, urge us on to prodigies of productivity, would have to direct their oratory to promoting quite different causes if ever it became fashionable to proceed, via the discovery of "demerit goods," to the estimating of those proportions of GNP that could reasonably be classified under such broad categories as "expendables," "luxuries," "regrettables," "frustratables," "inimicals" and "neo-garbage" ' [85, p 18].

It should be added that this view is very much contrary to that of more conventional economists; indeed *they* believe that cost-of-living indices contain an upwards bias, by reason of the technological improvements in underlying goods and services (as reported by Gross [54, p 22]).

5 It can be seen that this is a generalised form of McGregor's 'Theory X,' without (perhaps) the further implications that suppliers, workers and customers have a natural in-built tendency to short change the enterprise, that this should be checked—and that the mode of the checking process will not much affect the future.

6 This implies that if a worker is paid weekly, a supplier of raw material monthly and a supplier of machine tools (say) every five years, all that is required is a matching of those periods with those payments either directly through inventory. In fact, the interaction between the enterprise and its workers and suppliers ensure that not only is some current service being given, but to some extent the worker is acquiring, attitudes, skills, and experience of the sort which are required (and *may* continue to be required) by the enterprise; similarly, the supplier will be encouraged towards the purchase of plant and labour capacity and other resources of the type needed to serve his customers. Moreover, the current capacity for either worker or supplier/retailer to render the current service is affected by the past history of their dealings with the enterprise.

7 Although their paper 'sets out possible methods of calculating a firm's value of human capital,' Lev and Schwartz seem to concur with this view:

> 'The major limitation in the concept and measurement procedures advanced above is that the firm's value of human capital is not necessarily equal to the portion of the firm's income contributed by the labor force. Specifically, labor is one of several inputs in the production process. . . . However, in real life, input factors are interdependent and there is probably no practical way of dividing the total contribution among them' [76, p 110].

This dilemma posed by the impossibility of attaching meaningful values to specific in-service assets (as opposed to the project on which they are engaged) in a world where isomorphic accounting is demanded, has been discussed in Chapter 1.

8 Brummet, Flamholtz and Pyle also look forward to a subsequent phase when the *use* of this data and the effects of its use on the human resources themselves could be measured. This is clearly an attempt to look beyond secondary effects to tertiary effects; the possibility of some circuitous 'feed-back' is also entertained. One must suppose that when one has abandoned not only 'duality,' but also any finite limit on the number of externality stages, one will be left with an interactive, dynamic model, of the type to be discussed in Chapter 8.

9 It would not be possible to refer to control systems in the areas of social policy without referring to the work of Forrester and the System Dynamics group at MIT. The technique of system dynamics has been extended from its original compass of purely micro-economic 'Industrial Dynamics' [40], to 'Urban Dynamics' [41] and more recently to 'World Dynamics' [42]. It is not necessary to enter into the controversy that arose over the publication of the last-named work; model-building is essentially the extention of one's own convictions (or even prejudices) in some rather rigorous fashion. Even where the resulting models are 'tested for fit' against historical time-series data, the coefficients that result tend to confirm the fit of the data, rather than the authenticity of the thinking behin the model. What Professor Forrester can say is that *if* one accepts the authenticity of various views (commonly enough held) as to the interaction of population growth, land use, exhaustion of resources, levels of pollution and so on with the 'quality of life' and the size of the population which can be supported, it would follow that the world was approaching some sort of limit to its development—unless some quite radical solutions (as yet unknown) can be adduced to alter the rules of the game. Essentially, the system dynamics approach to feed-back systems sees them as sets of interrelated states of 'levels,' which rise or fall at 'rates' per unit of time and which reflect the net inflow or outflow of the level during that period. These rates are determined by equations whose coefficients are either constants, or other rates and levels existing in the system at the beginning of the period, or alternatively externally introduced lists of data. Most systems are seeking some 'steady state' or direction of growth, so a series of feed-back loops is formed, whereby an 'actual' level is compared to its desired (or perhaps permitted) level, and the rate of flow is then adjusted in such a way as to reduce the difference between them. In fact, the desired state itself on the state of other parts of the system, and hence on state of the actual level it is trying to control (see the diagram). In the illustration the solid arrows represent flows and the broken lines the passage of data. Of course, various constants and functions are needed to make most models; the technique will be discussed again in Chapter 8.

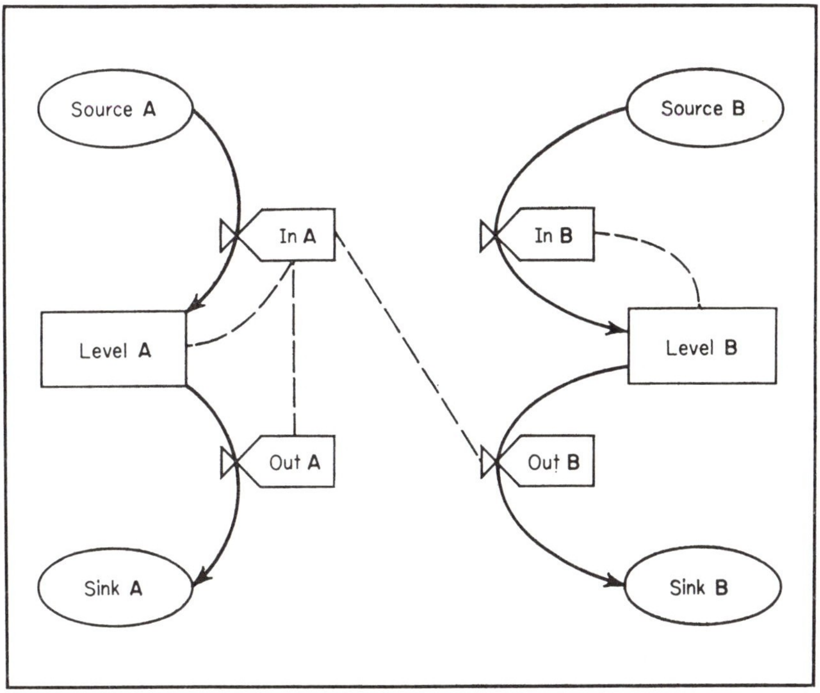

10 This idea is anathema to the formalist, no doubt. In part, the point was discussed in Chapter 3; the formalist *does* see welfare in terms of simple aggregation of flows. This psychic externality provides the additional element which the substantivist finds from the society's own institutional structure.

11 For example, health and security are necessary for the enjoyment of material prosperity; a millionaire who is always panic-stricken about atmospheric pollution, robbery and murder, is truly poor. The odd thing is that pollution and down-town ghettoes are not the product of general laissez-faire, but rather the outcome of activities that many men planned and slaved for, according to their lights.

12 A similar problem can be also observed in developed countries in their agricultural sectors. A 300-acre farm in England represents an investment of several hundreds of thousands of pounds, while producing a transferable annual income of no more than £5000 to £6000 for its proprietor and very low wages for its employees. Nevertheless, a farmer with 300 acres of arable land is likely to be a more substantial figure than anyone earning £5000 to £6000 in an industrial enterprise, even if he owned a non-interest bearing investment equal to the value of the farm. (This was also, of course, the conclusion of the Mexican villagers in Acheson's study.)

13 I cannot obtain any benefit directly from the Nigerian cultures by owning shares in Unilever. However, my shares in Unilever would not be unaffected by the existence of the Nigerian cultures: the density or sparsity of these cultures might make Nigerians less or more concerned about the size of the share of the *transferable* added value arising from Unilever's activities which went to stockholders overseas. At the same time their cultural wealth or poverty might make them more or less disposed to concern themselves with Unilever at all.

14 Both the superiors and subordinates probably welcome the controlled use of this device, which obviates the need to turn a conscious blind eye to minimal and statistically insignificant variances. Obviously, a calculation of the probabilities of statistical variance would achieve the same end (and prevent possible regression to fraudulent conversion), but most people seem happier to report (and hear) that performance is right on target, rather than the news that it is no more than reasonably off it.

15 Using the example from Chapter 2, suppose the employees of Company *A* 'wasted' £2000 worth of material, purchased from Company *B*. If they had not wasted it, Company *A* could have made and sold another £4000 worth of goods for household consumption. However, the employees would have demanded another £4500 in remuneration for doing this. If the goods were made, the National Income would be increased by £4000; wages would increase by £4500 and dividends or retained earnings would fall by £500. *Provided the choice has been presented rationally to the parties*, the 'waste' has a psychic value of £4000. This would be true even if the additional wages demanded would only be £3500, but the owners declined to insist on it because they preferred a more relaxed atmosphere to an additional profit of £500.

16 It seems reasonable to distinguish accounting from decision-making in this area. When a piece of plant is built, the enterprise creates a contingent liability to pollute the atmosphere to some degree. As time passes, this continent liability either becomes a real liability or can be written back to profit. The book-keeping might appear as follows:

ASSET ACCOUNT

		£			£
19×1	Cost of plant	100 000	19×1	Depreciation	24 000
	Contingent liability for pollution	20 000		(1/5×120 000) (Annually to 19×5)	
		£120 000			£120 000

CONTINGENT LIABILITY ACCOUNT

		£			£
19×1	Damages, etc	6 000	19×1	Asset Account	20 000
19×3	,,	4 000			
19×4	,,	4 000			
19×5	Profit and loss account (unclaimed damages)	6 000			
		£20 000			£20 000

DAMAGES, COSTS OF AMELIORATION, ETC

		£			£
19×1	Cash payments	6 000	19×1	Contingent liability	6 000
19×3	,,	4 000	19×3	,,	4 000
19×4	,,	£4 000	19×4	,,	£4 000

The point to note is that while it might be proper to record the fact of a process's prospective damage to the health and amenity of the surrounding community in this way, the figures should *not* be used to justify the installation in the first instance.

17 It should be noted that the mere fact of the existence of monetary penalties and rewards for the creation of external diseconomies or economies may not of itself bring about an optimal arrangement of affairs. Pigou proposed such a system as a means of achieving equality in the private and social net products. Turvey and Wellisz, among others, have debated the strict validity of the claim; Ralph Estes's recent paper in *Accounting Review* summarises these arguments, and also lists some attempts measuring the effects of the more direct externalities of this type [39]. The difficulties that prevent a purely 'economic' solution to these problems reinforce the argument for a more comprehensive 'societal' approach.

18 Many accountants would deny flatly that it was any part of the work of the accountant to deal with data that cannot be measured directly. Here, for example, is Norton Bedford (the 'Mr Bevis' was the author of a paper in the August 1958 number of the *Journal of Accounting*):

> 'In general Mr Bevis' restriction of the accounting function to measured data seems plausible. It eliminates from the scope of the accounting function unmeasured data, particularly data based on a feel, hunch, or intuition derived from past experience. The criterion of measurement would have meaning to and acceptance by the general public as a general notion of the basic unchanged nature of accounting data' [15, pp 27–8].

It may be that there is more 'feeling' in the most conventional accounting presentation than these authors and the general public believe.

6 Societal Aspects of Macro-Accounting

6.1 Macro-economics and societal wealth

Having, to some degree, established the possibility of various forms of societal income and wealth, it is necessary to examine any evidence for its existence in the real world. For the most part, this is to be found at the macro-level; one should not be surprised at this, since societal wealth and income, by definition, is not capable of individual ownership, or enjoyment, apart from as a member of the society as a whole. To the extent that the society is reasonably enclosed, such as a nation-state, it would be quite possible to construct some sort of accounts to record its societal wealth, if one could discover some convincing method of evaluating it. *Prima facie*, this might not seem to be a rewarding exercise, (a) because the accounts would appear as a quite separate system from the economic accounts, and (b) because the trade-off between the two systems seems largely subjective. On the other hand, there can be little doubt that the economic national accounts are much more 'subjective' than one might at first suppose (see Chapters 2 and 3) and it may prove helpful to consider the existence of a parallel system of societal macro-accounts, when dealing with these problems where data from conventional economic macro-accounts are normally employed.

Before considering the possible form of these accounts it will be helpful to list the likely sources of their content. Largely, this material will be found in a number of topics in macro-economics where the debate mostly concerns the reliability of monetary data, either in its own terms or as a measure of human happiness.[1]

There are (a) certain aspects of the 'economics of growth,' (b) certain aspects of 'Credit and banking,' (c) Planning-programming-budgetary systems (PPBS), (d) 'Cost-benefit analysis' and (e) the 'Social indicators.' All these matters have been the subject of expert enquiry in their own field; as usual the object here is merely to provide a summary (plus an initiatory bibliography) which will introduce the topic and give some framework for the extension of the tentative 'Theory of macro-accounting' set out in Chapter 2 and modified in Chapter 3. Subsequently an attempt will be made to break down this macro-theory into a similarly extended micro-theory.

Following the arguments at the conclusion of Chapter 5 it is unlikely that these discussions will turn up much in the way of hard statistics. Rather, they set out various models which their authors have put forward to explain observed macro-economic phenomena. It will be observed that their models are all rather hard to validate; little research had been done on human happiness, it would seem, and it is only very recently that people have suggested the possibility of trying to measure it empirically. Nor are these attempts receiving any general acceptance, mainly because the models being discussed tend to be only partial models of the whole system and so contain basic assumptions about the remainder which may be described as tendentious.

6.2 Economic growth and societal wealth

The problems of economic growth are the subject of dispute among economists, for example Mishan [85] and Beckerman [14]. Here too this book has no business either with the economic theory, or with the moralising that underlies so much of what can be said on this topic. One can only agree with Beckerman that much of the worry over economic growth proceeds from an unlikely alliance of people who were comfortably placed under the old regime and those who oppose the extension of private enterprise firms on quite different grounds. At the same time, the exponential growth of population in some countries and of the economic base in others clearly produce problems that are as ill-suited for study in terms of traditional economic accounting, as in terms of nostalgia and class-hatred.

Something was said about one aspect of this in the previous chapter, to the extent that economic growth is likely to bring about increased levels of pollution. It was pointed out that most industrial pollution seemed akin to the economic transfer of (in this case unwanted, non-) 'goods' to sections of the community, than to any effects on the social structure through externalities. When *X* Limited pollutes the atmosphere it is doing compulsory business with another 'firm'—a partnership of 'The Victims of *X* Limited,' which accepts its negative goods and may or may not pay a negative price for them. As such, these transactions can perfectly well be comprehended in the essentially 'economic' micro-accounts, even although this is rarely done at present, in the absence of distinct obligations to make good damage of this type.

On the other hand growth can have other effects which involve neither the transfer of negative goods (into forms of pollution, etc) nor even externality effects on other economic activities; these arise where growth affects the quality of life in some way, as was also described in the previous chapter.

To take Beckerman's example of a British shorthand-typist's holiday on the Costa Brava, the girl herself will usually obtain a very pleasant holiday, which 'is well worth the money' in most cases. Against this a large area of Southern England and the Iberian Peninsular are sprayed with aviation fuel and even less desirable substances, while Spaniards whose work is quite unconnected with the tourist industry find their economic prosperity enhanced by this influx of foreign currency. These are some of the more obvious macro-effects of the holiday. However, no matter how gregarious the young lady may be, the continuous eruption of hotels along the coast will eventually bring her to the view that 'It's just like Blackpool,' while the quite unavoidable double-booking scandals, which bedevil this industry, will demonstrate that its economic base is too flimsy to support such rapid growth. These are the purely societal aspects. The overall effects of the holiday are clearly complex; more so because at least two very different societies are involved. It can hardly be possible to assess this, and hence come to a sensible national and international recreation policy, without adequate accounting in both the societal and economic system.

The argument revolves (largely) around the conditions that would have to apply (or perhaps the assumption that would have to be made) before one could safely assume that any increase in real wealth *must* be accompanied by an increase in welfare, or happiness.[2] We are already familiar with the problem; the first-order transactions, whether requited or unrequited are always a series of dualities, but the externalities are not. It is worth considering why 'growth' might be expected to accentuate these externality effects, whether to the net benefit or detrimentally. Externalities have been described as the multipliers in a dynamic feedback system. Without disturbance of some kind, viable systems may be expected to reach a 'steady state,' but its introduction brings about oscillations while the system hunts about for some new steady state. Continually reinforced disturbance could easily keep the oscillations 'all one way' and so economic growth could produce the results for either good or ill, which Beckerman *or* Mishan suggest.

6.3 'Super-bezzle'

Apart from the purely societal wealth which may be omitted from the presently conceived national accounts, it is necessary to enquire further whether they measure even the economic income with an accepted degree of accuracy. The statistical aspects of this question were dealt with in an earlier chapter, but it should be appreciated that that discussion nevertheless assumed that the micro-accounts upon which the national accounts were based fairly represented the aggregate effect of the underlying economic activities. It is possible that this may not be the case and the reasons for this can be described as being of a societal nature.

A key area where this might be done is credit and banking. Although they have been mentioned in the earlier chapters, very little was said about them at that time; indeed, their operation was usually assumed to be completely covered somewhere in the 'Savings and investment account.' As was illustrated in Chapter 2, more detailed analysis is provided by the preparation of a National Flow-of-funds Statement, which showed the sources of the finance needed to carry out the operations disclosed in the rest of the (economic) macro-accounts.[3]

Extended discussion in this area would entail entry into an aspect of economic theory that is the subject of debate between the 'Keynesians' and the 'New Monetarists'—as to the role of money and banking in economic life. It is not the purpose of this book to contribute to the theory of other disciplines, but one is sometimes impressed by the apparently greater success of these disputants in demolishing each other's arguments than in supporting their own.

Perhaps a more clear appreciation of the fact that economic, separable wealth is not the only form of wealth, that other forms of wealth are just as real as economic wealth, and that these flows of wealth are not directly interconnected might be of some assistance to the disputants. Man is the only monkey who goes around attempting to observe himself. It follows that attempts to mislead observers are an inescapable part of the system and have a considerable effect upon its functioning.[4] 'Organisational slack' was discussed in the previous chapter; the more calvinistically inclined reader may already have concluded that the creation of this 'slack' sometimes carries the name of 'embezzlement.'

In his popular history of the New York Stock Exchange crash of 1929 [44], Galbraith says:

> To the economist embezzlement is the most interesting of crimes. Alone among the various forms of larceny it has a time parameter. Weeks, months or years may elapse between the commission of the crime and its discovery. (This is a period, incidentally, when the embezzler has his gain and the man who has been embezzled, oddly enough, feels no loss. There is a net increase in psychic wealth.) At any time there exists an inventory of undiscovered embezzlement in—or more precisely not in—the country's businesses and banks. This inventory—it should perhaps be called the bezzle—amounts at any moment to many millions of dollars.[5] It also varies with the business cycle. In good times people are relaxed, trusting, and money is plentiful. But though money is plentiful, there are always people who need more. Under these circumstances the rate of embezzlement grows, the rate of discovery falls off, and the bezzle increases rapidly. In depression all this is reversed. Money is watched with a narrow suspicious eye. The man who handles money is assumed to be dishonest until he proves himself otherwise. Audits are penetrating and meticulous. Commercial morality is enormously improved. The Bezzle shrinks [44, pp 152–3, Pelican edition].

Galbraith's thesis was, of course, that the universality of embezzlement meant that the attempts to find scapegoats for the Great Depression of 1929–32 amongst the more spectacular defaulters uncovered by the Stock Exchange crash itself were not well founded; the size of their speculation was due to the bull market and was not its cause. It is not within the author's capacity to confirm or deny this statement. However, if Galbraith is correct in saying that the 'bezzle' at any one time amounts 'to many millions of dollars,' this fact should be of considerable interest to the national income accountant, since it suggests that an amount which is both substantial and unstable may be affecting our ideas of national income, consumption and investment.

It follows that embezzlement is just one extreme of a larger spectrum of 'biased reporting within hierarchical structures.' Essentially the crime involves the fraudulent diversion of assets held in trust, usually by some fairly cerebral process which, given luck, will enable the property to be replaced at some later date. This distinguishes it from an ordinary 'inside job' of larceny, and puts it in a category of cases where, for one reason or another, reported results differ from reality.

Another example, of less certainly criminal content, is the 'bad debt.' This is the 'breaking and entering' equivalent of embezzlement and shares the other features noted by Galbraith. The debtor receives goods and services and either at that moment, or at some later time, he decides to default. The creditor will usually become aware of this decision quite independently and at a rather later date—here too there is a temporary increase in psychic wealth. Moreover, goods are not often obtained on credit with an original intent to defraud, but rather in the belief that if all goes well (but not otherwise) it will be possible to pay for them.

A further type of biased reporting which is seen as being even less tainted with criminality is the secret reserve. Although these are specifically forbidden in corporate accounting by the British Companies Acts, there is no reason to think they are less common, as opposed to less apparent, than in the years before 1948. Some typical examples were referred to in the writer's inaugural lecture [46]. Seed has also given some very entertaining transatlantic examples [102]. In fact the phenomenon is inevitable in any hierarchical system of management, where a subordinate is as unwilling to report undue success as he is to report failure, lest his superiors should then insist on him repeating an above-average performance.

This means that the problem is especially acute where the superior has some definite opinion about what is an average performance, namely where some degree of planning or budgeting is employed. For this reason, the secret reserve has much concerned writers on Soviet economic affairs (see Granick [53] and Campbell [25]).[6]

In all countries, the object of the game is to retain undisclosed inventories of stores and materials or excessive provisions and liabilities during favourable periods, with a view to letting these 'reserves' run down again in the unfavourable periods. This clearly represents a smoothing technique, and it could sometimes be argued that the practice merely eliminates quite meaningless statistical noise in the system. The danger is that it encourages employees to tell deliberate lies to their superiors and frequently leads on to attempts to cover up downright inefficiencies and frauds by the same means. Unfortunately it is not true to say that these reserves have to be self-correcting over time, since the losses carried forward in this way can eventually be allowed to fall into a period when a fire or a strike would make some loss inevitable. It is not unknown for managers to bring about disasters of this type to provide an opportunity to straighten the records.

Secret reserves are the reverse of the embezzlement and the bad debt, although all three arise in boom conditions. The former involves the non-disclosure of assets which are available to the enterprise, while the latter occur when the absence of assets is disguised in some way. However, it should be noted that the phenomena are complementary; assets which do not appear in the books are very readily misappropriated, and it is very easy to default on a debt when the creditor has already made a premature provision against its non-collection.

A fourth type of bias requires neither theft nor the creation of a reserve, so that the reported result is literally correct. However, the cost itself is inflated above what it need have been. This is the 'organisational slack'[7] as defined in the previous chapter. It is the difference between the technologically necessary cost, or 'rack cost,' and the accepted standard, or normal cost.

It is submitted that these four elements comprise what might be called the 'super-bezzle' in both micro- and macro-accounting. That is to say a measure of the difference, almost certainly a shortfall, between the apparent economic position and the real position. The signs of this structural model might be expected to behave as follows:

1 Criminal embezzlement is bound to be negative, since it is hard to imagine a situation in which an employee is moved to introduce his own funds into the enterprise in a clandestine way.[8]
2 Similarly, it is not very likely that a debtor would be so overcome with prosperity that he would press additional payments upon his creditors. Of course, sensible creditors will make provision for possible bad debts, which will reduce the shortfall between the expectations and the outcome, and an over-provision might conceivably be made. However, it should be observed that this point will be bound up with the whole problem of secret reserves; over-provision and low rates of default will be experienced in boom-periods, while slumps encourage both bad debts *and* under-provision.
3 Biased reporting does not involve abstraction of assets but can take the form of an under-statement or an over-statement of the true position. To the extent that secret reserves are in fact manipulated to smooth statistical noise in the system, it does not seem unreasonable to suppose that at any one time the amounts set aside in this way in the various enterprises of a country should themselves cancel out and be a largely neutral element in the super-bezzle. On the other hand, the firm may also attempt to smooth the effects of the trade-cycle in this fashion and so produce an under-statement of assets in the boom and an over-statement in the slump. Since the true bezzle and the bad debts are essentially negative, the effect of bias will be to reduce the super-bezzle in boom periods and accentuate it in the slumps. In short, embezzlements and bad debts are items that should be available to the enterprise and are recorded in its records as present, but have in fact been misappropriated. Biased reporting relates to assets that should be there, in fact are there, but are under- or over-valued in the books. Organisational slack involves resources that should be available, i.e. if the organisation was operating at maximum efficiency, but which are not in fact present and are not recorded as present.

Depending on how one defines 'actual,' one would probably say that this super-bezzle does not result in any discrepancy between the reported position and the actual position. On the other hand it clearly represents some divergence between the actual position and the correct one. Items are being shown as part of the inter-industry transactions which are really part of the added value and final consumption, from the national income point of view.[9]

It is now necessary to consider the various ways in which these different parts of the super-bezzle might affect the overall national accounts. It might be best to take as an example the two-firm economy from Chapter 2. These can best be viewed as a set of journal entries adjusting the original example:

1 Embezzlement

An employee of Company *A* has fraudulently converted £2000 of goods purchased from Company *B*

			£	£
a	In Company *A*'s records:			
	Wages	Dr	2000	
	To purchases from *B*			2000
b	In Company *B*'s records:			
	Sales to *A*	Dr	2000	
	Sales to householder			2000
c	In the household sector records:			
	Household consumption	Dr	2000	
	To factor payments			2000

2 Bad debt

Company *B* does not pay for goods purchased from Company *A* for £6000

			£	£
a	In Company *A*'s records:			
	Retained earnings	Dr	6000	
	To *B*'s debtor account			6000
b	In Company *B*'s records:			
	A's creditors' account	Dr	6000	
	To retained earnings			6000

(Clearly this results in no more than a transfer within the item 'Corporate saving.')

3 Secret reserve

A supervisor in Company *A* has constantly overstated his department's usages of raw material and so built up an undisclosed inventory costing £3000

			£	£
a	In Company *A*'s records:			
	Inventories	Dr	3000	
	To retained earnings			3000
b	In the savings and investment account:			
	Changes in inventories	Dr	3000	
	To retained earnings			3000

4 *Organisation slack*
Employees of Company *A* make 'excessive' usages of raw material amounting to £4000

a If this excess usage is equated to consumption of the goods by the employees concerned the accounting transactions will be identical to those for embezzlement, and will increase household consumption and factor payment by £4000.

b Alternatively if one considers that the increased usages are nevertheless avoidable, the transaction would be viewed as the conversion of retained earnings into factor payments, without any increase in household consumption.

Obviously these journal entries only reflect the direct transfer of goods, services and cash, and ignore the externality effects involved. £4000 taken out in organisational slack does not have the same welfare effect as £4000 in wages; £4000 paid in wages does not have the same effect as £4000 in retained earnings.

It remains to inquire what is the possibility of measuring the overall size of the super-bezzle at any one time and hence of estimating its effects on the reported national income and national investment. The more criminal parts of the sum might be estimated fairly roughly. Convictions for embezzlement and insolvency proceedings of the more formal sort are the subject of official record, and it might be possible to make some judgement of the proportion these detected cases bear to the total incidence. Of course, it would be necessary to bear in mind the point made by Galbraith originally; these deficiencies are almost winked at in good times and prosecuted in bad times. Not only will the detection rate be higher in bad times (if this hypothesis be true) but also a fair proportion of the sums involved will relate to earlier and more prosperous years.

The effect of biased reporting will prove more difficult to assess. It might be that to the extent that statistics of real business activity showed divergent trends from reported profits, it would be possible to argue that this provided some measure of the extent to which executives were sandbagging or lightening their reports to their superiors. Of course, this assumes that the returns of real activity are not capable of adjustment.

Organisational slack provides the most interesting and least readily measurable element in the super-bezzle. One could say that until wage negotiators (and cost negotiators) are able to admit that what they are really arguing about is not matters of absolute truth or absolute justice, but just how a cake should be divided between the collaborators in an enterprise, they are not able to admit that any slack exists at all, even probably to themselves. And yet everyone to whom the writer has mentioned the concept has readily agreed to the existence of the phenomenon—everywhere except in his own situation.[10]

6.4 PPBS and cost benefit analysis

It seems appropriate to say something about cost benefit analysis and the so-called PPBS at this point. Probably, as with many techniques introduced for the amelioration of social problems, the direct value of these techniques has been heavily overstated—as a necessary step towards getting them adopted and accepted in the first instance. However, once it is accepted that any organisation may have multi-dimensional objectives, with a heavy emphasis on such potentially vague criteria as 'quality of life,' it becomes more than usually necessary to install very formal procedures for establishing these objectives, evaluating the costs and results of different strategies in a uniform fashion, and subsequently controlling their implementation.

The paper by Carlson [26] sets out these basic parts of the PPBS.

1 Program structures. 'This is a grouping of agency activities into objective-oriented classifications so that programs with common objectives or common outputs are considered together, along with the cost of each' [p 617].

2 Issue letters. 'These are letters from the budget director to the agency heads defining major issues which should receive attention during the current planning and budgeting cycle' [p 618].

3 Program memoranda. 'The program memorandum for a selected major category is intended to be a brief document summarising the decisions made by an agency on major issues in the program category and articulating the reasons for them' [p 619].

4 Special analytic studies. '. . . Such studies could be economic analyses, sociological evaluations, data collection efforts, development of useful techniques, mathematical models, or almost anything else . . .' [p 618].

5 *Program and financial plans.* 'This document lays out, by program

category, and for the next five years, the funds committed to various program areas by past decisions, and, wherever possible, projected program outputs for the same period . . .' [p 619].

The techniques thus place heavy emphasis on formal statements (1, 2, 3 above) which attempt to discover the basic objectives of the various programs being undertaken, both with a view to eliminating duplications of effort and to finding any aspects of the problem which are not being covered at all. The need for all programs to have some measurable 'output' is also stressed, both as an aid to cost control and to provide some measure of the success being achieved. The fact that previous decisions have substantially pre-empted a substantial proportion of the budget is recognised as well; the very limited room for current manoeuver is often overlooked in operations of this type.

Turning to the application of the techniques to industrial enterprises, it is obvious that more firms are becoming concerned over the social and environmental effects of their activities, if only because the activities of 'ginger groups'[11] draw their attention to them. No doubt studies and memoranda are already prepared, but this governmental experience should be taken into account—the need for a really well-conceived objective, to avoid duplication or omission, to establish significant output measure are equally present at the enterprise level.[12]

However, the reasons for this latter-day disenchantment are simply the known weaknesses of the quantification technique which underlies the whole PPBS structure—cost-benefit analysis. These can be summarised by a few quotations from the well-known review article by Prest and Turvey [95]:

> There are two very general limitations of principle which must be recognised at the outset. First, cost-benefit analysis as generally understood is only a technique for taking decisions within a framework which has to be decided upon in advance, and which involves a wide range of considerations, many of them of a political or social character. Secondly, cost-benefit techniques as so far developed are least relevant and serviceable for what one might call large-scale investments decisions [p 685].

The first caveat is simply the point that has already made its appearance more than once so far; it is necessary to know what it is that the society in question is trying to do, then find the best of the strategies acceptable to it. It follows that this 'political or social' prejudice is what determines the answer obtained, since the rest of the operation must work within the limits set down by it. The second point is one which will be returned to in Chapter 8; we commonly make the assumption that it must be possible to isolate and solve subproblems. This assumes that the various prices and constraints used are not themselves affected by the decision to be taken. In small matters this may be near enough to the truth, but where a large public works programme is proposed for a small developing country the whole constellation of prices and outputs may need recalculation by some general equilibrium model.

In fact, the technique is the familiar net present value discounting procedure of conventional capital decision-making. Thus:

> This formulation is very general but it does at least enable us to set out a series of questions, the answers to which constitute the general principles of cost-benefit analysis:
>
> 1 Which costs and which benefits are to be included?
> 2 How are they to be valued?
> 3 At which interest rate are they to be discounted?
> 4 What are the relevant constraints? [p 686].

The answers to all of these questions are of necessity less than clear-cut. Most of the projects evaluated in this way have both direct and indirect effects; the problems of externalities have already been discussed in Chapter 5. Prest and Turvey continue:

> . . . Progenitors of the public investment *should* take into account the external effects of their actions in so far as they alter the physical production possibilities of other producers, or the satisfaction that consumers get from given resources; they *should not* take side effects into account if the sole effect is via prices of products or factors [p 688].

The argument is that to include both the additional traffic and the increased rental value of sites for filling-stations and restaurants near motorways is to count a single benefit twice. They observe:

> No one can pretend that this distinction is a simple one in practice; there may well be results from an investment which are partially technological and partial pecuniary.

The valuation of costs and benefits, once enumerated, is an equally debatable procedure. The prices used should not take account of general changes in the overall price level, but should include those specifically induced by the proposed change. From the viewpoint of private individuals and enterprises, it is clear that taxes and controls are factors which must be included, but it is important that the public authorities should work in terms of real resources only. Similarly, many examples arise where goods or services are exchanged at conventional prices which do not clear the market (i.e. leave unsatisfied demand at that price); where market imperfections lead to the inclusion of some monopoly price element; where collective goods are supplied free or at arbitrarily-fixed prices:

> The relevance of this discussion for our purpose is that where commodities are supplied at zero price or at non-market clearing prices which bear no relationship to consumer preferences, there is no basis for arriving at investment decisions by computing the present value of sales [p 696].

Finally, some undoubtedly and important effects are strictly intangible either because they cannot be quantified in any meaningful way, or because even though quantifiable, 'they cannot be valued in any market sense.' In general, the exercise of too much ingenuity in the solution of valuation problems of this sort is unsound, because it compounds the general problem of the need to accept some politically determined framework of reference, with further idiosyncracies of the valuer's own personal prejudices. This problem is also discussed again in Chapter 8.

The question of the interest rates to be used is one of baffling theoretical difficulty but of no great practical note at all. Turvey and Prest say:

> Discussion of social rates of time preference, social opportunity cost, etc, do not cut very much ice in most empirical work. . . . In practice, the most usual kind of procedure is to select an interest rate or rates on the basis of observed rates ruling at the time, for calculating present values, etc [pp 699–700].

As well as the obvious physical constraints which must be taken in these exercises, there will also be quite artificial legal or budgetary limitations on action which must be observed. Finally, there may be what are described as 'distributional' constraints, governing the extent, if any, to which the proposed change or investment is permitted to alter the distribution of income throughout the population.

6.5 Social indicators and the state of the nation

The previous section described some techniques that seem either to ignore second-order, 'externality' effects, or assume that they can be readily identified and measured if they are of real importance. As affluence grows (at least in developed countries) technological developments press more heavily upon the environment and so leave less slack of any sort to absorb the social effects of what we do. It is becoming apparent that what are apparently purely economic activities have social side-effects of considerable complexity.[13] Unfortunately our present expertise in building and manipulating complex interactive models is not great, so that any great sensitivity to these matters has, in the past, tended to be at the expense of any attempt at long-range centralised planning. An American writer, Bauer, remarks:

> As the opposite pole from the Soviet position of tight centralised, rather long-range planning, is the historic British doctrine of 'muddling through.' In a sense, this doctrine appears to be the antithesis of planning. But note that the doctrine of muddling through is based on an elaborate concern for second-order consequences of actions. It assumes that social systems and processes are very complex . . . [11, p 7].

Of course, concern for these second-order consequences is not new; indeed the phrase 'the state of the nation' which is often used in discussions in this area refers to the American President's annual report with the title 'The State of the Union Message,' and dates from Washington himself. What is new is an awareness that the phenomena are consequences of policy pursued elsewhere, and a desire to establish some 'social indicators' leading to a 'social systems accounting,' and the use of quantifiable models to achieve a sort of 'social engineering' aimed at improving the quality of life. Biderman's paper in *Social Indicators* [17, p 93] tabulates the frequency with which this Presidential Message makes specific reference to quantified social indicators of various types; a simple list of the indicators will suffice for the immediate purpose:

Economic indicators

- Total activity and income statistics
- Markets and production
- Income distribution
- Productive resources
- 'Sound' currency
- Employment rates
- Treasury surpluses
- Debts
- Sale of public lands

Non-economic indicators

- Population
- Technological advances
- Education
- Military appropriations
- Utilities and transportation
- Governmental growth
- Natural resources
- Welfare
- Other

In 1933, and again in 1960, President's Commissions have produced statements on the American 'National Goals.' Biderman's paper also contains the following list of 'goal areas,' combined from the two *Reports* [p 88]:

The individual
Equality
Democratic process
Education
Arts and Sciences
Health and Welfare
Democratic economy
Economic growth
Technological change
Agriculture
Living conditions

These goal areas contain 81 specific goals, for which some social indicators exist in only 48 cases. These detailed goals will be discussed in the next chapter, when an attempt will be made to relate the goals and indicators to the accounting activity of an individual enterprise. Readers may remark that this section contains very few figures. This is not by accident, since although substantial tabulation of data exists for a wide variety of social phenomena, they are of a type which have more appeal for the politician—and perhaps the econometrician—than for the accountant or the sociologist/anthropologist. The reasons will be discussed at length in Chapter 8, but this quotation from Bauer [*op cit*] is revealing:

> . . . no system of social indicators designed for general utility will ever be ideal for study in any one program. . . . The system to be developed must be a reasonable compromise for the range of phenomena that one can anticipate as being of importance [pp 39–40].

A criticism of this approach to data collection is that it clearly presupposes that no theoretical model has been devised to explain the causal relationships which it is believed exist within the system being studied; at the best we seem to be looking for some credible regression-line to be interpolated into a set of rather randomly selected time-series.[14] The unsatisfactory nature of this approach to what is bound to be an expensive data-collection operation will become clear in the next chapter, since enterprises will be required to provide data for both the national models and their own versions, and the unstructured nature of the model-building process becomes apparent.

6.6 Towards a societal theory of macro-accounting

The previous reference to any basic principles of accounting was in

Chapter 4, where Mattessich's assumptions were reconciled with a number of cultural variables. It remains to consider how the resulting five major assumptions are affected, or extended by the macro-accounting material discussed in the present chapter.

1 There are a system of valuation and a set of values, which are ranked in a purposive fashion. This assumption clearly looks towards a multi-dimensional system; the PPBS is an attempt at purposive ranking within such a system. PPBS has not, to the author's knowledge, been applied outside the governmental sector, presumably because multi-dimensional accounting has not been given practical consideration at the enterprise level. No doubt the technique would become necessary if it ever were. This assumption seems adequate at the macro-level.

2 There are data held to be material to these values, which are located in a period of time and at some within it. In general, the assumption of location at some point *within* a period seems less strongly held as to macro-accounting. However, the existence of the super-bezzle may also indicate the need for some revision of this assumption; although this chapter has shown some journal entries which purport to represent the effect of various parts of this phenomena, the text has suggested that by their nature the items are not strictly observable. Other classes of phenomena are observable, but only in a subjective fashion. Similarly, Chapter 3 referred to the greater importance of 'imputed items' of all kinds in macro-accounting, which were equally un-amenable to scientific measurement. The difficulty is not unique; one is told that the electron is a particle which can be located, or measured, but not both. . . . It will be suggested in Chapter 8 that all these items can be measured *by inference* in an entirely significant fashion. Perhaps one could amend and extend the assumption like this:

> . . . Which *may be* located in time a period of time and *may be* located at some point within it. *There is also a causal model which is held to explain the working of the system or subsystem and provides estimates of the dimensions of a number of coefficients which are also material to the values.*

3 The data . . . can be classified so as to suggest a significant structure. Chapter 2 showed that macro-accounting makes full use of the facilities offered by this assumption. The production, the household and Government sectors all comprise the same group of people, acting in various capacities at different times. Again, the quotation from Odd Aukrust in Chapter 5 suggested that data could be classified by reference to effects on other parts of the system, as well as in more obvious ways.

4 The relationship between the objects or agents is seen either as a single direct flow at one point in time, or as some more complex relationship involving direct or indirect effects over a period of time. Aukrust also drew attention to 'requited' and 'unrequited' flows, where a pair (or more) of direct flows are causally related. However, the material discussed in this chapter about 'economic growth' and 'social indicators' suggests that it is becoming increasingly difficult to avoid giving more and more formal recognition to externality effects, certainly at the macro-level. Probably what is usually meant by 'economic activity' is adequately reflected by a record of the underlying requited and unrequited flows; to the extent that the whole labour-force of a country was (or has been supposed to have been) totally involved in such activity for the major part of its waking life, one may suppose that it was not unreasonable to confine 'accounting' to the direct flows only. Affluence, and a technology that seems likely to press hard on the limits of the world's natural resources, seems to be bringing about a society in which both leisure takes up a much greater part of the time of the labour-force and also many able-bodied citizens are likely to be permanently unemployed. Purely 'economic accounting' has nothing to say about leisure and unemployment; these are reflected as simple transfer payments. Social policy to regulate this non-economic activity needs a societal accounting; this accounting will deal for the most part in externalities, whose dimensions (as has been pointed out) can only be inferred from social indicators. The wording of the assumption seems generally adequate; perhaps one should emphasize the difficulty of fitting societal accounting into the conventional discrete time periods by adding:

The second-order effects of direct flows may not be confined to those time periods in which they themselves are located.

5 . . . *humans are seen as collaborators in various ways for the purposive pursuit of values. Human collaborators can be grouped and regrouped so as to reflect varying mutual interests.* This grouping and regrouping will be considered in the next chapter, since it affects micro-accounting rather than macro-accounting. The distinctly attenuated nature of the 'entity' or 'proprietorship' being accounted to in macro-accounting has been discussed in an earlier chapter. Realisation and recognition of data do not seem to present any features which are peculiar to macro-accounting.

6.7 Notes

1 As might be expected from what was said about the contrast between the micro-(formalist) and the macro-(substantivist) approaches to the subject, it is much more respectable to consider societal matters at the macro-level.

2 Thus Mishan summarises his conditions:

'. . . the set of conditions that, if met, would ensure a positive relation between economic growth and welfare.

'*First*, that the economy be highly competitive in structure in all its branches, or else so organised that in all sectors the outputs of goods are such that their prices tend to equal their corresponding marginal costs. (*Note*: Perhaps it should be repeated that these conditions are sufficient, though *not* necessary. Necessary conditions would be more difficult to specify . . .)

'*Second*, that all the measurable effects on other people or firms arising in the production or use of any goods—other than the effects which already register on the market mechanism in the form of alterations in product or factor prices—be brought into the cost calculus.

'*Third*, that in increasing *per capita* output over time the process of growth does not bring about a less equitable distribution of income.

'*Fourth*, that the consuming public be fully conversant with the comparative qualities and performance of all new goods coming on to the market.

'*Fifth*, that the public, organised as producers, become no worse off in adapting themselves to new techniques or production.

'*Sixth*, that the so-called relative income hypothesis does not hold; or less stringently, that an overall increase in real income *per capita* will have more than negligible effects in making some people better off without making others feel worse off.

'*Seventh*, that the welfare experienced by men from sources other than goods produced by the economic system is small enough to be neglected' [84, pp 171–2].

3 The way in which economic enterprises are usually organised makes this aspect of macro-accounting of very great importance to their successful operation. These enterprises are almost invariably 'self-financing' and thus their basic objective of survival and perhaps growth tends to be expressed in terms of solvency. The need to generate

the required funds means that 'money and banking' provide a brake on the activities of such enterprises, which for the most part is no doubt salutary. Less justifiably perhaps, this criterion also provides a largely unanswerable evidence of the 'success' of any enterprise which in fact is able to make money from its activities.

And yet the existence of societal wealth, with its interface both through the mazeways of its collaborators and externality effects with economic activity, provides the possibility that a financially unsuccessful firm *might* be a net creator of wealth, while a financially viable firm could contribute a net reduction. Obviously, this effect is what governments attempt to redress by systems of subsidy and taxation, although its success in achieving this is rather debatable, as was described in note 16 of Chapter 5. However, subsidy and taxation *can only effect a redistribution of economic wealth*, and to the extent that they are employed for this purpose, it is usually seen as an essentially temporary arrangement until some Pareto optimum situation can be restored. The foregoing analysis suggests that subsidies, etc, are supposed in fact to serve as *conversions* of one form of wealth into another, for the purpose of enabling an enterprise to continue to operate its self-financing control. Since the systems are not directly interconnected, there seems little reason why subventions of this sort should not continue so long as a positive trade-off between the two can be observed.

4 It can be seen that the writer disagrees with the distinguished members of the American Accounting Association's Committee on Foundations of Accounting Measurement, who say in their report [1, p 48]:

> 'Thus may we envisage the possibility of reducing, in time, *the foundations of most scientific disciplines to the foundation of more elementary disciplines*. The ideal would be to express the foundations of accounting measurement in terms of economic and administrative behaviour, to express the foundations of the latter in terms of psychology and sociology, the foundations of these again in terms of biology, then in terms of chemistry, and finally in terms of physics.
>
> 'This, indeed, could be regarded as the ultimate goal of a superscience. Obviously, we are far away from this *Utopia*.'

One might suspect that it will not be strictly possible to build the bridge which this Committee sees as linking 'psychology and sociology' with 'biology,' and thence on into the natural sciences. We are monkeys who observe one another, and modify our behaviour because some other monkey is *watching*; in this way we differ from phenomena in the physical sciences which can be said to 'do their thing' whether anyone is watching or not. Also, we have rejected the idea of the possibility of fragmenting the social sciences, at least prior to the development of a general theory. This would prevent the possibility of viewing psychology, etc, as the foundation of economics. Finally, it does not seem reasonable to describe 'accounting measurement' as a more advanced discipline than, say, economics; it is the technique by which we make both *ex post* and *ex ante* assessments of the effectiveness of our actions in achieving those states of 'feeling-tone' which we value.

5 One might suppose that it would not be any easy matter to measure the bezzle since it is a crime which, if successful, is not even noticed by the victim, let alone reported to or solved by the police. This is just another aspect of the basic problems noted above—we are laboratory animals who have to observe one another, and by and large we do this by asking the subjects of our investigations to tell us what they have been doing rather than by watching them do it. Obviously, the subject may tell us downright lies, but even if he does try and tell us the truth, the interposition of his mental processes will introduce a greater or lesser degree of subjectivity into his reports.

6 The 'sovietologists' cited here remark on the activities of the *tolkachi* (or 'fixers') in Soviet industry who oil the wheels of the bureaucratic planning in a variety of enterprising ways—all involving the creation and disposal of 'organisational slack.' It is interesting to see how a Soviet writer sees things:

> 'The greatest development in the falsification of the data of accounting has been reached in the epoch of modern monopoly capitalism, when the competition between monopoly capitalists and the struggle for world domination has become highly accentuated' [34, pp 9–10].

7 The concept of organisational slack described previously does not coincide precisely with that of Cyert and March [33]. They view the firm as a coalition of members; organisational slack consists in payments to members of the coalition in excess of what is required to maintain the organisation [*op cit*, p 37]. At any one time, one supposes, there will be an element of leeway over and above the rack cost without which a member might decline to collaborate; Cyert and March refer to any surpluses beyond this level as the organisational slack, but from the point of view of ascertaining the amount of the super-bezzle the total excess over the rack cost seems to be more significant.

8 But not impossible; branch managers *have* been known to do this to prevent the closure of a shop or plant which would otherwise have appeared to be non-viable. Their resources for counter-embezzlement are not likely to equal those available for conversion in the more usual direction, however.

9 Presumably it makes us happier to waste say £5 worth of electricity than to save the electricity and have £5 added to our pay; presumably our employer is happy to leave it that way because he believes that if we were made to save the electricity, we would therefore demand more than £5 in additional wages. This suggests that a firm which appeared to pay miserable wages and negligible dividends might in fact be making a fair contribution to the national income, so long as it is *capable* of doing 'better,' but likes things the way they are. Alternatively, five weeks on the Costa Brava and a power-boat at the weekends may barely compensate for having to act as an efficient zombie for the rest of the working year.

10 A few more interesting points could be made about this aspect of the super-bezzle:

(a) It is necessary to have a job before you can share in the organisation's slack, so the unemployed tend to be doubly deprived.

(b) Moreover, it is only human collaborators who need organisational slack; machines work perfectly well without it and may even become less effective if they are over supplied. This means that a very highly automated factory has very little slack.

(c) A productivity agreement whereby the workers agree to increased automation and the redundancy of some employees is likely to pay for itself even if very high wages have to be paid to the surviving employees. Not only will the survivors find their working rhythm more closely enforced by the machines, but both the wages *and the necessary slack* of the redundant work-force will be saved.

(d) It is a truism that human beings obtain status and even entertainment from the performance of socially acceptable labour. If we ever reach a stage where it was necessary to face the fact that it was no longer necessary for every able-bodied man to be gainfully employed, it would become necessary to supply the unemployed not only with the equivalent of their wages, but also the equivalent of the slack they have to forego.

11 It would be unfortunate if the current radicalisation of sections of industrial workers and young people led the business world to see sociological (or societal) accounting as an opportunity either for a 'public relations exercise'—or a 'counter-insurgency drive,' or even as indicating a need for wearing a hair-shirt of some kind.

A recent paper to the Scottish Institute's Summer School by Louwers of NV Phillips, Eindhoven [78], entitled 'Sincerity in financial reporting,' gives hints of the emergence of all three viewpoints:

> '[Many people] believe that the large industrial enterprise is a kind of business that services the community in much the same way as Bonnie and Clyde used to service banks. It is the task of both today's business leaders and their advisers, the accountants, to explain and justify their policies to the public.
>
> 'The dominant concept is that a company holds a franchise from society, and management must therefore consider itself accountable towards a larger universe than shareholder interests. . . .
>
> 'Concealing bad news by ignoring it or sandwiching it between optimistic statements can and will generate a credibility gap between the reader of the Report and the company. Issues such as ecology, pollution control, civil rights and consumerism were never referred to in annual reports in the past. It is now considered corporate responsibility that these and many more such subjects be examined and reported on.'

What Louwers and others concerned with the preparation of the reports of large enterprises are up against can be judged from the activities of an organisation 'Counter information services.' This body issues very well produced facsimiles of the reports of companies (to date Rio Tinto-Zinc and the General Electric Company), whose content may be assessed from the following quotation from the press release which accompanied the latter 'Anti-report' [32]:

> 'Three areas heavily affected by GEC's redundancies, Harlow, Woolwich and Lincoln were visited by CIS researchers, and the text includes first-hand comments from trade union officials and GEC workers affected by the 'Weinstock Axe' [pp 17–24).

The role of the Labour Government in fostering the merger and accepting the redundancies that followed is criticised; so also is the role of the national trade union officials in tacitly co-operating in the GEC strategy of massive redundancies, a role made easier by the absence of any effective national combine committee [p 25]. There is a detailed factual run-down on the company's sub-divisions, with a full list of all its factories and figures on the sales and profits of each product division (p. 3). A full list of directors, with their names and addresses, shareholdings and other directorships, is included [p 8–9].

Further sections expose little-known aspects of the group's involvement in the arms trade including equipment for US aircraft in Vietnam [pp 27–9] and South Africa where the company pays black workers the minimum rates for the electrical industry. . . . The report concludes:

> 'If "the national interest" means anything more than the interests of the shareholders of GEC, then it is patently absurd on economic, social and moral grounds that more and more workers should be added to the enormous pool of unemployed to swell the profits of a tiny minority of the community' [pp 30–5].

Rousing stuff, containing many inconvenient points for the company's managers; but one must still ask 'Does the *Anti*-report give a true and fair view of the GEC, either?' If one reads both the Report and the Anti-report together, would one have an adequate (as opposed, perhaps, to a balanced) view? In the absence of a convincing model of the workings of our society it just is not possible to say what data are significant, and so impossible to win any argument. As things are, one can rightly take GEC to task over its wage policy towards black Africans, but one ought to allow the company to speculate on the fate of those Africans if the plant were to close down, and they were to be returned to some remote Bantustan. . . .

12 In short, the irreverent could claim that PPBS is simply an attempt to place a sham façade of precision around a type of activity which is essentially imprecise; certainly the full formalities as described by Carlson are more rarely to be met with at the present time. In 1969 the US Bureau of the Budget examined sixteen Federal agencies (after three years' experience with PPBS to find 'that most agencies do not perform the planning, programming and budgeting functions much differently than they did before the introduction of PPBS.'

13 This is simply because the market-mechanism becomes less capable of providing acceptable allocations of welfare under these conditions. Consider these extracts from the Brooks Report of the OECD [100]:

'However, once the stage of relieving economic scarcity for the majority of the members of society is passed, the accuracy and sensitivity of the market mechanism as an indicator of the aspirations of society can be called in question. The transformations generated by economic growth in the market sector of the economy have given birth to a range of new needs that are not readily expressible as market demand. These are collective needs—essentially indivisible benefits enjoyed in some measure by all members of society whether they pay for them or not, e.g. clean air and water, aesthetically satisfying urban surroundings, the amenities of nature.

'In addition, there is a trend towards supplying certain types of needs as a matter of right to all citizens, even though these needs were formally treated as goods or services to be sold on the market. Examples are universal education, health care, parks and recreation areas, public housing, social welfare services and the preservation of civil order' [p 27].

'Collective needs' differ profoundly in their behaviour from those satisfied by the market; the former have to be aggregated vertically rather than horizontally (see the diagram).

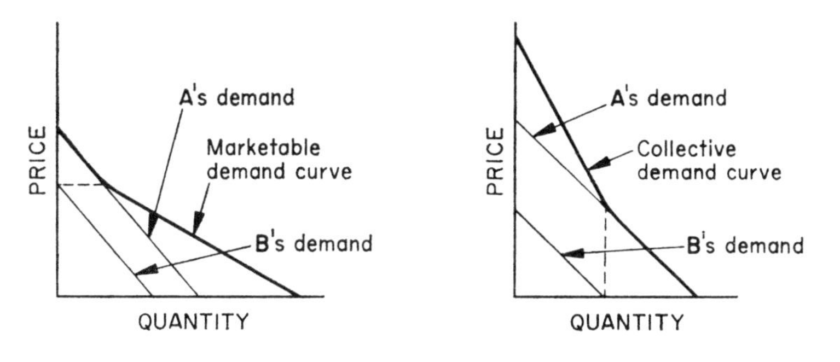

Once needs become 'social ends' rather than matters of personal preference, a 'policy' is needed to determine allocation; the Report also points out:

'Furthermore, even if there is a consensus on the value to be attached to certain social ends, this is not sufficient to determine the programmes that can meet them. Many of our social goals are stated in too generalised terms to be readily translatable into concrete applied research tasks—at least in the present state of basic understanding. Moreover, we are dealing not with a single, simple goal but with a complex of mutually dependent and interacting goals . . . [*op cit*, p 56].

14 A recent paper in *European Business* by Cazares provides a very useful summary of the present state of the discussions over social indicators; moreover, it provides evidence of publications in the area other than in the English language. Cazares rightly warns against allowing recognition of the need for some over-arching theory to justify the collection of social data, to be used as grounds for doing nothing at all. He also writes (even in translation) with a Gallic precision which is eminently quotable:

'. . . the progress achieved since 1966 has been somewhat less than modest. For what reason? Unquestionably, one is that the difficulties of the operation had been underestimated, and that a good many illusions had been entertained about the potentially fast emergence of a new social quantification. It strikes me that all this is reflected in the time lag between the appearance of the two main trends in the interpretation of the nature and role of social indicators: the first trend to emerge—of "normative" inspiration and action-geared—was also the most ambitious one; the second, more scientific and more realistic, showed up later on . . .

The first school contains those like Gross who seek to build 'social accounts' on the lines of existing economic ones; the second feel that measurable social phenomena are but a small part of the considerations which ought to be taken into account. Cazares goes on to point out that in any case compilers of social indicators tend to exclude all subjective measures of welfare:

'Angus Campbell, the director of the University of Michigan's Institute of Social Research, takes a sharply defined stand with respect to the role of social indicators. He fails to share Mrs Sheldon's purism with regard to recourse to social quantification for elaborating a policy. However, against the other school of thought—that of the "normativists"—he levels a criticism that I have encountered in no other observer, to the effect that so far, the advocates of social indicators have concerned themselves only with the so-called objective dimensions of welfare, those that are apprehended via the intermediary of the physical environment (consumer durable or non-durables, social overhead capital), or, at least, by the intermediary of behaviour patterns (in health matters—the death rate, chronic disability, temporary incapacitations), totally disregarding data related to satisfactions or aspirations . . .' [pp 47–50].

7 Societal Aspects of Micro-Accounting

7.1 Mini-accounting, micro-accounting and macro-accounting

Following the usual custom, the prefixes 'micro' and 'macro' have been used to refer to enterprise-level and national-level activities, respectively. It might be noted in passing that 'governmental accounting' is essentially micro-accounting; central and local government departments are simply budget-financed enterprises whose results are aggregated into the national accounts in the normal way.

However, macro-accounts include sectoral accounts for 'households,' which are assumed to be an aggregation of the income and expenditure of private citizens during the relevant period. Clearly, these activities of private households are most unlikely to be matters of formal record, and it will be remembered from Chapter 3 that an assumption that a man's interior 'psychic accounts' could be cast in conventional ledger form is rather unrealistic. Accordingly, it might seem unnecessary to take much time over consideration of what these accounts (which might be described as 'mini-accounts') might comprise if they did in fact exist. On the other hand, it could be argued that their aggregation into the 'household sector' account is only one use, and perhaps the less important use of the putative mini-accounts.

The behavioural Theory of the Firm claims that the 'firm' has no separate corporate essence, but comprises a number of individuals who enter into a coalition, in which they continue as long as they receive compensation which (in some sense) satisfies them. It follows that although some collaborators can hold titles like 'managing director' and 'head of department' while others have to make do with those of 'cleaner' or 'warehouseman,' it is not likely that in fact either at this time or in previous times that the 'Objectives' and decisions of the firm simply reflect that personal preferences of the managing director, let alone such simplistic concepts as the 'maximisation of profit' or anything of that sort.

This analysis suggests that the micro-accounts of the firm could bear the same relationship to the putative mini-accounts of its collaborators as do the macro-accounts to the micro-accounts. It might be possible to restate the accounts of a company, so that they were seen to be, in effect, the mini-accounts of the individual proprietors, rentiers and workers, plus a statement of their collective transactions with the 'rest of the world,' which in this case would include other enterprises and government departments in their own country as well as foreigners. It will be remembered from Chapter 2 that the 'production boundary' lies between the 'household sector' and the 'production sector.' This demarcation must also exist in the mini-accounts.[1] Accordingly, the (household) mini-accounts of the various families might be distinguished from the (production) mini-accounts of any member of these households who happen to be workers, rentiers or proprietors. Since the mini-accounts are supposed to be capable of consolidation into conventional micro- and macro-accounting statements, they may be assumed to contain only the normal economic transactions,[2] and to take no account of the other societal items discussed in the two previous chapters. However, it may be useful to attempt to construct a set of mini-accounts to illustrate possible interfaces between transferable economic wealth and cultural wealth (see the diagram opposite).

Of course, this diagram is one appropriate to a Western capitalist society. Note 1 refers to the artificial, culturally-ordained nature of the production boundary. It follows that the diagram for the same industrial complex in the Soviet Union, for example, would be different. Using the same personnel in a Soviet context, suppose that Tom Smith, Jean Brown and Bill Brown in fact take out directors' salaries and not dividends, etc, while Company *A* is a ballet company, and Edith Black and her Government Services are also treated as non-productive transfers.[3] The diagram would become as shown on page 180.

A society that did not seek to exploit its environment would not have a production boundary and so would not be able to construct micro- or macro-accounts, even if it wanted to, because the mini-accounts could not exist.

The effect of consolidating these production mini-accounts into the original micro-account form is to present the data from the viewpoint

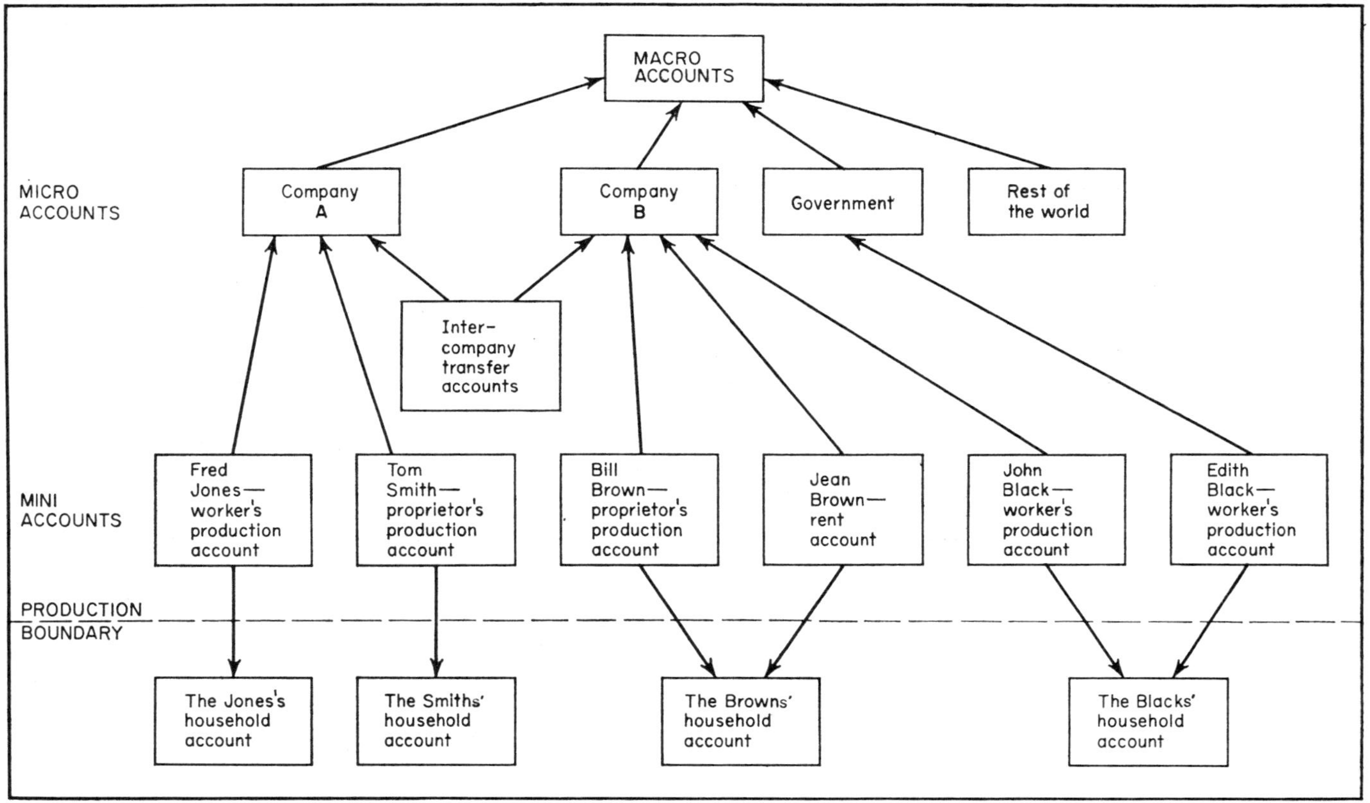
MACRO ACCOUNTS
MICRO ACCOUNTS
Company A
Company B
Government
Rest of the world
Inter-company transfer accounts
MINI ACCOUNTS
Fred Jones— worker's production account
Tom Smith— proprietor's production account
Bill Brown— proprietor's production account
Jean Brown— rent account
John Black— worker's production account
Edith Black— worker's production account
PRODUCTION BOUNDARY
The Jones's household account
The Smiths' household account
The Browns' household account
The Blacks' household account

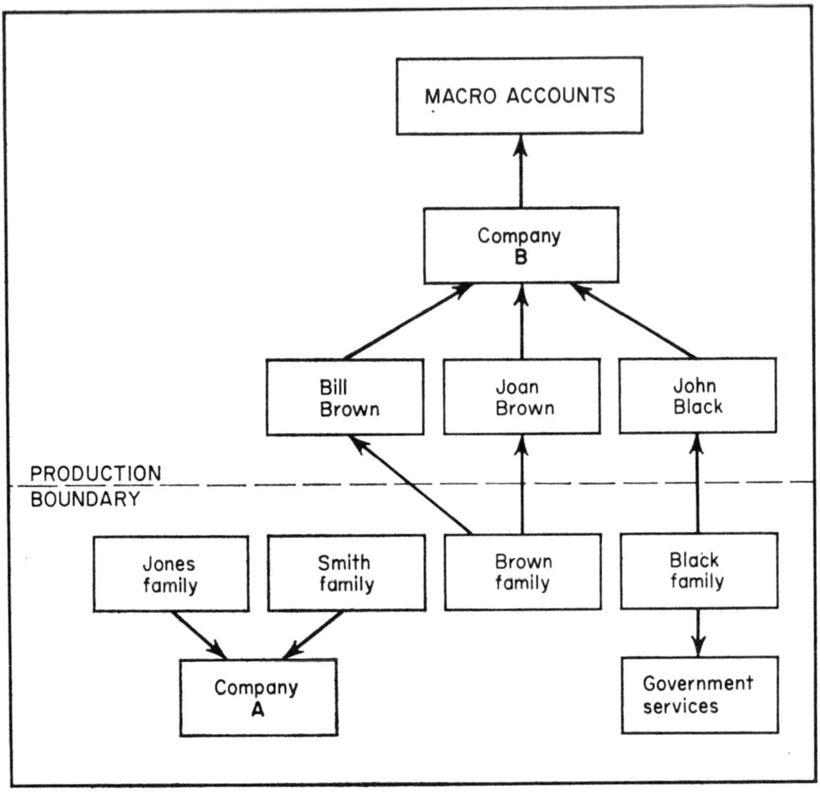

of an entity which is 'the firm.' This is parallel with the effect of consolidating groups of micro-accounts, which then show the affairs of the group of enterprises, but from the point of view of the shareholders in the holding company only. If the analysis in the first two chapters is accepted, conventionally interpreted accounting theory (of any variety) relates only to the intermediate micro-accounting stage; it can apply neither to the mini-accounts of the collaborators nor to the macro-accounts of the society to which they belong. The mini-accounts seem to be as neutral in content as the macro-accounts themselves, because only wages, dividends and proprietors' drawings for the business are shown in the production mini-accounts. It is assumed that the retained earnings of sole traders and partnerships remain in the micro-accounts as corporate savings. Since (in national macro-accounting) retained earnings and provisions for depreciation are normally run together as 'corporate savings' it can be seen that considerations of 'divisible profit' have been excluded from the mini-accounts altogether. One must now inquire whether this conclusion is reasonable; to what extent are proprietors (including shareholders) influenced by the possession of a growth stock? A substantial literature has grown up on this topic; a recent paper by Gonedes [49] provides the reader with an initial bibliography. In general, this material is 'formal' rather than 'substantive' in its approach and so does not pay much attention either to individual behaviour or the effect of specific social organisation (for example, a paper by Lerner and Rappaport [75]).

This treatment (which takes account of direct flow transactions only) in the household accounts is in accord with the overall treatment afforded to these items in macro-accounting. Psychic income is sought, if at all, in another system of reckoning. The various types of saving are seen either as 'forced saving' (to the extent that the holders of cash claims were *unable* to spend them on the consumer goods they actually desired) or as the investments made in the expectation of some future benefit which is more highly valued than an equivalent current act of consumption. Chapter 4 contained some discussion of the differing cultural approaches to the time-value of money. Perhaps the machinery for this valuation can be viewed as a type of externality which links the observation of the 'investment' with the psychic wealth of the man who has title to it.

It might be argued that this approach did not possess even a theoretical validity. In the first place the mini-accounts are almost never prepared,[4] and instead the micro-accounts are extracted from a mass of data produced by the firm itself as a by-product of its own control systems. Similarly, the macro-accounts are not, in practice, consolidations of the micro-accounts. Indeed, it could be argued since that the macro-accounts are in many respects prepared directly from raw data closely resembling the mini-accounts, the micro-accounts themselves could be looked upon not as an intermediate stage between an individual's mini-accounting and the society's macro-accounting, but rather as a completely separate system of records. The distinction at first seems to be between a view of the social accounts as a solid hierarchy of sub-accounts, wherein every detail of the subsidiary accounts is an integral, if undistinguishable, part of the overall picture, and the concept of a series of increasingly comprehensive précis, where the connection of the detail and the final picture is quite indirect. The concept of group dynamics discussed in Chapter 4 must lead to the acceptance of both propositions. The traditional economic accounts (at macro- and micro-level) *can* be arrived at by the aggregation of the various direct flows relating to the individuals who comprise them. Superimposed on this simple system of flows is the more complex network of secondary effects.

Although the 'direct flow' economic accounting is, in theory, a straightforward aggregation from the mini-level, it can be seen that many of the flows will be 'contra-ed out,' and so become redundant at the micro- and macro-levels. Similar redundancy occurs in the second-order system. This is because the acceptance of a Behavioural Theory of the Firm does not of itself invalidate the theory of classical macro-economics. The latter is defended by pointing out that matters may be of overriding importance in the individual case but may have no significance at all at an aggregate level.[5]

All sorts of personal quirks may incline an individual to decide to purchase or defer purchasing an automobile; if one wanted to know how the individual's decision is made it would be necessary to take account of these details. However, many of these personal influences are likely to be counter-balanced in the overall picture by contrary attitudes in other members of the society. For example, the man who loves to drive up to the country club in a car of the latest model is offset by the little old lady who has so much trouble getting the hang of her present vehicle that she intends to drive it until it falls apart. Such divergent attitudes are inevitable in any population and can probably be considered as deviations about some central trend. The trend itself may be sensitive to essentially macro influences such as population growth and the general level of prosperity.

The multiplier type of externality, as might be expected, is subject to an averaging process in larger groups, rather than aggregation. However, it should not be supposed that this results in a simple arithmetic average of the reading for each member. The internal structure of this group will mean that some members are more influential than others, so that greater weight is given to what *they* believe. It was also noted in Chapter 4 that groups are less cautious than individuals, so that one must suppose that greater weight will also be given to those extreme positions which favour the general trend of sentiment in the group.

Finally it must be observed that the mini-accounts illustrated above comprise only the *cash* flows of *individuals* and ignore the existence of commonly owned flows of any sort. Returning to the first diagram, the *psychic* income of the various families will comprise:

	The Joneses	*The Smiths*	*The Browns*	*The Blacks*
a Household consumption (per note 2)	£900	£6000	£6500	£1400
b Value of personal savings	?	?	?	?
c Value of corporate saving		Company *A* ?	Company *B* ?	
d Government services	———	£4800		———
e Value of government saving	———	?		———
f Effect of individual multipliers	?	?	?	?
g Effect of group multipliers (including organisational slack)	— Company *A*? —		— Company *B*? — Government?	
h Effect of general multipliers	———	?		———

7.2 Interface of cultural wealth and transferable wealth

In the foregoing chapters concepts of cultural wealth and income were discussed in a rather abstract fashion; for the most part the reference was to 'accounting' in the most general sense, and if any particular type of account was envisaged at all, this was probably the mini-accounts of the individual member of a society. The link between these mini-accounts and the conglomerate of individual collaborators which comprise the micro-accounts of the enterprise has been discussed in the previous section. However well argued a case may have been made for that analysis, it must be admitted that few people commonly see the accounts of an enterprise in that fashion. It is much more usual to see the firm as an entity which has dealings with its members, which has the facility of circumventing a number of very difficult problems. By looking at problems from the point of view of the enterprise as an entity, it is possible to say 'Business is business—the culture can look after itself; our job is to maximise transferable income.' In fact this is a short-sighted policy since it is possible to identify an interface between the profits (and transferable income) of any enterprise and the cultural wealth of both the group of its own collaborators and the larger society of which they are a part. This is through the organisational slack discussed in Chapter 5, where the budget-setting operation within the enterprise was shown to be a bargaining session between the plant supervisors (and other subordinates) with the budget controller over the allocation of the organisational slack. The negotiations are of a type known to economists as 'bargaining under conditions of bilateral monopoly.'

Following the analysis of Fouraker and Siegel, this type of negotiation will normally maintain the *status quo ante*, except to the extent that this is disturbed by an element which I call ψ, which will be a function of the following:[6]

1 The relative deprivation of the bargainer as against his peers. This will be complicated by the fact that most of these negotiations are part of a series where each supervisor has to negotiate on behalf of his subordinates, and then renegotiate a further distribution with them, as has been discussed. It seems reasonable to suppose that the 'deprivation' to be considered here will be that of the collective subordinates, as well as that of the supervisor himself. One might wonder whether the deprivation to be taken into account here is solely deprivation of material, transferable wealth; prima facie, one cannot have *relative* deprivation of non-transferable, or cultural, wealth by definition. However, to the extent that the primary groups engaged in the negotiation are not homogeneous, relative deprivation could well exist, although how it should be measured is a debatable matter, for the reasons discussed in Chapter 3.

2 Another related factor will be the relative importance attached to transferable wealth as opposed to cultural wealth. At this point it will be necessary to discuss whether the organisational slack is transferable material wealth, or non-transferable cultural wealth. In fact, it will fall into a curious intermediate category, since (i) it is clearly transferable in the sense that it can be bargained over, and assigned to some one group within the firm, but (ii) once it has been assigned finally, it is not capable of personal exclusive ownership by a single individual member of the group.[7] In part ψ represents feedback from past experience; in part the psychological changes which are seen to occur within the group.

3 The level of the negotiants will be an important factor for a variety of reasons. The taxonomy of organisational slack in Chapter 5 shows it is taking a variety of forms, some of which directly benefit the primary group while others directly or indirectly benefit the larger groups as a whole and more particularly, the supervisors and managers of the larger groups. The existence of slack lower down in the hierarchy means that subordinates are less likely to report inadequate performance, and so benefit the supervisors at each level by giving him less bad news to report upwards and less compulsion to take disciplinary action of some sort against those below him. However, a manager might well hold back from negotiating away all the slack available to him, at least in the first instance so that he could build up a secret reserve not only from his superiors but even from his subordinates. Again some forms of slack (which can be described as 'technological slack') are available directly to managers; typically this arises when they opt for some less demanding or risky technology or market than the most profitable one open to them.

4 Another factor in the negotiation will be the perceived status of the negotiating group. With equal illogicality a society may traditionally pay more than the norm for similar work performed by an Old Etonian and less than the norm if the job goes to a woman; they are paid more or less because they are expected to work for more or less. Of course, this effect is complicated by a sort of hysteresis, or stickiness, so that jobs that are frequently performed by women or Old Etonians are poorly or well paid, whoever in fact holds one. Clearly a change in the perceived status of the bargainers has the effect of shifting the agreed cost from the *status quo*.

5 The personal leadership qualities of the bargainers will also effect the outcome in another way. One might suppose in theory the manager who has the senior post in the hierarchy should have more 'leadership quality' than his subordinates. Even if this were in fact so, it is important to realise that his part in the negotiation is quite different from that of the subordinates, and at any level it is likely to be the relative possession of these qualities by the various subordinates negotiating with any one manager which is important. The manager's own qualities are neutral here since he just 'holds the ring' and tries to find a just, or at least feasible, division of the available organisational slack between all his subordinates. Of course his own qualities count (as against those of his peers) in the superior negotiations which he has just completed to produce the slack he is now asked to divide.

It is not easy to hypothesise the strength or even the direction of the trade-off between transferable wealth and cultural wealth. As far as the internal cultural wealth of a primary work group may be assumed to consist solely of the organisational slack they have been able to acquire, one may suppose that there is some trade-off between this and their transferable wealth, as evidenced by their pay rates. However, one ought to beware of the essentially 'Theory *X*' assumption that the relationship is inverse; people might well prefer to work in conditions where high standards of work were expected, to others where greater slackness is permissible, but the real purposes of collaboration are less well defined. It is even less likely that a direct relationship exists between wage demands and the richness of the general culture of which the employees and entrepreneurs are a part. One cannot say 'Let them eat their culture'; on the other hand, as has been explained, culture is not used here to describe only non-material benefits, but all those items of value which are enjoyed in common by the community. Acquisitive exploiting cultures are likely to underestimate the value of these benefits, but one might suppose that the greater the perceived value of the cultural wealth, the less importance will be attached to wages [see (2) above]. This perception will depend largely upon the relative strength of the primary and altruistic values of the culture itself.[8]

To the extent that one accepts the notion of a negotiated budget, it seems reasonable to examine the forces which may have an influence on the course of the negotiations. It is suggested that the degree of cultural enrichment, in a broad sense, may have a profound effect upon the trade-off of industrial discipline and transferable wage-income, and hence that the behaviour of money costs is affected by the surrounding cultural level.

7.3 Societal accounting within the enterprise

In a chapter that deals with sociological wealth and micro-accounting it seems appropriate to discuss a phenomenon that has been remarked by many who have worked for very large companies: the externally most aggressively capitalistic firm has an entirely collectivist internal organisation (see Horwitz [61] and Gorelik [52] on the resemblance of the Soviet 'enterprise' to the Western 'division'). That it to say, there is a plan, and a budget (which may be a flexible budget, of course) and the internal transactions of the enterprise are conducted in accordance with that budget. However, as was seen in the previous section, the budgets themselves are evolved by procedures that are extremely susceptible to social pressures, or at least to those pressures exerted by the collaborators who comprise the enterprise. This is a further example of the phenomenon discussed in the opening chapters, since the interpretation placed upon the same accounting information will vary as to whether it is viewed by an individual in the capacity of an employee, or otherwise. Note that this distinction lies between an employee and others, and not between collaborators and others; stockholders are, of course, also collaborators.

Thus the theory of accounting applied internally will be the fund theory. It will be recollected that this placed emphasis on the creation of funds to meet budgets and the encumbrancing of those funds by placing orders against them. As a result a typical accounting report can be seen externally as a report on the managerial processes which went into the establishment of the budget, but internally as a report upon the disbursement of the budget itself. This distinction may, at first, seem to be mere formal logic-chopping, but it may be that its use in analysis may help towards making some more practical statements about the operations of groups of companies which claim to exercise 'commercial autonomy' between subsidiaries or divisions. It may even shed some light upon the difficult problems of the so-called multi-national firm, and the assessment of its activities outside its country of origin.

Interdivisional transactions can be conveniently divided into (a) contracts for (intermediate) goods or materials for further processing or merchandising, (b) 'Make or buy' decisions of all kinds and (c) management services and engineering services agreements. The general analysis of type (a) dealings is well established from Hirschleifer [58] and others[9]; essentially this is a special case of bilateral monopoly (as are the cost negotiations themselves), where economic analysis suggests a range of prices rather than a single price as the outcome of the bargaining process. The point which distinguishes type (a) transactions from type (b) and some type (c) transactions is the monopoly/monopsony element; a British Leyland assembly division must buy British Leyland bodies, which the body division has to sell to them. However, where the intermediate product is undifferentiated (say a chemical compound) the possibility of buying *or* selling externally is always present. Even where the goods are specialised, a contract may be given to an independent firm for their manufacture; this is done by British Leyland, for example, with its electrical components. Generally one would not expect the latter type of make or buy decision to be reversed as a short-term measure, because of the formidable capital investment required for which probably no alternative use could be found. Again the decision-making techniques are fairly well established.

A number of divisionalised firms make genuine attempts to give divisional directors full autonomy over make or buy decisions of both classes; one may suppose that a prime consideration is a fear that if managers are not allowed initiative in this very sensitive area, they will be able to disclaim final responsibility for the results of their division; and yet at the same time it becomes necessary, at intervals, to draw divisions' attention to the desirability of buying internally within the group. The series of events which leads to this situation is along these lines. Outside suppliers seem to find these large divisions very attractive customers, and often quote prices and deliveries which are better than those obtainable within the group. One must ask in such cases why the group should wish to interfere with an arrangement which supplies intermediate materials more cheaply than it can manufacture them itself. In general one must suppose that the group's own plant has a certain 'sunk cost' and probably also either has to be kept in operation as a matter of policy, or cannot be phased out immediately. Under these circumstances, internal supply will be preferable so long as the marginal cost of production lies below the bought-in price. Moreover, the outside suppliers may sometimes be suspected of 'dumping' surplus capacity themselves by means of offering excessive discounts, and so represent a source that cannot be relied upon at all times. And yet the transfer price should reflect the fair market price, if this can be ascertained.[10]

Type (c) service contracts are often simply a device for re-naming some part of the transfer price of the goods themselves; this occurs where a holding company extracts a 'management fee' from its subsidiary. Alternatively, it may be a general service function which the subsidiary may use or not at its own discretion as the need arises. The former contracts follow the transfer-pricing analysis, and the latter seems to be examples of the make or buy decision. However, the internal collectivisation of the enterprise can produce odd results in practice.

Several combinations of circumstances could be achieved.

1 The total budgets for the service raised by user divisions might fall short of the total budgeted costs of the management services division.
2 The user divisions might decide subsequently not to expend their full budget in this area.
3 The user divisions may not be able to utilise their full budgets, because the service division cannot provide the required service for some reason.

An interesting, if rather wayward, description of the problems is provided by Goetz [47].

It is necessary to consider how this system of interlocking fund accounts fits into what was said in Chapter 1 about the accounting theories, which may be applied to such accounts. Clearly combination (1) will be avoided if the divisional budgets are subject to rationalisation; an interesting paper by Ronen and McKinney suggests how this might be attempted [96]. Combinations (2) and (3) are examples of discrepancies between the *ex ante* and the *ex post* situation, whose theoretical analysis has been considered by Demski [35]. Our immediate concern with these solutions is not with their detailed operation, but whether their use is truly consistent with the idea of divisional autonomy.

It is probably significant that the discussion of internal accounting theory so often returns to the question of autonomy. 'Autonomy' seems to imply a right to pursue one's own immediate interests in total indifference to the secondary effect of one's actions, even on the community of which one is oneself a member.[11]

In general, an enterprise, or even a group, is a true commonwealth; Assumption 7 of Mattessich's scheme (. . . there exists a custom to enter *debts* with the understanding to *redeem them* . . .) does not strictly apply. It usually matters little whether the members of a group are solvent as between themselves, and cash resources are moved to suit considerations of currency fluctuations, taxation or internal needs. Thus, at least internally the member of a group is freed from the self-financing principle; he is therefore not concerned with the need to maintain his capital and so be is less concerned with 'profit' and more concerned with the correct disbursement of funds in accordance with an agreed plan. The desire to prevent infantile behaviour by introducing autonomy clearly produces problems which demonstrate (were this needed) the difficulties which taking into account of externalities must always produce for the self-financing enterprise.

7.4 Social indicators and micro-accounting

The concept of indicators of the social condition was discussed, at the macro-level, in the previous chapter. Following the assumptions that underlie this book, we now turn to micro-aspects of national indicators that would have relevance at the enterprise level, because they usually need to be taken into account by management in its own direct dealings with its employees, customers and the community at large. The following items have been selected from the paper by Biderman [17], which was referred to in the previous chapter [pp 147–52]:

Equality

—of race		—access to education
—of sex	in	—access to employment
—of religion		—access to occupation and promotion

Community participation

Democratic process
Use of advertising media
Use of pressure groups
Political areas of operation

Education
Adult education

Arts and sciences
Support of research
Support of humanistic and social science
Foreign language skills

Democratic economy
Collective bargaining
Labour relations
Trade associations
Pension rights
Employment of older workers

Economic growth
Maintenance of full employment

Technological change
Relocation of industry

Severance pay
Retraining of employees
Use of scientific manpower

Living conditions
Provision of housing
Use of road transport
Use of land
Pollution

Health and welfare
Sickness and absenteeism
Industrial accidents

These are all fairly sensitive areas with respect to 'the state of the nation,' and it may be that the enterprise should maintain a number of statistics to explain its dealings in each of them. Many are already required by law, as with industrial accidents much of the data would simply be further analysis of existing financial accounting material. It can be seen readily enough that it might be useful for an enterprise to be able to explain its activity in these areas, especially in the current atmosphere of concern (and pressure, where 'questions are raised' at annual general meetings and the like). Governmental and individual bodies of all kinds collect a great deal of information about major companies, who need to be well armed to counter the arguments they put forward. A good British example is provided by the Anti-report GEC, which has been referred to already in note 11 of Chapter 6, and one of the controversial provisions of the *Industrial Relations Act, 1971*,[12] requires disclosure to trade union representatives and employees. However, it must be admitted that the preparation of ammunition for use in debate is not what is usually implied by the provision of management information. Nor is it supposed that many managements are entirely unaffected by these considerations of social welfare which follow from their own decisions, even if their concern is solely the avoidance of governmental intervention, bad publicity, riot-damage and the like. Nevertheless, there seems to be very little uniformity over the nature or precise content of the records needed, at least where they are not required by law. This situation can be contrasted with their financial cost and accounting systems, where the procedures are stylised and well-known. The reason for the contrast is obvious; the issues involved in financial and economic decision making are themselves well known, but this is not the case with the societal issues. In short, well-defined quantifiable 'models' exist for the former, but not for the latter. More will be said about this problem in Chapter 8, but it is obvious that neither comprehensive data collection nor truly logical argument can occur in an area in which accepted models do not exist. It follows that little purpose would be served by elaborating upon the micro-indicators that might be used for decision making in the areas described by Biderman, in the absence of a well-defined model of social behaviour at that level.

7.5 Towards a societal theory of micro-accounting

The material discussed in this chapter falls into two classes, firstly, what are simply the micro-aspects of macro-phenomena already discussed in Chapter 6. Obviously this is the case with the social indicators discussed in the last section, whileorganisational slack is just the principal micro-form of the super-bezzle. Although what was said in section 7.3 about the interior accounting of enterprises and groups probably echoes something of what was said about PPBS and cost-benefit analysis at the macro-level, this topic, and the concept of mini-accounts, is an attempt to move nearer to a substantivist theory of accounting. This has been done by taking the 'Behavioural Theory of the Firm' to its logical conclusion and assuming that micro-accounts are consolidations of the 'accounts' of the individual collaborators. Although this assumption limits the mini-accounts to first-order transactions, when sub-groups of collaborators are considered, an odd fact emerges: such groups do not have to settle their debts in any sense which supports Assumption 7.

In Chapter 4, Assumption 7 was assimilated into Assumption *E*, because it involves general concepts of self—others and the like. Assumption *E* reads: 'The human environment is distinguished from the non-human environment, in that humans are seen as collaborating in various ways for the purposive pursuit of values. Human collaborators can be grouped and regrouped so as to reflect varying mutual interests.'

This formulation does not make specific reference to the settlement of debts; clearly it is an optional extra demanded by the conventions of self-financing rather than the purposive pursuit of values. Self-finance is a very common device, but it is limited to the micro-level only and rarely applies in a meaningful way at the mini- OR macro-levels. Perhaps the reason could be expressed as follows: Collaboration in a firm and membership of a nation are continuing relationships which cannot be brought to an end except in some fairly cataclysmic fashion. Members may join and leave, but not very often, and while the organisation continues, they cannot insist upon a final settlement of 'debts,' which relate to the collectivity rather than themselves as individual members. This can be contrasted with the relationship of customers and suppliers, and who can and do cease to collaborate at will. Finally it may be the fact that employee-employer collaborators can plan their future (at least internal affairs), which makes settlement unnecessary between them.

One might add to Assumption *E*: 'This pursuit of values will give rise to a variety of debtor and creditor relationships: some will accrue to individual, others only jointly to groups and sub groups. Conventional settlement procedures may be adopted, especially in respect of debts between individuals and groups who have no continuing plannable relations.'

7.6 Notes

1 The justification for this 'hierarchic' approach to social accounting might be adduced from the natural way in which the mini-accounts faithfully reflect the particular bias of the society at large. They have been divided into an individual production account and an individual household account, and this division will lie along whatever production frontier is observed by the society in question. It seems reasonable to suppose that the production account is a doubly 'artificial' creation. A social group that simply existed in its environment and did not seek to change it would have only household accounts, at both mini-level and macro-level. In such a society, not only would micro-accounts be unlikely to be prepared, but there would be nothing to prepare them from. Notice that the existence of trading and manufacture does not guarantee that the people who act in those ways effectively separate the act of production from the act of consumption, and so define a production boundary. In section 1.1 it was observed that merchants kept account books for several centuries without preparing final accounts. In part this might have been due to the universality of 'sole trading,' but this confusion of business and private expense suggested that a concept of a boundary between them was not fully recognised. Of course, the content of the production mini-account would depend upon the principal objective pursued by the particular society. A Western mini-account would relegate everything except consumption, and transfers of consumption, into the production account. A Soviet mini-account, on the other hand, would only segregate social production activities. This might imply that a Russian ballet-dancer (or policeman) would only have an individual household account, but since the sectorisation of Soviet national accounts provides a 'non-productive sphere' (see Chapter 3) to cover activities of this type, it might be best to provide them with 'service activity' mini-accounts, plus appropriate micro-accounts which will clear themselves as transfer payments.

2 The transactions on some of these accounts might be:

HOUSEHOLD ACCOUNTS

	THE JONESES	THE SMITHS	THE BROWNS	THE BLACKS
Production accounts	£	£	£	£
Fred	1 000			
Tom		7 000		
Bill			11 000	
Jean			600	
John				1 200
Edith				800
	£1 000	£7 000	£11 600	£2 000

	THE JONESES	THE SMITHS	THE BROWNS	THE BLACKS
	£	£	£	£
Personal taxation	200	1 500	2 500	400
Household consumption	900	6 000	6 500	1 400
Saving/dis-saving	−100	−500	2 600	200
	£1 000	£7 000	£11 600	£2 000

MICRO-ACCOUNTS (assuming no changes in inventories, etc)

	GOVERNMENT	COMPANY A	COMPANY B
	£	£	£
Purchases	4 500	8 000	11 000
Wages and salaries	800	5 000	7 200
Rents			600
Dividends		3 000	5 000
Corporate taxation		3 000	4 200
Corporate savings including depreciation		1 000	2 000
	£5 300	£20 000	£30 000

	GOVERNMENT	COMPANY A	COMPANY B
	£	£	£
Sales			
Government		1 000	3 500
A			8 000
B		11 000	
Households		5 300	9 500
Rest of world		2 700	9 000
Government services	5 300		
	£5 300	£20 000	£30 000

PRODUCTION ACCOUNTS

	FRED JONES	TOM SMITH	BILL BROWN	JEAN BROWN	JOHN BLACK	EDITH BLACK
	£	£	£	£	£	£
Wages and salaries	1 000	4 000	6 000	600	1 200	800
Rents received	—	—	—	—	—	—
Dividends received		3 000	5 000			
	£1 000	£7 000	£11 000	£600	£1 200	£800

	FRED JONES	TOM SMITH	BILL BROWN	JEAN BROWN	JOHN BLACK	EDITH BLACK
	£	£	£	£	£	£
Household accounts	1 000	7 000	11 000	600	1 200	800
	£1 000	£7 000	£11 000	£600	£1 200	£800

2 (*continued*)

NATIONAL ACCOUNTS (assuming no production for capital investment)

	PRODUCTION		HOUSEHOLDS		GOVERNMENT		REST OF THE WORLD		SAVINGS AND INVESTMENT	
	£	£	£	£	£	£	£	£	£	£
Wages	13 000			13 000						
Rents	600			600						
Dividends	8 000			8 000						
Corporate taxation	7 200					7 200				
Corporate savings	3 000									3 000
Exports		11 700					11 700			
Personal taxation			4 600			4 600				
Household consumption		14 800	14 800							
Government services		5 300			5 300					
Foreign savings							–11 700			–11 700
Personal savings			2 200							2 200
Governmental saving					6 500					6 500
	£31 800	£31 800	£21 600	£21 600	£11 800	£11 800	—	—	—	—

3 The national accounts would become:

	PRODUCTION		NON-PRODUCTIVE SPHERE		HOUSEHOLDS		GOVERNMENT		REST OF THE WORLD		SAVINGS AND INVESTMENTS	
Wages and salaries	12 800		8 800			21 600						
Corporate taxation	4 200		3 000					7 200				
Corporate savings	2 000		1 000									3 000
Exports		9 000		2 700					11 700			
Personal taxation					4 600			4 600				
Household consumption		9 500		5 300	14 800							
Personal saving					2 200							2 200
Government expenditure		3 500		1 800			5 300					
Government savings							6 500					6 500
Non-production sales/ expenditure		—3 000	8 000	11 000								
Foreign saving										11 700		–11 700
	£19 000	£19 000	£20 800	£20 800	£21 600	£21 600	£11 800	£11 800	£11 700	£11 700	—	—

4 However, Nancy and Richard Ruggles refer quite extensively to increasing use of what they call 'micro-data':

> 'A more promising method of integrating economic and social data is the creation of special sets of micro-data. For many sets of aggregate data it is possible to establish a representative sample of individual reporting units showing the micro-data on which the aggregates are based. For example for the household sector of the economy it should be possible to construct a sample of households such that the total of the income of all households, weighted by the appropriate sample weights, would be equal to the total personal income of the economy as a whole. If the sample is representative, a distribution of the individuals in it by occupation and industry would yield the employee compensation paid by industry. . . .
>
> 'An initial start in this direction has been made by the (American) Bureau of the Census in their 1-in-1000 sample of the US population. This sample contains information on approximately 10 000 households, and contains over forty items of information for each household' [98, p 72].

5 This problem is central to the use of any 'model' of underlying reality. Some degree of abstraction is inevitable, and it would be naïve to expect too great an accuracy from using a model for the purpose of forecasting; its principal use may often be in the analysis of complex situations on the basis of historical data.

On the other hand, accounting is not itself a phenomenon (except perhaps to the student of the history of accounting), but rather it is a methodology for examining and evaluating phenomena. It seems more reasonable to consider the individual's mini-account and mini-system of externalities as the foundation for all subsequent accounting because any ideas which we possess about accounting theory are interior to us and it is our own standing as against the rest of creation which is most concretely present to us. The view which we take of the situations of the various sub-groups of which we are members will be more abstracted and subject to group processes of various sorts.

6 It seems reasonable to suggest that cultural 'enrichment' or 'impoverishment' may affect such changes and hence the transferable costs themselves. The bargaining was described as a trade-off between industrial discipline and money wages, which seem to fit in well enough with the suggestion made here.

7 Of course, it would be possible for an individual to insist on a further negotiation so that some part of the slack of a larger group was personally assigned to him, but if this is in fact feasible, it is apparent that the group could not have been a primary group in the first place. Perhaps a primary group could be defined, at least for the present purpose, as one to where further subdivision of slack is infeasible, either because it is physically indivisible beyond that point, or because the members of the group feel no desire to divide it. It would follow that organisational slack will have the attributes of transferable wealth at levels above that of the primary group, but of cultural wealth to the group itself.

8 The greater importance of non-transferable welfare to developing societies was mentioned in Chapter 1, and it was also suggested that increasing expectations of wealth may mean that the citizens of developed countries are demanding more for this source. However, another problem faces the developed country; many of its citizens are so unskilled technically that they cannot make a contribution to the transferable income of the nation which is equivalent to the minimum ('poverty line') standard of acceptable consumption. When these citizens form a social class, or worse still an ethnic group, the social problems become acute, because in a democratic and affluent society, the implication is that anyone could improve himself, so that a failure to do so must proceed either from personal unworthiness or some injustices in society itself.

It is possible (although I do not guarantee it!) that an investigation of the sources and distribution of cultural wealth might make it easier to understand and even to remedy this problem. 'The Protestant Ethic' can relate only to transferable wealth.

9 As was pointed out in Chapter 3, problems of transfer-pricing are often experienced in peculiarly aggravated forms in developing countries, where foreign mining operations tend to form semi-independent 'enclaves' in the host economy.

The enclave economy problem is as simple to analyse as it is intractable in solution. Just as we have suggested that any cost can vary between a lower rack cost and an upper maximum cost, it is apparent that the 'cost' of an extractive product can lie anywhere between the cost of the miners' wages and equipment, and that cost plus the whole of the net surplus arising in the subsequent manufacture of the finished product. There is no right answer here, and the price must be arrived at by bargaining operations of the type already described for cost or divisional transfer-price negotiations. Extractive operations will give rise to highly sensitive situations, since the ecological effects are bound to be considerable, and moreover represent an irreplacable diminution in the local resources; these problems will be reinforced where the mining occurs in a developing country, since not only does it provide a prospect of enormous wealth in the midst of comparative poverty, but it is likely to be the sole source of such wealth in the region.

10 Obviously, what is required are some ground rules (along the lines discussed by Whinston [123] which might be hoped to defend the internal supplier division against unfair competition without subsidising inefficient operation. Since this is also the intention of most international tariff policies, one must suppose that the result will not be very easy to achieve. A peculiar danger, in practice, is that these ground rules tend to create areas of tolerance within which the internal or external supply will be used, together with cut off points at which a change of policy becomes mandatory. Unless the system of ordering, lead-times and stock-holding is very fully understood, these sudden reversals are likely to prove exceedingly expensive. In fact, the interactions of these systems across several divisions will set up a highly complex series of feed-back loops, which probably will not prove easy for intuitive analysis. Here too a 'System Dynamics' simulation, along the lines developed by Forrester, may enable a group at least to avoid some of the more unprofitable combinations.

11 The basis of this approach is well described by Tawney [111]:

> 'The moral self-sufficiency of the Puritan nerved his will, but it corroded his source of social solidarity. For if each individual's destiny hangs on a private transaction between himself and his Maker, what room is left for human intervention? A servant of Jehovah more than of Christ, he revered God as a judge rather than loved him as a Father, and was moved less by compassion for his arising between them by impatient indignation at the blindness of vessels of wrath who "sinned their mercies." A spiritual aristocrat who sacrified fraternity to liberty, he drew from his idealisation of personal responsibility a theory of individual rights, which secularised and generalised, was to be among the most potent explosives that the world has known' [p 230].

12 A useful summary of the accounting provisions of this Act is in an article by Dyson [38]: 'This Act required employers to disclose information to trade union representatives for the purpose of collective bargaining (s56) as well as to employees where at any time during a financial year more than 350 people are employed (s57). Section 56 has not yet come into operation, even though the Commission on Industrial Relations has presented its report on the type of information that should be available to trade union representatives. This will not be easy, as another section of the Act (s158) allows employers to withhold any information the disclosure of which would be seriously prejudicial to the interests of the employer's undertaking for reasons other than its effect on collective bargaining (s158).

'*Let-out clause?* This looks like a let-out clause, although it is doubtful whether it is really meant to be so, for the Industrial Relations Code of Practice makes clear that management are expected to meet all reasonable requests from trade unions for information which is relevant to the negotiations in hand (para 97). What is relevant? That we shall not know until the Commission's report has been accepted and agreement has been reached with interested parties. The Secretary of State will then amend the Code of Practice, and therefore accountants will undoubtedly find themselves trying to dig out information that may not be readily available (always assuming that in principle management do not object to disclosing it to trade union representatives). The range of information demanded is very wide: the TUC's "shopping list" includes items not shown in published company accounts. For example, distribution and sale costs, production costs, administrative and overhead costs, costs of materials, labour costs including social security payments, as well as details of prospective closedowns, mergers and take-overs. There is no doubt that such information would put union negotiators in a very strong position, but this seems to be the Government's intention. The Code of Practice states quite coldly that "collective bargaining can be conducted responsibly only if management and unions have adequate information on the matter being negotiated" (para 96). If anyone imagines that the repeal of the *Industrial Relations Act 1971* is imminent, and that therefore these sort of disclosures will never see the light of day, he should be reminded that under the Labour Government similar proposals were put forward in the *Industrial Relations Bill 1970*.

'Indeed, some of the clauses in the Act seem to have been lifted straight out of that earlier Bill. It would appear that whatever the political complexion of the Government, "undertakings" will be expected to disclose quite detailed information to trade union negotiators. The accountants' "Bible" is, therefore, going to be not only the *Companies Acts 1948 and 1967*, but also the *Industrial Relations Act 1971*. Disclosure of information to employees is another matter. Details are not outlined in the Act. All we know is, that employers are expected to issue in respect of that financial year, i.e. if on any date during a financial year more than 350 persons are employed, a statement . . . (s57 [1]). And, "every such statement shall be issued not later than six months after the end of the financial year to which it relates" (s57 [2]).

'*Confidentiality*. Further "every such statement shall be in writing and (subject to section 158 of this Act) shall contain all such information as may be required in accordance with regulations made by the Secretary of State . . ." (s57 [3]). Section 158 deals with the confidentiality of information.'

It is significant that although Dyson (and the TUC's 'shopping list') seem to see the information to be disclosed as accounting information only, the Act itself does not always limit its scope in this way.

8 A Generalised Theory of Accounting

8.1 The 'general problem' of existence

In the closing chapter of such a book it is difficult to avoid some rather 'large' statements which may seem to be by way of philosophising over the condition of man. And yet, as was promised in the preface, it is not the intention here to take sides, or commend any particular course of action, but merely to set out the close interconnection between any sort of accounting statement and the social system within which it is found.

A plant or an animal was seen not to be trying to enhance anything at all; they simply exist as part of an ecological cycle. To the extent that a human society was content to exist in the same cycles of production and consumption as their fathers, one might expect it to reach a sort of 'steady state' with nature, and so form part of a pattern which changed at an evolutionary rate. Following the expanded definition of accounting theory developed in Chapter 4, this society would not have an accounting theory, but one might ask whether such a society had anything that they would recognise as a 'problem' that needed solution. The lilies of the field in fact take no thought of the morrow, and if their means of sustenence fails—they wither away quietly. It is human societies which, in their more advanced stages, seek to beat the system, and so face the problem of which strategies should be employed to meet the current situation.

In fact, people attempt to solve this problem by subdividing and simplifying it in various ways.[1] This approach is not strictly feasible, since attempts to solve sub-problems in isolation are likely to produce less satisfactory solutions for the overall problem. Thus, for a start, we tend to try and solve things for our own benefit, or those of our company, tribe or nation, rather than for humanity as a whole. Often enough we may succeed in obtaining benefit at the expense of others, but as we have seen, we do have various altruistic values which may be infringed by this approach. Alternatively, short-term success of this type may bring about long-term political disadvantages; we may even set off a series of externality effects which feed back, adversely, into our own situation.

It may be that accounting, as it has developed, has contributed to the institutionalisation of this limitation of concern. This might follow on the acceptance of the ideas of Sombart, whose quotation opened the first chapter of the book; however, just as we have seen that societies with no knowledge of written book-keeping may possess 'theories of accounting,' this final chapter will try to show that it is the confinement of accounting in any form to direct flows of goods and service, rather than the specific technique of double-entry book-keeping which secures this limiting effect. It will also be suggested that it is the reform and further development of accounting which offers the most hopeful prospect of resolving many of the most pressing problems of our societies. In short, this accounting-inspired desire for limitation of responsibility has shaped the whole development of 'the social sciences,' as they are commonly termed.

8.2 Accounting and taxonomy

Social *Science* is a science, but still in a primitive, Aristotelian form. It is often referred to in the plural as 'the Social Sciences,' because of a very noticeable reluctance towards attempts to construct over-arching theories to explain social phenomena. As a result, those social scientists who tend to look at all at the outward form of things, devote time and effort to explaining how a limited number of phenomena in existing institutions actually work. Thus they lay themselves open to the charge of being like aeronautical engineers who assure a bumble-bee that it can fly, while making only the vaguest suggestions of how it can fly right.[2]

A practical example of the difficulty has already been discussed at length in an earlier chapter with respect to the use of 'social indicators.' There is evidence of doubt over the utility of such indicators until it is possible to be sure what they are indicative of; this cannot be ascertained without the use of some model of how society (as a whole) is supposed to be operating. Another discussion of this point, by Johnson, suggests that empirical work commonly founders on the dubious nature of the classification or taxonomy used in it [64]. He says:

> Since taxonomy is a system of concepts, it is not strictly equivalent to a theory, which is a system of propositions. But out of taxonomy, hypotheses may come for empirical research. In this sense, the target of this paper is a 'theory of theories in accounting research...' [p 64].[3]

Thus valid empiricism waits upon a valid taxonomy, which in turn demands some comprehensive *Weltanschauung*, or theory regarding the relationships of the immediate phenomena to the world outside.

This concern with small corners and flabby taxonomy is not confined to empirical accounting theorists, or indeed to accounting as a whole. A common jest is to the effect that the pessimist sees a half-empty bottle where the optimist sees one which is half full; it seems possible that we use differing taxonomic systems to classify the same objective phenomena. As a result 'Social Science' is sub-divided into a number of virtually independent sections—primarily economic on the one hand and a tangle of 'behavioural sciences' on the other.

One of Nature's 'hard men' might favour one approach, the clinician or the politician quite others, but one would not feel confidence in the outcome, if it was taxonomic inexactitude alone which made this possible. It may be that if one were to ask one of the poorer inhabitants of some great city what were his economic problems, his political problems, his psychological problems, and so on, he would almost certainly answer 'I've just got problems.' This answer would not proceed from linguistic naïvity, because very few subjects seem able to sort out *their own* problems into these categories. They seem instead to be convenient terms which social scientists have developed to file away *other people's* problems. Also, the sub-division of problems in this way may suggest possibilities of local solution, which would be much less convincing when viewed in the context of the whole social phenomena, within which the subject has to conduct his affairs. This is another aspect of the conflict of 'emic' and 'etic' views of a society discussed in Chapter 4; the insider is always denied the convenience of oversimplification.

Quite apart from its stultifying effect on development in Social Science, the existence of conflicting modes of classifying social phenomena makes life difficult for the accountant. This is because it is in his sphere of activities that the inconsistencies of the various approaches become most obvious. In a perfect world, accounting would combine social statistics to provide a technique for analysing, measuring and perhaps controlling social phenomena. Moreover, as was suggested at the close of Chapter 7, such a world would tend to be a perfectly planned world in which financial settlement would play a minor role. Most enterprises are either self-financing, or at least seek to 'balance their budgets,' because it is convenient to control their activities by this means. This has the effect of locking the accountant into an 'economic' mode of thought, which concerns itself primarily with direct flows and sees other effects as much less significant 'externalities.'

Thus, once one steps beyond the simple mechanics of book-keeping (or statistics) it becomes necessary to adopt one or the other of the modes of analysis of the social scientist; the phenomena have to be categorised as 'economic,' 'political,' 'sociological' and so on. Because these divisions are largely meaningless, this can only be done by playing down those bits of the data which do not fit into the selected taxonomy. Unfortunately the accountant (to a greater extent even than the social statistician) is essentially part of the field he is investigating; this is because he is part of the management team to which he reports, as a result he and his colleagues have to live with the results of the ensuing decisions, which they take on the evidence of fragmented and possibly contradicting taxonomies. The accountant therefore has to operate at the interface of the 'emic' and 'etic' views, where it becomes much more obvious both to himself and to others that (a) he cannot provide much of the information which the theorists want and (b) that what he does produce is a tendentious and incomplete picture of what is occurring. This seems to leave the blame for all the deficiencies in the quantification of social phenomena with the accountant, since the possibility that he may be being invited to attempt the impossible is not often entertained.

The confusion does not stop here. Accounting has a much longer history than the conscious, systematic investigation of social problems, as has been discussed in the opening chapter of this book. This has caused accounting to develop as a quasi-social science in its own right, especially in those countries such as Britain and the USA, where substantial organisations of professional accountants were in being before 'the social sciences' were developed as disciplines.[4] Even where the accountant does make an effort to adopt the taxonomies of the present social sciences, he commonly obtains little credit thereby. Becker's comment '. . . most, if not all, the experiments performed by accountants . . . add nothing to knowledge in behavioural science' is well known—and frequently echoed. The reason is simply that, as has been seen, the accountant has to take social costs and economic costs as they are really ascertained and ascertainable. Theoretical social scientists have the advantage of using more abstract concepts, and perhaps of standing further away from the phenomena, so that accountants very often appear as laborious fellows[5] who are struggling to validate something which has already been demonstrated quite satisfactorily elsewhere.

However, it is important not to imagine that there is anything inevitable about its operations of economic phenomena, which do not occur for the same reason that physical phenomena occur. One may have a variety of theories about the behaviour of atomic particles, but clearly they may be said to 'do their thing' whatever theory the observer may currently entertain about them. Moreover, they will certainly continue to do their thing until very definite steps are taken to deflect them from their normal courses. The situation with human institutions is quite contrary, where the subjects of the investigation *themselves* devise the machinery and the rules of their own game. These have to function within the limits laid down by physical laws, but since, as we have seen, the players also supply their own criteria of success, and have facilities for filtering out data which run contrary to their expectations, it is at least conceivable that people could be entirely happy while doing things that are by no means physically efficient. In earlier chapters it was shown how, for example, the values and the institutions of the Papago Indians differed from those of the Western man; in another place it was pointed out that inter-cultural comparisons of welfare were meaningless.

8.3 Basic assumption of the principles of self-finance

Nevertheless, the impossibility of saying that any one society is better or worse off than another, does not mean that every social order must therefore be beyond criticism. It remains possible to claim that given the values entertained by society and the resources available to it, the institutions it has developed fail to produce the most satisfactory return, even in terms of its own values. This was the point discussed by Lerner and Rappaport [75] in a paper explaining why the DCF approach to capital budgeting is not universally accepted; the use of conventional accounting techniques can produce violent fluctuations in the reported earnings for companies whose DCF calculations would show steady and profitable investment in an optional portfolio. This paper has led Williams to comment:

> The lack of understanding of even the most elementary economic concepts has perpetuated a financial system which is blatantly inefficient and irrational. Their [accountants and analysts] lack of imagination in effecting more realistic procedures of data supply and interpretation has encouraged wasteful speculation and unnecessary economic instability. In an era of increased communicative and analytical skills, the professions of accountancy and security analysis remain as economic anachronisms.
>
> Fortunately both professions are blessed with farsighted members, particularly within the academic community. Hopefully, these individuals will be able to convince (or replace) the conservative powers (the establishment of accounting and finance) so that the old ways can be amended and the existing old wives' tales eliminated. Perhaps the economist will then be able to return to solving the plethora of problems posed by nature (the scarcity of resources) without having to worry about the problems posed by man (the allocation of resources) [124].

At one level this quotation merely illustrates the point made a little earlier, to the effect that accountants are held to blame for failure to produce the data that economic sciences suggest should be available. However, to the extent that he also claims that this fact has 'perpetuated a financial system which is blatantly inefficient and irrational,' he may be making a more revolutionary statement than he had thought to do.[6]

It would be possible to argue that the art of accounting has perpetuated a financial system that is at least worthy of critical examination, if not 'blatantly inefficient and irrational.' The general acceptance of the self-financing enterprise throughout the world has been discussed in a previous chapter; it survives under a wide variety of political and social systems. No doubt the origin of the device was that an individual capitalist could do what he liked with his own wealth, but personal ownership is incidental to the working system; the essence is that the business should conduct itself in such a way as to maintain its own capital, whoever owns it. The obvious dangers of suboptimisation that the system contains have already been discussed, but one might nevertheless feel some intestinal conviction of the 'rightness' of a device which places final reliance upon the long-term recovery of costs. A capital deficit in a company is similar to deficit financing at the national level, in that it puts purchasing power into circulation for which no corresponding supply of goods and services exists. We have seen that the equation of factor payments to purchasing power is not so direct; the propensity to save, changes in the terms of trade, the supply of money, the supply of goods which have to be traded for money, and more besides, all serve to complicate the machinery. On the other hand, in Chapter 7 it was observed that the compulsion to settle debts was a convention rather than a natural law. It would be quite possible to have a balanced budget and every company operating at a profit and declaring legal dividends, and still find conditions of inflation or deflation existing. Not even the law specifically enjoins the self-financing ethos; insolvency is defined as 'the inability to meet one's debts as they fall due.' It follows that a capital deficiency does not always imply insolvency—nor does a surplus guarantee solvency either, as anyone with experience of bankruptcy practice will know. Why then do we insist on keeping the accounts in credit? The answer must be in some conviction that (a) it permits businesses to run pretty well independently so long as they remain (super) solvent; if they could 'go into the red,' it would be necessary to enquire much more closely into the societal justifications for what they were doing, and (b) one might also suppose that the need to pay up in cash and maintain capital also serves to prevent fraud within the enterprise, at least in the long term.[7]

Another argument that can be adduced for the self-financing enterprise is that it is dedicated to making a profit or at least breaking even; since 'nasty shocks' are more common than 'nice surprises,' even the latter can be best assured by aiming to make a profit on everything. It follows that 'the profit motive' could be said to provide an unequalled incentive to action and initiative. Some quotations from a very interesting paper written many years ago by Sir Basil Smallpeice cover this aspect of the problem very effectively:

> It is necessary . . . to be clear about what is meant by the profit motive. Applied to the individual in industry it is personal incentive; it is local in its effect, and can be used to stimulate a man's efforts in any given direction. As usually understood, it takes the form of private profit as the reward for individual enterprise.
>
> But the profit motive applied to industry . . . is a different thing altogether. It is independent of personal incentive. It is in fact not so much an incentive as a directive.
>
> . . . every decision . . . that has financial consequences must be justified by the expectation of profit or the avoidance of loss.
>
> This does not apply only at the highest level of authority. It runs right down through every level at which decisions are taken in industry, from the general manager to the foreman and section head. In fact, the lower the level at which the decision is reached, the stricter must be the adherence to the 'profit rule' (which is a better phrase to use in this connection, being more exact and less susceptible to misinterpretation than 'profit motive').
>
> Now in the profit rule we have at hand, as a guide in making decisions, a rough and ready rule of thumb which is both convenient in use and readily understandable by even the meanest intelligence.
>
> In the economic sphere I think there can be little doubt that, if industry is left to make its own decisions on the basis of what appears to its separate units to pay better in terms of £sd, it cannot, in present circumstances, satisfactorily provide the whole community with the necessities and frills of modern life [107].

The distinction that this writer draws between profit motive (on the personal level) and profit rule (on the institutional level) is important and valid. We have already discussed the inevitability of some system of values in any culture, and pointed out that man, like any energy-conserving organism, only responds to appeals for action in terms of these values. Of course, the nature of the value entertained can vary greatly, which means that 'profit' must be interpreted in the broadest sense as any increment in positive values or decrement in negative values; in this way the profit motive can be seen to be universal in its application. This cannot be claimed for the profit rule; there profit must mean accruals-based accounting profit, because it is to be applied institutionally, without reference to the personal reward of the decision maker. To return to the example used by Acheson [5], the Tarascan villagers probably adhered to cash-flow concepts of profitability as much because the profit *rule* was opaque to them, as from a disinclination to place much value on future income. The profit *motive* was very clearly understood. Thus the profit motive, broadly defined, cannot be removed; it *is* 'a fact of life.' On the other hand, the profit rule is a piece of technique which has been developed, like any other tool, for achieving some end. It is unlikely that the end to be achieved is simply the use or refinement of the tool itself.[8]

8.4 Accounting for a social system

Just as the present-day aversion to 'over-arching theories' prevents the useful further development of social indicators, the absence of such theories provides a justification for continuing to use the self-financing corporation. Any thinking man can see that a firm's activities have social costs and social effects that feed back to the firm itself; it is very hard to present absolutely convincing estimates of what those effects might be, precisely because we do not have theories about how the whole society works. Therefore the profit rule and the maintenance of capital provide a sensible framework for perpetuating the firm under conditions of extreme uncertainty. If one did attach credence to any one over-arching theory, one could then proceed to produce a comprehensive taxonomy of the variables needed to describe the issues facing society, and so produce accounting statements that would tell us more clearly how existing institutions were supposed to be affecting that society. From thence one might proceed to consider whether some reorganisation of those institutions might improve their capacity to add value to the society. It might be useful to conclude the book by examining one or two over-arching theories, in spite of their obvious imperfections, to see what taxonomies and institutions would follow upon their acceptance.

The indefatigable Professor Forrester[9] provides some theories which may or may not be correct but, since they have the advantage of being presented at several levels of aggregation, they will suit this purpose very well. His three books *World Dynamics* [42] *Urban Dynamics* [41] and *Industrial Dynamics* [40] are dedicated to the proposition that the problems facing the world are a series of interlocking feedback systems, and the technique of 'systems dynamics' is used to analyse them. The material has been criticised extensively, but to the extent that it purports to explain the operation of the whole system under examination, it provides explicit taxonomies for the data needed to produce a quantified model of that system. The model consists of a number of 'levels,' whose net change in value is determined by various 'rates (-of-flow)'; in turn the rates are determined by the interaction of the value of the levels in various parts of the system with a number of 'constants.'

System dynamics is a large topic, and readers are referred to the original texts for the details of the techniques, and of the models themselves. However, it may help the argument of the current work to consider what variables and constants are used in the various models. The system for 'World dynamics' makes use of five level variables: population, natural resources, capital investment, capital investment in agriculture fraction, and pollution. The taxonomy can be illustrated by the following schema (the intermediate steps in calculating the rates are described as 'auxiliaries':

LEVELS	RATES	(FIRST GENERATION) AUXILIARIES	(FIRST GENERATION) CONSTANTS
1 Population	(a) Birthrate	(i) Birthrate from material (standard of living) multiplier (ii) Birthrate from food multiplier (iii) Birthrate from crowding multiplier (iv) Birthrate from pollution multiplier	*A* Birthrate normal

LEVELS	RATES	(FIRST GENERATION) AUXILIARIES	(FIRST GENERATION CONSTANTS
	(b) Deathrate	(i) Deathrate from material (standard of living) multiplier (ii) Deathrate from food multiplier (iii) Deathrate from crowding multiplier (iv) Deathrate from pollution multiplier	*B* Deathrate normal
2 Natural resources	(a) Natural resources usage rate	(i) Natural resources from material (standard of living) multiplier	*A* Natural resources usage normal
3 Capital investment	(a) Capital investment generation	(i) Capital investment (from standard of living) multiplier	*A* Capital investment generation normal
	(b) Capital investment discard		*A* Capital investment discard normal
4 Capital investment in agriculture fraction	—	(i) Capital investment from quality (of life) ratio	*A* Capital investment in agriculture fraction adjustment time
		(ii) Capital fraction indicated by food ratio	
5 Pollution	(a) Pollution generation	(i) Pollution from capital (investment) multiplier	*A* Pollution normal
	(b) Pollution absorption	(ii) Pollution absorption time	

The foregoing portion of the schema shows the levels, their relevant rates and the auxiliaries and constants which feed directly into those rates. The general idea is clear; there is assumed to be some constant normal 'rate of flow' per head of population or other unit, which is accelerated or decelerated by one or more multipliers. These multipliers are not themselves constant, but vary in response to the value of further auxiliaries measuring the material standard of living, the availability of food, the degree of crowding, the level of pollution and the level of capital investment. In turn, these secondary auxiliaries are also built up from constants and tertiary auxiliary measures:

TERTIARY AUXILIARY	CONSTANTS	FURTHER AUXILIARY SYSTEMS
(i) Material standard of living	*A* Effective capital investment ratio normal	(a) Effective capital investment ratio
(ii) (Availability of) food ratio	*A* Food normal *B* Food coefficient	(a) Food from crowding multipliers (b) Food potential from capital investment (c) Food from pollution multipliers

TERTIARY AUXILIARY	CONSTANTS	FURTHER AUXILIARY SYSTEMS
(iii) Crowding ratio	*A* Land area *B* Population density normal	
(iv) Pollution ratio	*A* Pollution standard	—
(v) Effective capital investment ratio	*A* Capital investment in agriculture fraction normal	(a) Natural resource extraction multipliers

These are the principal auxiliary measures that affect the flows in Forrester's system. However, there are further series of auxiliaries which give 'the quality of life':

(vi) Quality of life	*A* Quality of life standard	(a) Quality of life from material standard of living (b) Quality of life from crowding (c) Quality of life from pollution (d) Quality of life from food

This then is the 'Little World of Professor Forrester'; readers of the original text will know that his conclusion is that the world will experience a substantial fall in the quality of life and in population early in the next millennium. If mankind were lemmings, of course, there would be no point in keeping records of the catastrophe (supposing the model were in fact correct). However, the man who wants to keep accounts believes he can 'beat the system'—either as a body, or at least by ensuring his own (or his posterity's) presence amongst the survivors. What records should be included in the (extended) macro-accounts of a nation which accepted this model? At the outset, it can be seen that one of the possible objections to this model is that it *seems* to make no allowance for social policy at all. In fact, most of the auxiliary measures listed above contain 'tables'; these give the effect of a sinusoidal or some other non-linear function as population or some other variable increases or decrease. Presumably these tables take account of social policy, but obviously in an ex-ante fashion. Thus, for example, Forrester says [p 43]:

Crowding is here assumed to include psychological effects, social stresses that cause crime and international conflict, the pressures that can lead to atomic war, epidemics, and any effects from too many people that are not more appropriately defined into the other influences that are represented in the model.

The figure shows the crowding effect that has been included....

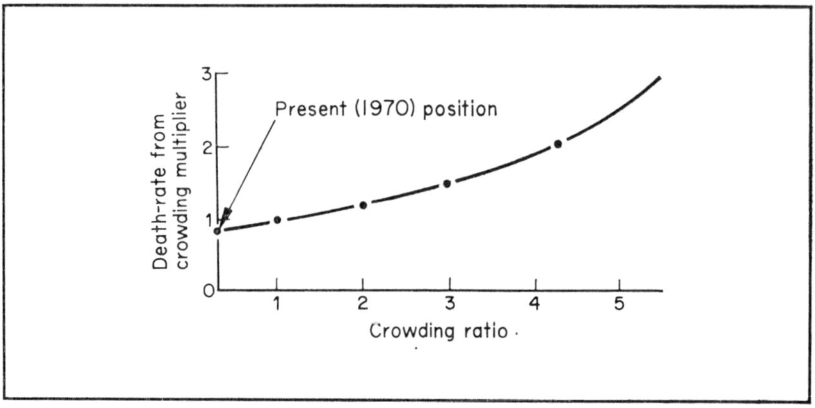

The reading of 1/1 is taken as the present-day (1970) position, given 1970 death-rates and levels of crowding. Forrester assumes that as crowding rises to five times the present population, the present deathrate would treble. It seems possible to claim that he does not consider the mechanics of these 'psychological effects' and 'social pressures' and whether some development in social engineering could ameliorate them; perhaps he feels that these effects follow even our best efforts in those directions.[10]

A number of features can be observed in this model:

1 The model contains feedback loops, and will tend to oscillate to a greater or lesser extent about some trend; it follows that any policy to be adopted should concern itself as much with controlling the size of the 'swings' about the trend as with securing a satisfactory trend-line overall. Especially when the issue at stake is something like 'the quality of life,' or even survival, it is apparent that no upswing can truly outweigh a really convincing down-swing. Returning to the material in Chapter 4, it can be seen that a society's attitude towards swings-versus-trends is likely to depend upon the weight given to future events of any sort.

2 It is also worth remarking that even as few as five interlocking flows (as in this model) can produce highly complex relationships, which cannot be understood intuitively. Nor can they readily be resolved by mathematical computation, at least to the extent of permitting direct calculation of the results of several changes in the constants or values attached to variables. For this reason, Forrester commends a simulation exercise, with graphic output, so that the system can be adjusted by a series of trial-and-error experiments.

3 This adds a further dimension to the claim in the previous chapters that a satisfactory taxonomy requires an over-arching theory. No doubt it does, but the complexity of the relationships required by any worthwhile model will still render a direct, mechanical solution very difficult. However, it does collect what are thought to be significant data into a single set of equations,and so overcomes the fragmentation (and probable sub-optimisation) referred to in the opening section of this chapter. If the model is accepted, any strategy for improving the situation must involve an attempt to change one of the constant parameters, or, at a more revolutionary level, to change the way in which the variables themselves are linked up in the equations. Again returning to Chapter 4, it can be seen that a society's willingness to attempt such changes will depend on whether they look upon these constants and variables as matters which it would be possible or proper to manipulate.

4 Finally, it is worth pointing out that the constants referred to here are to be distinguished from what are commonly called 'Acts of God.' The former are measures and ratios from the world of physics, or from the biological make-up of man; as such they are not readily changed by taking thought. The latter are random disturbances seen as coming from outside the system, and for which the model does not attempt to supply any remedy, beyond some sort of reserve for contingencies. The extent to which people look for an orderly, explicable universe has also been seen to be an aspect of their cultural development. The search for order is not necessarily 'a good thing'; indeed its excessive pursuit is commonly a sympton of considerable mental disturbance.

8.5 A generalised theory of accounting

The foregoing example, and the examination of the considerations proceeding from it confirm the point made more than once in the book; decisions are made on the basis of the decision-maker's mazeway, either individually or collectively. The 'model' put forward by Forrester *is* a proposal for a formal, collective mazeway at a highly aggregated level. The thing to note is that, once accepted as correct, and followed to its logical conclusion, it provides a definitive forecast of the future as it will be if no policy changes are made. Note that it *should* also have provided a convincing explanation of the *past* behaviour of the system as well. Thus we can and do test the validity of such models, to see whether they produce results from past data which provide a reasonable 'fit' to our observance of past events.

It follows that the sole management purpose of preparing any accounts (except for some attest or stewardship function) is to provide a continual series of test data to compare with the expected values of the data which the model has produced. In such a case we will only keep data that are capable of comparison, so that our taxonomy of data will be dictated by the model. Of course, to the extent that we believe the model itself to be faulty, or we are faced with situations for which no model exists, we may start to keep 'likely' data in the hope that by examining them we may devise a suitable model. Returning to Forrester's model as described in the last section, it is apparent that one would keep data on the various *flows* and *levels* listed—birthrates and deathrates, natural resource extraction, capital investment generation/discarding and pollution generation/absorption. The constants may be demonstrable by laboratory experimentation (or accepted as an act of faith). It is not possible to find data that *directly* prove or disprove the accuracy of the *auxiliaries*[11]—the multipliers, ratios and absorption times. The equations and their parameters are artificial constructs, arrived at very much along the lines described by Forrester in his text; they are logically *plausible*, but they acquire their *validity* only indirectly, to the extent that the completed model succeeds in forecasting or explaining what can be measured directly.

As we have seen in Chapter 4, the mazeway or culture provides a set of values and (one hopes) some rules for settling conflicts of value where they occur. These are described as 'feeling-tones' associated with a number of dichotomies.

In short, accountants are faced with the task of making objective measurements, which in the final analysis are to be judged subjectively.[12] This places great importance on section 3 ['Techniques—(images of ways of manipulating objects in order to experience desired end-status or values)'] of Wallace's schema. These are especially significant when constructing group or cultural mazeways, which must agree some acceptable bench-mark[13] for assessing opportunities and performances.

Now the mountain has brought forth its mouse: externality effects are very important. The proposal of this book is that accounting theory *and practice* need to be adjusted to include the various examples discussed in the last four chapters. It has been suggested that an abandonment of the convention of recording only direct transfers of goods and cash might lead to a reconsideration of business organisation itself, to the extent that super-solvency may be less significant than we now believe. Perhaps the continuum 'Specificity/diffusion' (or 'Unique/general') can be expanded on these lines:

1 Recognition of direct flows only.
2 Recognition of linked flows—'requited,' 'unrequited,' etc.
3 Recognition of simple regression—overhead rates.
4 Recognition of multiple regression.
5 Recognition of reciprocal overhead relationships—Churchill, Williams and Griffin *et al.*
6 Recognition of the existence of dynamic systems.

This continuum is the complement of 'Universal/particular' (or 'Unitary/pluralistic'); it is a step forward in sophistication of thought to recognise set-structure, but at first people are unable to add thereto the full complexity of the relationships that link the sets into the dynamic whole. Until this is achieved they tend to use a record of direct, visible transfers as a surrogate for the dynamic principal.

The current interest in 'behavioural' and 'social' aspects of accounting and business organisation merely reflect the fact that an increasing sophistication has now overtaken current accounting practice and theory. People are becoming more aware that summaries of direct flows (however adjusted) fail to present 'a true and fair view' of the enterprise's activity; the 'generally accepted accounting principles' are therefore no longer generally acceptable. One must not fall into the trap of supposing that any overwhelming virtue must reside in the fact that direct flows can be audited by calling over, ticking and stamping. Once a taxonomy of the necessary multipliers and other auxiliary coefficients has been established by the selection of acceptable models, their audit becomes an entirely straightforward operation: the standard tests of econometric model-building. The auditor would see whether the existing model still provided a reasonable 'fit' between the expected flow and level results and the actual measurements which have been observed. Undoubtedly there are disputed areas in these techniques, but they are not necessarily more frequent or insoluble than those already encountered in traditional practice.

Finally, these considerations might justify a rather stronger restatement of the Assumptions of Accounting Theory as developed in Chapter 4, and extended in Chapters 6 and 7:

1 In any exploitive society there are a system of valuation and a set of values which are ranked in a purposive fashion.
2 There are data held to be material which may be located in a period of time and may be located at some point within it. There is also a causal model which is held to explain the workings of the system or subsystem and contain estimates of the dimensions of a number of coefficients which are material to the values. These estimates seek their justification through the closeness with which the expected dimensions of the dependent variables in the model (using the data on the independent variables) correspond with the observed dimensions of the dependent variables given by the data.
3 The data which are seen as relating to the human and non-human environments can be classified so as to demonstrate a significant structure, which underlies the causal model. Data can be aggregated into these classes, and the classes themselves can be grouped and regrouped in a significant fashion.
4 There is also a set of relationships linking the classes which form the human/non-human environments. The relationships are expressed either in a crude surrogate form as a single direct flow at one point in

time (or some other more complex but essentially static fashion), or as a dynamic representation of the causal model, which may involve direct or indirect effects over a period of time.

5 The human environment is distinguished from the non-human environment, in that humans are seen as collaborating in various ways for the purposive pursuit of values.

Human collaborators can be grouped and regrouped so as to reflect varying mutual interests. . . . This pursuit of values will give rise to net differences between the direct flows of goods which find expression as a variety of debtor and creditor real relationships: some will accrue to individuals, others only jointly to groups or subgroups. Conventional settlement procedures may be adopted, especially in respect of debts between individuals and groups who have no continuing planable relations. These settlement procedures may form constraints upon the optimal operation of the system as a whole.[14]

6 There are criteria for deciding when material data may be recognised for classification in its appropriate categories.

8.6 Notes

1 It seems likely that it is not only self-interest that leads to this desire for some limitations of the scope of decision making. Boulding has suggested [22]: 'We all suffer from some degree of agrophobia, that is the fear of open spaces, especially open spaces in the mind. As a result we all tend to retreat into the cosy closed spaces of limited agenda and responsibilities.'

Of course, the retreat from large problems is not entirely attributed to small mindedness! Quite pedestrian administrative and commercial problems involve quantities of variables, constraints and data that are beyond the capacity of present-day computational equipment. A paper by Wenke [121] gives some idea of the problem of very large-scale data processing; another by Terleckyj [112] demonstrates the complexities of multi-dimensional planning in social areas.

2 A splendid simile from the discussion of a paper in the 1968 *Empirical Studies in Accounting* by Justin Trueblood; 'As a CPA my first reaction to Mr Beaver's excellent paper is to feel like a bumble bee confronted by an aeronautical engineer. The engineer has just proved to the bumblebee that the bumblebee can fly. The bumblebee is outraged: he knew he could fly all this time . . .' [114, p 99]. It would be a pity to appear to attack the current popularity of empirical studies in these areas, specially since the previous concern with mere philosophical approaches was hardly more fruitful. The problem is the Kantian dilemma of 'percept without concept' and 'concept without percept'; the former producing chaos and the latter a void.

3 Another quotation runs: 'Since all things came from somewhere, go somewhere, have associations, and have discernible parts, some general taxonomic principles might be (respectively) genetic, teleologic, ecologic, and morphologic. Only morphology implies classification on the basis of similarities and differences among objects themselves considered in their own right. The other three imply relationships to things outside the universe being ordered: origins, consequences, and functions' [*op cit*, p 65]. This statement can be compared with the views of Aukrust (quoted in section 5.2) on classification. The assumption of duality is essentially morphologic and so very limiting.

4 This dichotomy between internally based and economics-based accounting theories has also been discussed in Chapter 1; the argument developed in that chapter suggests that the internally based theories accept the taxonomies which have been made traditionally (because they are particularly easy categories for book-keepers to provide). They look for some internally evidenced and consistent 'accepted principles of accounting,' whose purpose is to prevent people being misled by accounts prepared along traditional lines.

5 There is an old 'anti-accountant' story of an Australian drover who asked his accountant how many sheep the latter could see from the window of the sheep-station. The accountant is supposed to have replied immediately '7006—six under that tree and about 7000 down by the creek.' Although accountants are not alone in the fault of inconsistently aggregating data of dubious accuracy (as Morgenstern has pointed out), this story does illustrate the common situation of the accountant; he is *on* the sheep-station, the drover *asks* him and *expects* him to have an *answer*, in turn the drover probably has his own technique for counting sheep and is merely asking his accountant to provide some check-figure. This is contrasted sharply with the economist who can, in effect, say 'Let x be the number of sheep,' and then as an afterthought add '$x \simeq 7000$' while the behaviourist is not expected to bother about the number of sheep at all, but rather to consider the 'level of aspiration' of the accountant and the drover, or something of that sort. In fact, the drover, the accountant and even the sheep are caught up in the interlocking systems of Australian ecology, economy and society. That is not to say that it is necessarily unprofitable to study subsections of those systems in isolation, but rather that it is essential to recognise that they are all part of the same grand system and so requiring analysis in terms of the same, or at least congruent taxonomies.

6 It is interesting to see that Professor Edwards also pays tribute to the power of cultural influence in what is conventionally thought to be very much a matter of 'the economic facts of life.' 'Old wives' tales' is a common synonym for 'folk-lore'; perhaps much of what is taught (and practised) as finance *has* something of that nature. That is not to say it is unimportant, let alone that it doesn't work—men have died of fright when a witch-doctor pointed his bone. It is also interesting that he sees some problems of economics as man-made, confirming that the fact that an institution is folk-loric does not ensure that it is helpful.

7 Howard Ross provides a comment upon these arguments (with reference to accounting disclosure, rather than organisation, of course); he says 'Authorities like the *A*(ccounting) *P*(rinciples) *B*(oard) and *S*(ecurities) and *E*(xchange) *C*(ommission) appear to be so intent on preventing anyone from issuing misleading information that they view with alarm any departure from customary forms of presentation. It is easy to understand their point of view, but surely the restrictions they insist upon are much less likely to keep the crooked promoter on the straight and narrow path of rectitude than to trip up the honest operator. . . . There is plenty of evidence that the dishonest businessman can find ways to beguile his public through use of generally accepted procedures . . .' [97, p 115].

Certainly much of the actual thinking in both these areas could be labelled '*naïve* Theory *X*.' Neither the enforcement of the self-financing system nor rigorous requirements to disclose how one has conformed thereto seems to prevent the perpetration of some astounding frauds.

8 Until quite recently the operation of washing cloth always involved some beating action—a stone, a dolly-peg, a wash-board; since the objective was to clean clothes and not to beat them, this technique is abandoned without many qualms wherever the new technology of the detergent comes into use. The self-financing corporation with its profit rule is not an objective in itself, as the profit motive is. Rather it is a very old-established tool which has worked effectively enough over the years, but lately has come into increasingly difficult conditions of working because of heightened sensibilities and expectations, and the growing awareness of the finite supply of much that was traditionally thought of as free goods. The purpose of the tool is to exploit the profit motive so as to bring about the production of positive values and the removal of negative values, and distribute the 'added value' in some fashion amongst the society at large. It might be very hard to conceive a better tool for the purpose, but there are no grounds for assuming that one might not exist.

9 By using as his illustrations the work of Forrester (and referring less extensively to that of Bonini) rather than constructing his own model, the author risks an accusation of being a gatherer of other men's flowers. In fact, the author is not very interested in the nature of the model itself (at this time), but in the need to have *some* model to reach *a meaningful taxonomy*.

10 In contrast, Bonini's book [20] describes a model that is based on a rather more general version contained in Cyert and March's work [*op cit*]: it includes a facility of changing the decision-parameters to cover societal variables such as '*loose*' *vs.* '*tight*' *industrial engineering department* (by which he means the chance of obtaining organisational slack in costs), *contagion of pressure* (signifying the build up of pressures within an hierarchy) and *sensitivity to pressure* (the point at which corrective action is taken by an executive) [pp 78–81]. Bonini contrasts this approach with that of Forrester, while emphasising that this comparison does not imply a criticism of that work; he says (at that date he is speaking of *Industrial Dynamics* only):

> '. . . there is a major difference between our "decision rules" and their counterparts in the Forrester systems (what Forrester has described . . . as "amplification"). These differences are:
>
> 1 Since we are interested in factors internal to the firm, the control system of the firm is of crucial importance, since it is the mechanism by which feed-back takes place. But any realistic approach to a control system cannot be content with mere "amplification" effect, but must include psychological and social factors. . . .
> 2 . . . we have made an attempt to relate our "decision rules" to accepted theory in economics or the behavioural sciences or to accepted business practice. Professor Forrester's "amplifications" tend to be more mechanistic. . . .
> 3 We have made our model in such a fashion that the decision rules themselves are amongst the subjects of study. . . . Forrester has not emphasised this approach [p 13].'

It is noticable that Forrester's other, later work has concerned itself very much with 'psychological and social factors'; perhaps the difference between his approach and Bonini's is essentially in the level of aggregation. At the urban and national levels the models have to take account of cultural matters, at the personal and smallish group level with social psychology, while a model of a large firm *may* well find it difficult to include any equivalent parameters.

11 It follows that concepts such as 'the quality of life,' 'welfare' and so on cannot be made the subject of direct data collection, and thus, as has been discussed in earlier chapters, models tend to give verifiable answers in terms of cash flows, housing, pollution levels or numbers of indictable offences. This is probably the reason for the need to create artificial 'production boundaries,' which was discussed in Chapter 2. Accounts can produce, as a surrogate, details of what is being produced in physical terms (including cash), but whether this production is truly equivalent to the principal of 'joy' as well is not guaranteed.

12 Although the auxiliaries in this model are essentially subjective, it is apparent that any techniques which are to be used to manipulate the situation have to be applied at those points. No refinement of the intellectual concepts in these equations can effect any change in the underlying activity; it follows that any attempts at manipulation must involve the construction of a more detailed (sub)model which includes one or more rates of flow which can be controlled in some way. This is why the exponents of PPBS place emphasis on the needs for measurable outputs from all programmes. Thus, returning to the detail of the model: one could consider, say, the 'Natural resource usage from material (standard-of-living) multiplier.' Are there any flows which could be adjusted so as to alter the relationship between the usage of resources and the material standard of living? In this connection, it should not be supposed that the fact that *techniques* can only be applied to physical flows of some sort, implies that only physical flows can be *measured*. Social psychology can now provide quite sophisticated and well-tried methodologies for the measurement of attitudes: in view of the inherent difficulties seen by Ijiri and others in measurement of any sort, it seems unlikely that attitudes are really more subjective than, say, inventory costs!

13 As Churchman has pointed out in the paper already cited, it is clear that this act of accepting a bench-mark effectively decides the course of action to be adopted [28]. Thus the items described as tertiary auxiliaries, which measure 'quality of life' in the Forrester model we are using as an illustration, must reflect the agreed 'priority systems among values' described by Wallace. If one does not accept them, presumably one substitutes other systems—and perhaps arrives at contrary conclusions.

14 The sting in the tail is this: if an exploitive society nevertheless wants its self-financing enterprises to take account of externalities in their decision-making, it will not be possible to insist upon them remaining solvent as well! Beneficent 'lame ducks' will need subvention, while maleficent 'blue chips' will have to be penalised. Both policies will require very adequate analysis of the interaction of social and economic wealth.

Bibliography

1 AAA, 'Report of the Committee on Foundations of Accounting Measurement,' *Accounting Review*, Supplement to vol 41, pp 1–48 (1971).
2 AAA, 'Report of the Committee on Non-financial Measures of Effectiveness,' *ibid*, Supplement to vol 46, pp 165–211 (1971).
3 AAA, 'Report of the Committee on Measures of Effectiveness for Social Programmes,' *ibid*, Supplement to vol 47, pp 337–96 (1972).
4 Abraham, W I, *National Income and Economic Accounting*, Prentice Hall, (1969).
5 Acheson, J M, 'Accounting Concepts and Economic Opportunities in a Tarascan Village: Emic and Etic Views,' *Human Organisation*, vol 31, pp 83–91 (1972).
6 Ady, P, 'Uses of National Accounts in Africa,' *in* Samuels, L H (Editor), *African Studies in Income and Wealth*, Bowes and Bowes, pp 52–65 (1963).
7 Ameiss, A P, 'Developing Nations and Tax-ordained Accounting Principles,' *International Journal of Accounting*, vol 6, pp 89–102 (1971).
8 Ando, A, 'An Econometrician Comments on the National Income and Product Accounts,' (*US Dept of Commerce*) *Survey of Current Business*, vol 51, part II, pp 1–3 (1971).
9 Ansoff, H I, *Corporate Strategy*, McGraw-Hill (1965).
10 Aukrust, O, *Nasjonalregnskap—Teoretiske Prinsipper* (Statistisk Sentralbyrå, Oslo) (1955); contains English summary.
11 Bauer, R B (Editor), *Social Indicators*, MIT (1966).
12 Becker, A S, *Soviet National Income 1958–64* (University of California), (1969).
13 Beckerman, W, *International Comparison of Real Incomes* (Development Centre of the OECD) (1966).
14 Beckerman, W, 'Why We Need Economic Growth,' *Lloyds Bank Review* (1971).
15 Bedford, N, *The Future of Accounting in a Changing Society* (University of Edinburgh—Arthur Andersen Lecture Series) (1969).
16 Bennett, M K, 'International Disparities in Consumption Levels,' *American Economic Review*, vol 41, pp 632–49 (1951).
17 Biderman, A D, 'Social Indicators and Goals,' in *Social Indicators*, edited by Bauer, R B, MIT, pp 68–153 (1966).
18 Billington, G C, 'A Minimum System of National Accounts for use by African Countries, and some Related Problems,' *in African Studies in Income and Wealth*, Samuels, L H (Editor), Bowes and Bowes, pp 1–51 (1963).
19 Boddewyn, J, 'The Cultural Approach to Business Behavior,' Chapter 11 *in Interdisciplinary Studies in Business Behavior*, edited by McGuire, J W, South Western Publishing, pp 189–206 (1962).
20 Bonini, C P, *Simulation of Information and Decision Systems in the Firm*, Prentice Hall (1963).
21 Boulding, K E, 'Economics and Accounting: the Uncongenial Twins,' *in Studies in Accounting Theory*, edited by Baxter, W T, and Davidson, S, Sweet and Maxwell, pp 44–55 (1962).

22 Boulding, K E, 'The Ethics of Rational Decision,' *Management Science*, vol 12, pp 161–9 (1960).
23 Brummet, R L, Flamholtz, E G and Pyle, W C, 'Human Resource Measurement—A Challenge for Accountants,' *Accounting Review*, vol 43, pp 217–24 (1968).
24 Bursch, E C, 'View your Customers as Investments,' *Harvard Business Review*, vol 44, pp 91–4 (May–June 1966).
25 Campbell, R W, *Accounting in Soviet Planning and Management*, Harvard (1963).
26 Carlson, J W, 'The Status and next Steps for Planning, Programming and Budgeting,' in *The Analysis and Evaluation of Public Expenditure* (US Joint Economic Committee), part IV (1969).
27 Chambers, R J, 'The Foundation of Financial Accounting,' *Berkeley Symposium on the Foundation of Financial Accounting* (University of California), pp 26–44 (1967).
28 Churchman, C W, 'On the Facility, Felicity and Morality of Measuring Social Change,' *Accounting Review*, vol 46, pp 30–5 (1971).
29 Clapp, C E, 'National Variations in Accounting Principles and Practices,' *International Journal of Accounting*, vol 3 (1967).
30 Collins, B E, and Guetzkow, H, *A Social Psychology of Group Processes for Decision Making*, Wiley (1964).
31 Cook, S, 'The Obsolete "Anti-market" Mentality: a Critique of the Substantive Approach to Economic Anthropology,' *American Anthropologist*, vol 68, pp 323–45 (1960).
32 Counter Information Services, *The General Electric Company Ltd: Anti-report*, CIS (1972).
33 Cyert, R M, and March, J G, *A Behavioral Theory of the Firm*, Prentice Hall (1963).
34 Dembinski, N V, *Teoriya Sovetskogo Bukhgalterskogo Ucheta*, State Publishing House, BSSR, Minsk (1957).
35 Demski, J I, 'An Accounting System Structured on a Linear Programming Model,' *Accounting Review*, vol 42, pp 701–12 (1967).
36 Devine, C T, 'A Behavioral Theory of the Firm: a Review Article,' *Journal Accounting Research*, vol 2, pp 197–220 (1964).
37 Dopuch, N, Birnberg, J G, and Demski, J, 'An Extension of Standard Cost-variance Analysis,' *Accounting Review*, vol 42, pp 526–36 (1967).
38 Dyson, J R, 'Who Will Be Entitled to Accounting Information?,' *The Accountants Weekly*, pp 24–5 (20 October 1972).
39 Estes, R W, 'Socio-Economic Accounting and External Diseconomies,' *Accounting Review*, vol 47, pp 284–90 (1972).
40 Forrester, J W, *Industrial Dynamics*, MIT (1961).
41 Forrester, J W, *Urban Dynamics*, MIT (1969).
42 Forrester, J W, *World Dynamics*, Wright-Allen Press (1971).
43 Frankel, S H, 'Psychic and "Accounting" Concepts of Income and Welfare,' from *Readings in the Concept and Measurement of Income*, edited by Parker, R H, and Harcourt, G E, CUP (1969).
44 Galbraith, J K, *The Great Crash 1929*, Hamish Hamilton (1955).
45 Gambling, T E, *Modern Accounting: Accounting as the Information System of Technological Change*.

46 Gambling, T E, *The Accountant, the Computer and the Abacus*, University of Birmingham: Inaugural Lecture (1969).
47 Goetz, B E, 'Transfer Prices: An Exercise in Relevancy and Goal Congruence,' *Accounting Review*, vol 42, pp 435–40 (1967).
48 Goldberg, L, *An Outline of Accounting*, Sweet and Maxwell (1957).
49 Gonedes, N J, 'Efficient Capital Markets and External Accounting,' *Accounting Review*, vol 47, pp 11–21 (1972).
50 Goodfellow, D M, *Principles of Economic Sociology*, Routledge (1939).
51 Gordon, M J, 'The Use of Administered Price Levels,' in *Management Controls: new directions in basic research*, edited by Bonini, C P, Jaedicke, R J, and Wagner, H M, McGraw Hill (1964).
52 Gorelik, G, 'Enterprise Profit and Profitability Measurements: Soviet-American Convergence,' *International Journal of Accounting*, vol 6, pp 1–14 (1971).
53 Granick, D, *Management of the Industrial Firm in the USSR*, Columbia (1954).
54 Gross, B M, 'The State of the Nation: Social Systems Accounting,' in *Social Indicators*, edited by Bauer, R M, MIT, pp 154–271 (1966).
55 Hall, E T, *The Silent Language*, Doubleday (1959).
56 Hambly, W D, *Source-book for African Anthropology*, Reprinted by Kraus Reprint (1968).
57 Hendriksen, E S, *Accounting Theory*, Irwin (revised edition 1970).
58 Hirschleifer, J, 'On the Economics of Transfer Pricing,' *Journal of Business*, vol 29, pp 173–84 (1956).
59 Hoffman, L R, 'Homogeneity of Member Personality and Its Effect on Group Problem Solving,' *Journal of Abnormal Social Psychology*, vol 58, pp 27–32 (1959).
60 Horngren, C T, *Cost Accounting: a Managerial Emphasis*, Prentice Hall, (1st edition, 1962).
61 Horwitz, B, *Accounting Controls and the Soviet Economic Reforms of 1966*, Studies in Accounting Research No 4: American Accounting Association (1970).
62 Ijiri, Y, *Foundations of Accounting Measurement: a Mathematical, Economic And Behavioral Inquiry*, Prentice Hall (1967).
63 Jacobsen, L E, 'The Ancient Inca Empire of Peru and the Double Entry Accounting Concept,' *Journal of Accounting Research*, vol 2, pp 221–8 (1964).
64 Johnson, O, 'On Taxonomy and Accounting Research,' *Accounting Review*, vol 47, pp 64–74 (1972).
65 Kaplan, D, 'The Formal-substantive Controversy in Economic Anthropology: Reflections on its Wider Implications,' *Southwestern Journal of Anthropology*, vol 24, pp 228–51 (1968).
66 Kennedy, T A, Ord, H W, and Walker, D, 'On the Calculation and Interpretation of National Accounting Material in East Africa,' in *African Studies in Income and Wealth*, edited by Samuels, L H, Bowes and Bowes, pp 350–432 (1963).
67 Kissack, W F, *Towards a Performance Economy*, Trans-España SA, Jaime III 144, Palma de Mallorca, Spain. Privately circulated paper, undated.

68 Kluckhohn, C, 'Towards a Comparison of Value Emphasis in Different Cultures,' in *The State of the Social Sciences*, edited by White, L, University of Chicago (1956).
69 Kosiol, E E, 'An Axiomatic Approach to the Patagoric Theory of Financial Income Determination,' *International Journal of Accounting*, vol 5, pp 1–28 (1970).
70 Kroeber, A L, and Kluckhohn, C, *Culture: a Critical Review of Concepts and Definition*, Random House (1963).
71 Kuznets, S, *National Income and its Composition 1919–1938*, National Bureau of Economic Research, vol II (1942).
72 Ladd, D R, *Contemporary Corporate Accounting and the Public*, Irwin (1963).
73 LeClaire Jr, E E, 'Economic Theory and Economic Anthropology,' *American Anthropologist*, vol 64, pp 1179–1203 (1962).
74 Lenin, V I, 'The State and Revolution,' in *Questions of the Socialist Organisation of the Economy*, Moscow, undated.
75 Lerner, E B, and Rappaport, A, 'Capital Budgeting and Reported Earnings to Shareholders,' paper to AAA Conference (1968).
76 Lev, B, and Schwartz, A, 'On the Use of the Economic Concept of Human Capital in Financial Statements,' *Accounting Review*, vol 46, pp 103–12 (1971).
77 Linowes, D, 'Socio-Economic Accounting,' *Journal of Accountancy*, pp 37–42 (November 1968).
78 Louwers, P, 'Sincerity in Financial Reporting,' Paper to the 20th Summer School of the Scottish Institute of Chartered Accountants, reported in *Accountancy*, vol 83, pp 6–7 (1972).
79 Mattessich, R, *Accounting and Analytical Methods*, Irwin (1964).
80 Mattessich, R, 'Methodological Preconditions and Problems of a General Theory of Accounting,' *Accounting Review*, vol 47, pp 469–87 (1972).
81 Mead, G C, 'A Managerial Approach to Governmental Accounting,' *Journal of Accountancy*, pp 50–5 (March 1970).
82 Mikesell, R M, and Hays, L E, *Governmental Accounting*, Irwin (4th edition, 1969).
83 Miner, H, 'Cultural Change Under Pressure: a Hausa Case,' *Human Organisation*, vol 19, pp 164–7 (1960).
84 Mishan, E J, *The Cost of Economic Growth*, Staples (1967).
85 Mishan, E J, 'Economic Growth: the Need for Scepticism,' *Lloyds Bank Review*, No 106, pp 1–26 (1972).
86 Mobley, S C, 'The Challenges of Socio-economic Accounting,' *Accounting Review*, vol 45, pp 762–8 (1970).
87 Moonitz, M, and Jordan, J H, *Accounting: an Analysis of its Problems*, vols I and II, Holt, Rinehart and Winston (revised edition, 1963).
88 Morgenstern, O, *On the Accuracy of Economic Observation*, Princeton, (2nd edition, 1963).
89 Most, K, 'An Accountant Looks at Social Accounting,' *Accounting and Business Research*, vol 2, pp 264–74 (1972).
90 Mueller, G G, 'Academic Research in International Accounting,' *International Journal of Accounting*, vol 6, pp 67–81 (1971).

91 Okigbo, P N C, *Nigerian National Accounts 1950–1957*, Federal Ministry of Development, Nigeria (1962).
92 Parsons, T, *The Social System*, Tavistock (1951).
93 Polyani, K, 'Anthropology and Economic Theory,' in *Readings in Anthropology*, edited by Fried, M H, Crowell, pp 161–84 (1959).
94 Powelson, J P, *National Income and Flow-of-funds Analysis*, McGraw-Hill (1960).
95 Prest, A R, and Turvey, R, 'Cost-benefit Analysis: A Survey,' *Economic Journal*, vol 75, pp 683–735 (1965).
96 Ronen, J, and McKinney, G, 'Transfer Pricing for Divisional Autonomy,' *Journal of Accounting Research*, vol 8, pp 99–112 (1970).
97 Ross, H, 'The Wonderful World of Accounting,' *Empirical Research in Accounting, Selected Studies*, pp 108–15 (1970).
98 Ruggles, N, and Ruggles, R, *The Design of Economic Accounts*, National Bureau of Economic Research (1970).
99 Scott, G M, 'A Business Economics Foundation for Accounting: the Dutch Experience,' *Accounting and Business Research*, vol 1, pp 309–31 (1971).
100 The Secretary-General's *Ad Hoc* Group on New Concepts of Science Policy, *Science, Growth and Society*, OECD [*The Brooks Report*] (1971).
101 Schiff, M, 'Accounting Tactics and the Theory of the Firm,' *Journal of Accounting Research*, vol 4, pp 62–7 (1966).
102 Seed III, A H, 'The Rational Abuse of Accounting Information,' *Management Accounting* (*NY*), vol 52, pp 9–11 (1972).
103 Seeff, G M, *Accounting: the Measurement of Organisational Effectiveness*, University of Birmingham: unpublished doctoral thesis (1973).
104 Seers, D and Joy, L, *Development in a Divided World*, Penguin Books (1970).
105 Simon, H A, *The Sciences of the Artificial*, MIT (1969).
106 Simpson, J R, 'Uses of Cultural Anthropology in Economic Analysis: a Papago Indian Case,' *Human Organisation*, vol 29, pp 162–8 (1970).
107 Smallpeice, B, 'The Profit Motive in Industry,' *The Christian News-letter*, Supplement to No 152 (23 September 1942).
108 Smith, M G, *The Economy of the Hausa Communities of Zaria*, Colonial Office Research Studies, parts I and III (1955).
109 Sombart, W, *Der Moderne Kapitalismus*, Humblot, vol 2.1 (6th edition, 1924).
110 Stuvel, G, *Systems of Social Accounts*, Clarendon Press (1965).
111 Tawney, R H, *Religion and the Rise of Capitalism*, John Murray (cheap edition, 1929).
112 Terleckyj, N E, 'Measuring Progress Towards Social Goals: Some Possibilities at National and Local Levels,' *Management Science*, vol 16, pp B765–B778 (1970).
113 Tritschler, C A, 'A Sociological Perspective on Accounting Innovation,' *International Journal of Accounting*, vol 5, pp 39–67 (1970).
114 Trueblood, H J, 'Discussion of the Information Content of Annual Earnings Announcements,' *Empirical Research in Accounting, Selected Studies*, pp 96–100 (1968).
115 UN Department of Economic and Social Affairs, *A System of National Accounts*, Studies in Methods, Series F, No 2, Rev 3, United Nations (1968).

116 UN Economic Commission for Europe, 'A Note on Some Aspects of National Accounting Methodology in Eastern Europe and the Soviet Union,' from *Readings in the Concept and Measurement of Income*, edited by Parker, R H, and Harcourt, G C, CUP (1969).
117 Van Arkadie, B, and Frank, C, *Economic Accounting and Development Planning*, OUP, Nairobi (1966).
118 Vatter, W J, *The Fund Theory of Accounting and its Implications for Financial Reports*, University of Chicago (1947).
119 Wallace, A F C, *Culture and Personality*, Random House (1961).
120 Wallach, M A, Kogan, N, and Bern, D, 'Group Influences on Individual Risk-Taking,' *Journal of Abnormal Psychology*, vol 65, pp 75–86 (1962).
121 Wenke, K, 'On the Analysis of Structural Properties of Large-scale Micro-economic Input-output Models,' *Management Science: Models and Techniques*, edited by Churchman, C W, and Verlust, M, Pergamon Press (1960).
122 Wheeler, J T, 'Accounting Theory and Research in Perspective,' *Accounting Review*, vol 45, pp 1–10 (1970).
123 Whinston, A, 'Price Guides in Decentralized Organisations,' in *New Perspectives in Organisation Research*, edited by Cooper, Leavett and Shelley, Wiley (1964).
124 Williams, E E, 'A Note on Accounting Practice, Investor Rationality and Capital Resource Allocation,' *Financial Analysists Journal*, vol 25, pp 37–40 (July/August 1969).
125 Winjum, J O, 'Accounting and the Rise of Capitalism: an Accountant's View' *Journal of Accounting Research*, vol 9, pp 333–50 (1971).
126 Yamey, B S, 'Accounting and the Rise of Capitalism: Further Notes on a Theme by Sombart,' *ibid.*, vol 2, pp 117–36 (1964).
127 Yanovsky, M, *Anatomy of Social Accounting Systems*, Chapman & Hall (1965).

Index

Index